I0755754

THE YEAR OF AN ARTIST

365 DAYS IN THE MIND'S EYE OF A PROFESSIONAL PAINTER & SCULPTOR

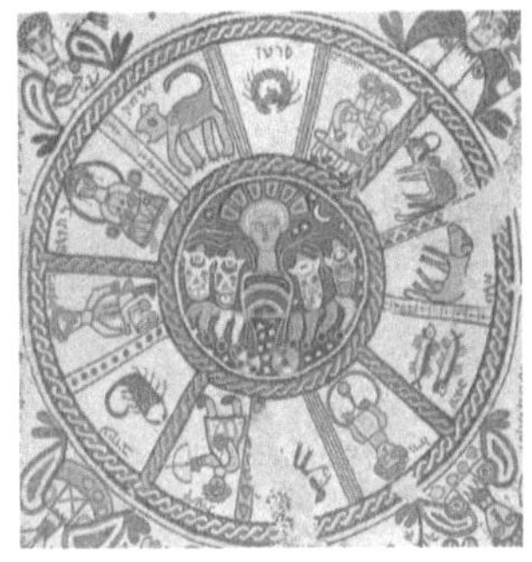

SANDY GARNETT

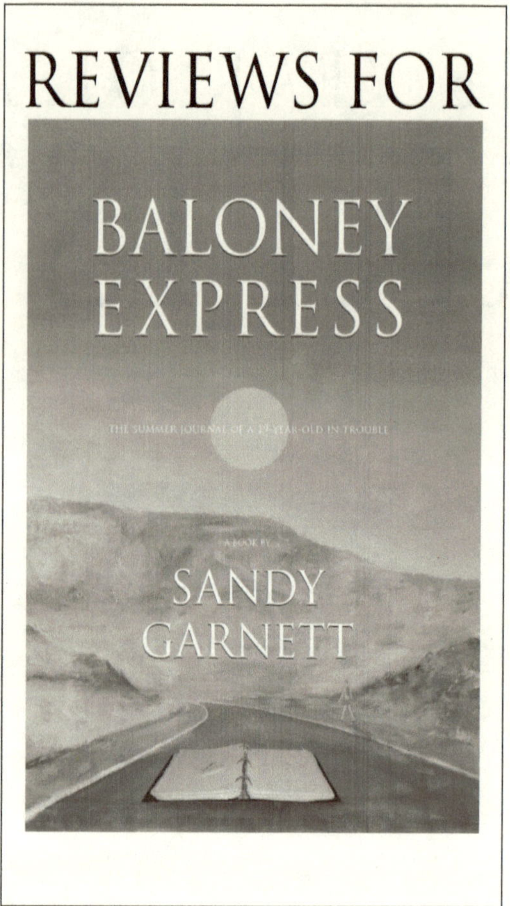

"It doesn't matter how long this project has been on the shelf. Go back to the old journal, start a new file, edit the document, make a book and get it out there. You need to publish this story."

- Deborah Shea, Senior Independent Advisor
for the first draft of Baloney Express
College Writing Professor, St. Lawrence University

"Baloney Express was impossible to put down. Garnett's artistic talents are as evident in his words as they are in his art; his phrasing and descriptions of people and places and feelings create profound visual images. I know that some family members may have been reluctant for him to share such private experiences, but I have to say I have only the greatest empathy and respect for his trials and the man he is today. Clearly, he loves and appreciates his parents and his brothers and the value of family and how close he came to wandering away from that gift." - V.F., College English Professor, 4 July 2011

"I am most amazed at what seems to be a very real view-point of the naturally self-absorbed teenager becoming aware of the rest of the world and evolving on each page. I was a child and family therapist and worked in methadone clinics and rehabilitation centers for years. I am reminded of the academic curiosity that is rarely satisfied in books of this nature that students read to prepare for their careers as therapists. Baloney Express should be read by students in therapy fields as well as by patients and their loved ones." - A.B., Professional Therapist, 29 April 2011

"Baloney Express is a real life, fly on the wall account of rehab and the growing pains of family. Unlike other reads in this genre, there are no whiny justifications and party days one-upmanship here. Enlightening and witty, Garnett's irreverent, candid, self-deprecating voice is so honest it begs the reader to take a look in the mirror. BE is a memoir, but the human experience in all its ugliness and glory is universal and this guy nails it." - Miles Carroll, 2 May 2011

"After reading Baloney Express I thought that we should all go to rehab to get over ourselves." - Kim Harris, Shippan Book Club, May 2010

"Baloney Express is one of the most powerful, brave and well written books of all that I have read." - 30 May 2011, P.F., Owner Consulting/Marketing Firm, Father, Grandfather

"Baloney Express seems to me to be absolutely free of the BS we all put out there to survive and make our ways in the world. It is, of course, a book about letting go of that BS and finding something true to pursue, to give us higher purpose in our lives, for a change." - B.B, award winning author of six books, 23 May 2011

"I loved Baloney Express. I read it in two days. The author completely understands what it feels like to be in here. I will read it again, a journal entry a day, as I go through my recovery. I will refer to this book now and in the future. Everyone at the clinic wants to read it. We need more copies." - B.D., Anonymous Patient in Recovery

"Earnest and amusing. A quick, insightful, enjoyable read. A three train ride book. Let me put it this way... that other whiny memoir I started long before I picked up Baloney two days ago sits in my trunk unread, where it will probably live all winter." - Christopher Peter, Astute Cultural Critic

"A timeless classic beach read with guts, humor and vision. What a debut book from this professional painter and sculptor. Baloney Express will make a riveting film." - Alan Abel, America's Most Famous Hoaxer (alanabel.com)

"Baloney Express is an amazing journal of a young man's recovery and return to the arms of a loving, deeply worried and scared family. I wept at the end of the book and the end of the Closer Chapter. The book is beautifully written and the growth of an angry young man from page one to the end is astounding." - S.N. , 29 April 2011

"I loved Baloney Express. Every entry is captivating. I did not want the book to end. What an amazing read." - I.W., MSW, Professional Therapist, March 2011

"An honest coming of age story, unlike some famous recovery books that are fictional and therefore disrespectful to their readers. I strongly recommend a slice of Baloney." - H.T., Anonymous Patient in Recovery

"Baloney Express came into my hands at exactly the right time. I am trying to find a therapeutic wilderness camp for my son this summer. Baloney Express is a comfort, showing that change and healing are really possible. I want to thank the author for writing his story and sharing it with me."
- Anonymous Reader, 20 May 2011

"Baloney Express is very strong, well-written, fast, fluid, funny and poignant without being self-conscious. This is a wonderful book, a coming of age story that everyone should read." - Annie Edgerton, Broadway Actress

"I've been meaning to write about how great and really inspirational Baloney Express is. Baloney was not only a pleasure to read as it is written very well, but Garnett's story is fascinating. The author's "journey" so to speak is amazing, how he turned everything around in his life. over the course of one short summer. Congratulations to the author on publishing his story and especially on what he does with his life as a professional artist. I can't wait to find out more about his artistic endeavors. I want to thank the author for sharing his story and for making it a delight to read." - P.W., artist and mother, 10 September 2011

"I blew through Baloney Express in less than two days though it looks like I've had it for years; complete with folded down corners on several pages. What an honest expression of the author and quite a journey he took in such a short amount of time. Many are in the same situation the author was in at the innocent age of 19, but few have the courage to admit it, do something about it and live it. We ought to all be in therapy. I will definitely be purchasing another copy; I have a 17 year old nephew who is headed down the same path the author was on and unfortunately has no idea how quickly he can screw up his life before it even begins. I'm hoping the raw honesty Garnett expressed in Baloney Express will turn the light on for him." - J.M. 4 August, 2011

Other Published Works

Books:

Baloney Express
ISBN - 978-0-9822348-3-9

Art Catalogues:

The First 1000 Paintings of Sandy Garnett
(Updated Periodically)
ISBN - 978-0-9822348-7-7

Sandy Garnett Paintings & Sculptures Inventory
(Annual Editions)
ISBN - 978-0-9822348-4-6

Children:

The Rainbow Riders
hardcover ISBN - 978-0-9822348-5-3
softcover ISBN - 978-0-9822348-1-5

The Rainbow Riders ABC Book
hardcover ISBN - 978-0-9822348-6-4
softcover ISBN - 978-0-9822348-2-2

More Rainbow Riders books and things can be found at
www.rainbowriderskids.com

Music:

Sandy Garnett's songs are available
at online music retailers

All of the above can be found at
www.sandygarnett.com

THE YEAR OF AN ARTIST

365 DAYS IN THE MIND'S EYE OF A PROFESSIONAL PAINTER & SCULPTOR

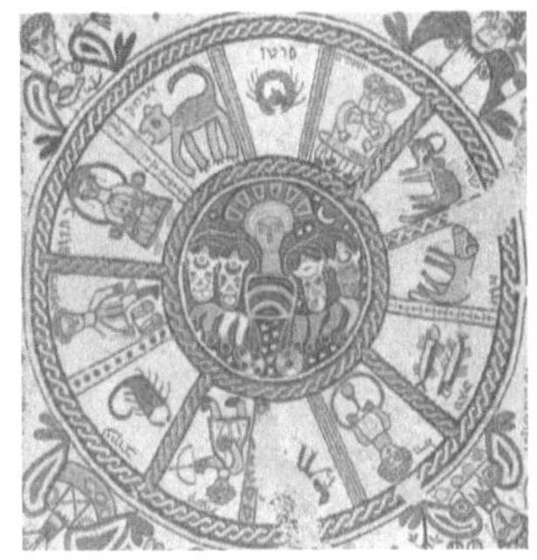

SANDY GARNETT

Printed in the United States of America.

ISBN 978-0-9822348-8-4 - hardcover

The Year of An Artist

Published by

Chelsea Press

A Division of Chelsea Multimedia
Graphics 2000 Inc.

For bulk orders and correspondence:

inquiries@chelseapress.com

www.sandygarnett.com

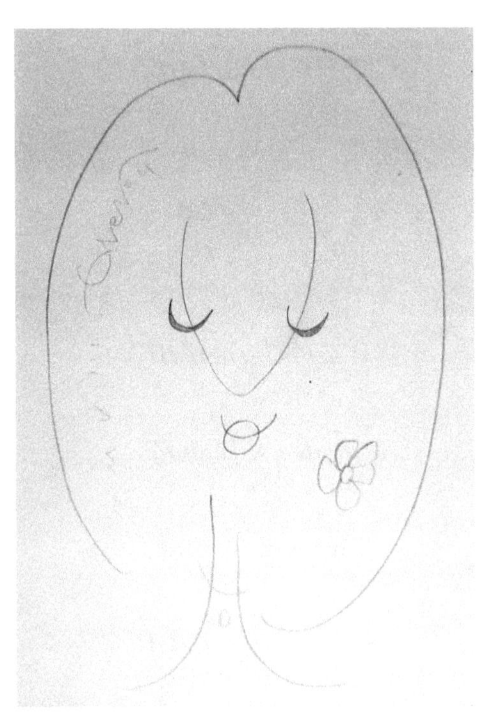

ACKNOWLEDGEMENTS

I would like to thank my Editorial Team :

A.Y.P. Garnett III

Sandee Kirchhoff

Annie Edgerton

Christopher Peter

This book is dedicated to
Artists in all arenas,

Who survive by the blood sport of art.

We hunt the art and mount the heads,
Deep vines which line our studios,

These rhyming, mirrored, former selves,
Our timeless spirit reference shelves.

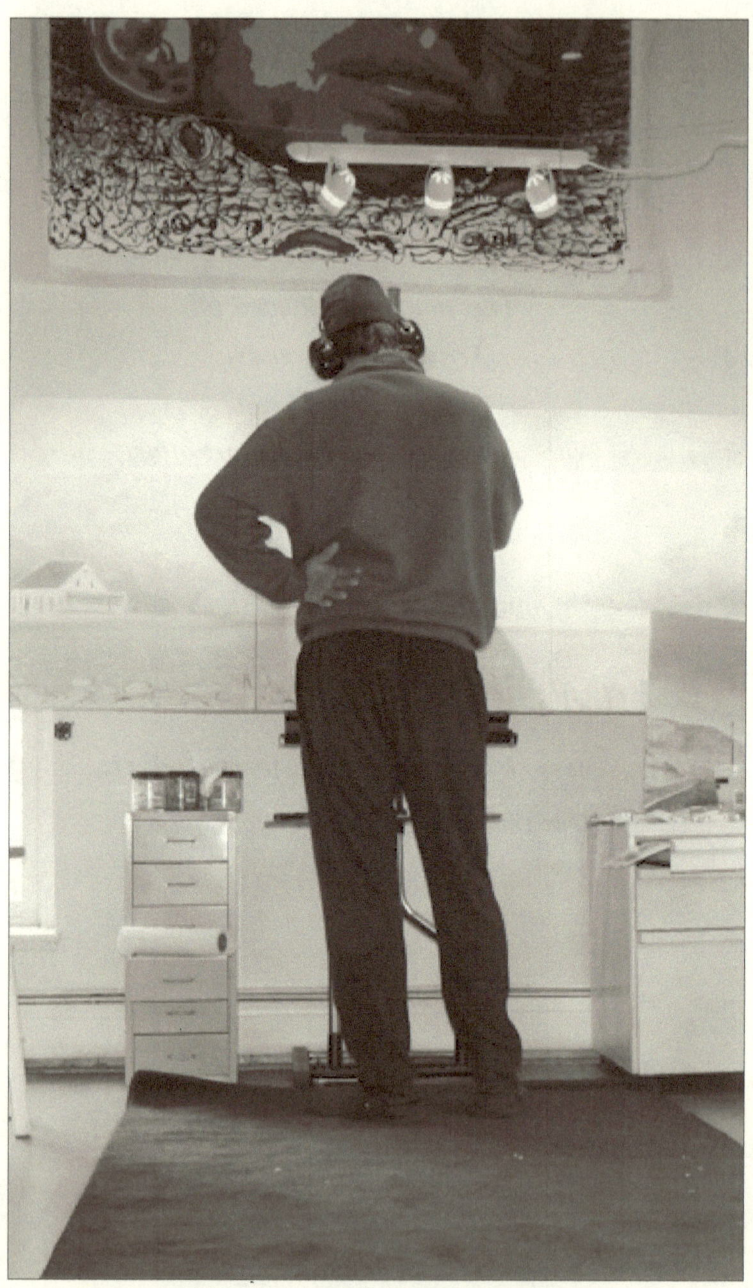

The solitary artist hunting in his studio

This book is the author's
365 journal entries
of a single calendar year.

Names used in this book
may have been changed.

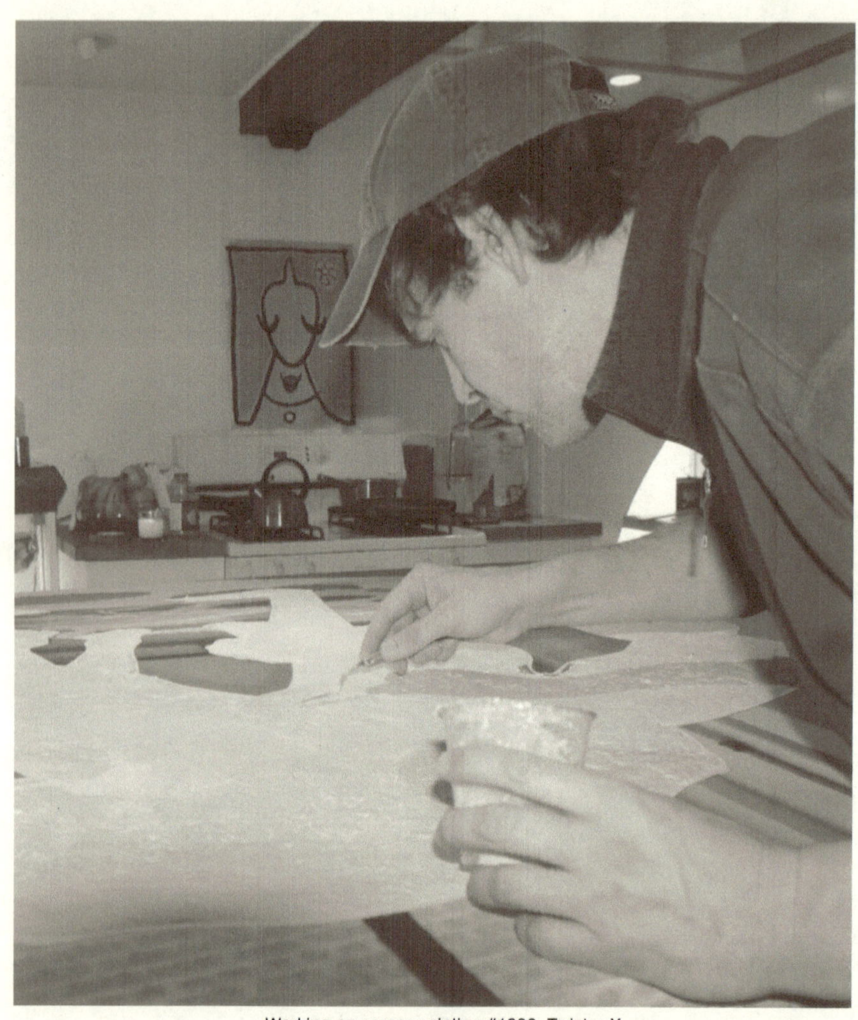

Working on career painting #1000, Twister X.

January 1 Saturday

I woke into a New Year at 6 am and went back to work on my 1000th painting.

Making art has been my only job since graduating from college, and now I've got my first 1000, a painting a week for 20 years.

In the first week of January I think about having survived another year by the old art sword. I am grateful for my lot in life and I hope this year will see me through as a full-time artist again. I never allowed any other career into the picture, never considered making money another way. You do something right out of the gate and suddenly you are years down the road doing that same thing, so it was art for me after my 19 year-old coming of age story *Baloney Express*.

I have to write an honest entry for the next 364 days to make this book work. If I candy-coat or glorify anything I will suck, which is why I'm not good at these two bullshit things. I lead with my self-effacing humor for better or worse, which comes in handy when you're getting your ass kicked 365 days a year in the art game, so we'll see how the year unfolds.

January 2 Sunday

Sundays are good studio days, particularly on the crest of large painting sales that capped December, which gives me a little room to stretch the limbs and freak out on a new project. I'm strongest when my mind can float for a spell, unburdened by financial pressures that can sap the most resilient spirits.

My life is pretty simple by design so my art can be rangy and complex. I navigate the choppy waters that come with the territory. I do the good work, I try to let any oncoming negative energy slide off my back, I do my best to stay in the light.

The artist often ruminates on what has not been made, what has not been achieved, what has yet to be accomplished. The world can always be new, renewed, rekindled, the creative spark can be around any corner, like my new painting, which has a sculptural component I am mesmerized by. I get to play with monochromatic texture like a kid in a sandbox this week.

January 3 Monday

Today a friend died too young. She has a son who now has a house filled with his mother's belongings, which include three of my paintings. One of these paintings in particular, a nautical nocturne, struck a chord with my audience, which found me new collectors years ago.

Death rains down around the living through life and we have to make peace with it. Becoming friends with death was one of the hardest things I ever learned how to do, but it makes living easier, if there is such a thing. Today I will make art with my friend in mind, thinking of her grieving family.

My collectors keep me alive and making things, so they are very important. I will miss your good energy Mimi.

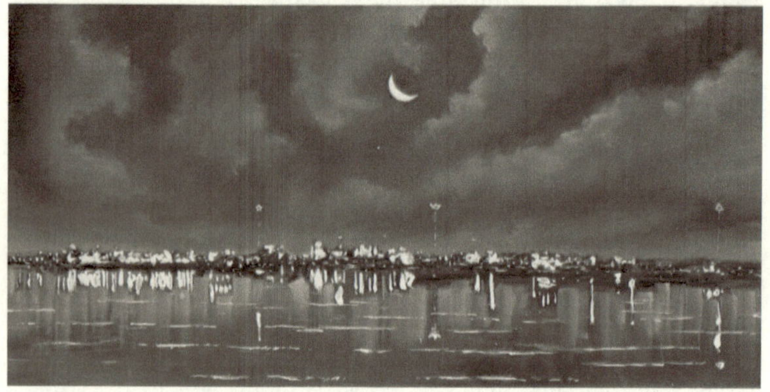

Rowayton New Year, oil on canvas, 12 x 24 inches, 2000, Private Collection.

January 4 Tuesday

Often times artists sound like they are speaking Alien to no one in particular, unless they find another artist who speaks the same dialect in the vicinity, after which point these two can speak Alien amongst themselves for the rest of the evening without having to translate to anyone.

January 5 Wednesday

Recently I came upon a huge aluminum sign next to the dumpster of an industrial building my friend Pam runs her business out of, who mentioned that the landlord would be happy to see his old, rusted sign disappear.

I took the aluminum over, flapping like a sail as it was longer than my jeep, to a local metal place, they cut it almost in half and sanded the edges. My friend Steve adhered wooden frames to the aluminum with a two-part epoxy. I prepared images that will be printed on vinyl adhesive, and this vinyl will be applied to the front of the aluminum panels. I will sculpt figures and paint on top of the vinyl.

I've only done one small version of this experiment, which is how it usually goes. You try a prototype, learn from your mistakes, then figure out a way to make the next ones smarter, larger, more powerful.

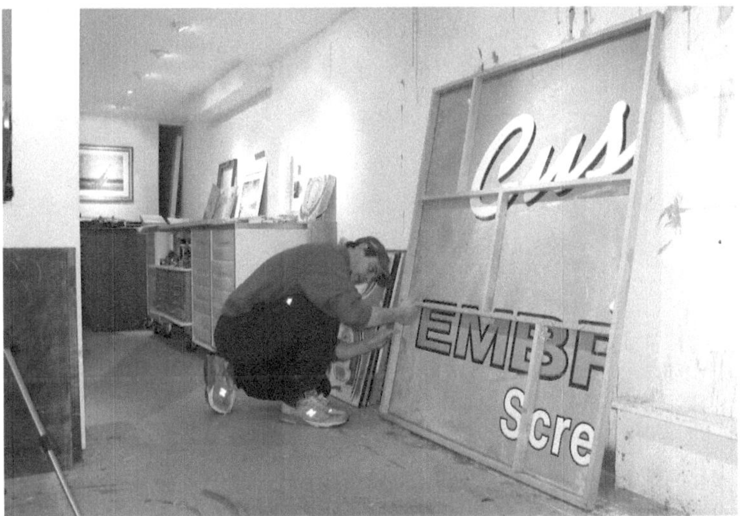

Prepping wooden-backed aluminum Twister #1000 support

January 6 Thursday

The Twister photograph on vinyl came in today. I adhered the vinyl to the 48x60 inch aluminum panel, which took several hours. I wrapped the vinyl around the wooden edges and made the corners as clean as possible. I should have had an extra set of hands and I should have softened the edges of the aluminum better. All in all I did a good job for my first large photograph-printed adhesive vinyl.

January 7 Friday

Half the fun of running my own little ship is research and development. I spent the day learning about and making paper maché. I will be using this medium to sculpt my Twister figures, so I found a woman who posted some comprehensive videos on the best maché she has developed over decades in the field. I have learned that I don't know anything, so I will take lessons from a wiser person when it comes to a new process.

I picked up supplies, made maché and got into a rhythm with the material as I shaped rough figures in my new painting. The aluminum was flat on the kitchen island I made with casters on it to roll around, which comes in handy. I spent the day walking around the work, applying maché with a palette knife. The palette knife was too big so I snipped it with metal snippers into shape and filed the rough metal down to work best with this new paper maché I've never worked with before.

Days like today are free and liberating.

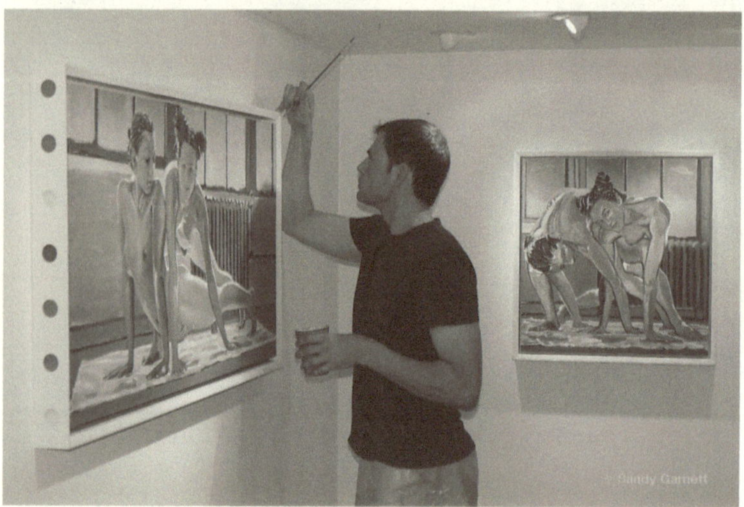

Painting routed Twister frames

January 8 Saturday

Today was my birthday. I spent the whole day making maché and sculpting figures in a state of blissful creativity.

I have a gallerist who wants some of these larger works. He wanted them last spring but they didn't come along fast enough. I was thinking that if he liked this series then maybe he could take some of the ten Twister paintings I already have, but he liked the new reliefs and wanted some large paintings. I was moving in this direction, but without a solo show offer or immediate collectors, the art had to come out of me organically.

In the evening I went for a warm, low-key birthday dinner

with my family. It was nice to get out of the studio for a couple hours. I am hook, line, and sinkered into this new Twister work, obsessed with the process, so while we sat, ate and laughed in family candlelight my mind drifted back to the surface.

January 9 Sunday

I spent another euphoric day sculpting my Twister work, movies running in the background as I mixed new batches of maché and built up the reliefs. The feeling of sculpting, material in my hands, raising these figures off the aluminum, off the photograph, felt otherworldly, which is what makes them unique. I have had this image, this art in my head for over a year, so the release of flow was like a shot of adrenalin, like a physical high, this sensation that all artists and creatives are after all the time, to be under the powerful influence of creativity.

I was early to bed and rise all weekend. My body needs to be worked out, but aside from this I continue to eat and sleep well. I need to return to the gym, which I let go of last year because of a right knee injury from sailing. I recommend that people do not fall through the bow hatch of any boat on a full sprint and hairline fracture their femurs.

January 10 Monday

Today I worked on the Twister relief, which is taking form, and I painted a smallish Garnett Girl. Painting in short bursts is a way to balance more complex portraits, Reconstruction series narratives, Fingerprint Portraits, moving between genres, then between loose pictures and tight pictures. A painting comes together by moving in and out, looking at a painting in every light, from far away and from up close. It is the micro-macro vision which helps me to weave paintings together, as often a painting looks different from three feet or 11 feet. There are plenty of paintings that look great at 15 feet which look like unfinished sketches at three feet. When I sign a painting I want the picture to be solid, stable in most lights and from most sight lines.

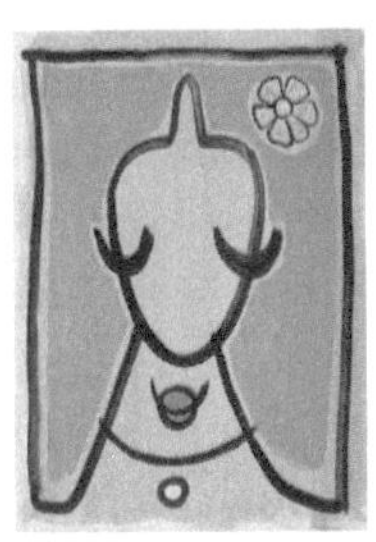

I have identical setups at each easel station on three studio floors. I use the same metal easel, the same rolling chair, I use a glass palette that sits on a swing arm, I have my oils on the left in a rolling cabinet and my acrylics on the right. The top drawer always has brushes, razor blades, tools, hanging hardware. The second drawer always has the paints. The third drawer is large and houses larger bottles, sprays, stretcher wedges, extension cords, paper towels, mediums. Having the same setup at every painting station allows me to move conceptually and visually between the easels to change things up if I need to refocus on a painting problem. Each easel has a different vibration to it as a result of the space it occupies and the light that easel receives. My upstairs easel is a good finishing and contemplation easel, the middle level easel is a good workhorse easel, and the basement easel is good for making a mess, or for working long hours on, or for signing a painting, when the energy is high and blood is in the water, which is how the air tastes when I'm circling the finish on a painting.

January 11 Tuesday

One of the best things about a home studio is that I wake up and I'm five paces from my computer, my music studio, my easel, my drawing table. This is one of those weeks when I will likely hang around the campfire, leaving the studio rarely. I am not a shut-in, but I am a workhorse and my best work is done in the comfort, peace, and privacy of my two studios. I chose this place because it is quiet, it is one minute to the two interstates that run down to New York City, a 45 minute drive to Houston Street on a good day. I have enough room, the prices to purchase were reasonable for the market, excellent food is right down the street, I am close to family, friends, and within a 60 mile radius of probably 50% of my collectors. I have collectors in maybe 35 states and ten countries who reach out to me, check in with me, buy work from afar, so the key thing for an artist who has built a professional career is to have the right space he can grow into for years. I know artists who move around a lot and this is a hard way to go. Sometimes artists move out of necessity, and sometimes they move because they can't stay put. I have learned that if one is moving things around establishing new space all the time one is not making as much studio art.

The same thing goes for a heavy social schedule. I have a lot of people in my life, and I would love to see them more, get out more, socialize more, see more art and theater and film, travel more. The more I am out of my studio the more opportunities can present themselves, but the opportunity cost of being out of the studio is running my body down and not making as much art as possible.

January 12 Wednesday

Today I purred away on several canvases, wandering from one easel to the next, to my drawing table, to my Twister relief. As I did not leave my studio I painted in my boxers all day.

I was up at 6 am and worked until 11 pm at a leisurely clip, deep in focus on various levels with multiple projects. This is my idea of a very productive day; tilling the land, a gardening of sorts, in the zone, ideas and visions and colors and compositions and arithmetic and paint and music and words flowing through the mind. There is power in this meditation, a rejuvenation of spirit. I sit quietly, I listen to my heart and to the wind, I open my eyes, hear the sounds and see the images drifting in, I am doing the work I was put here to do. Sometimes this is my greatest peace, tapping into something eternal, a space that no energy can take from me, a place all my own. In this place I can produce artifacts that are physical manifestations of these energies, objects that people want to live with, are inspired by. In this way art can be magic, a wellspring of goodness and an affirmation of life.

January 13 Thursday

I had another fluid painting day, moving between the easels. If only my studio flowed like this all the time. When I have cushions like this my body repairs itself, my spirit roams and grows, I meditate on the right things, I relax into the art. When the studio is flowing I am juggling feathers instead of lead weights, a much more frantic business. When times are tumultuous and I am seeking the next answer to sustain my studio, I know from experience that more peaceful time is ahead of me at some point in the future.

January 14 Friday

I am getting close with several paintings that have been hanging around for so long they have grown into stubborn creatures which bristle at the notion of leaving my studio for the walls of collectors.

January 15 Saturday

I opened a Tupperware container of paper maché to see that

it had turned colors that did not appeal to my senses. I thought the maché would be fine as long as it was sealed. Either the seal was not true or the maché just turns from a nice natural color to green if you don't use it fast enough.

While making another batch of maché I burned out the cheap mixer, so I had to go out for another one. This maché is an odd and original recipe; wood glue, toilet paper, drywall compound, linseed oil, flour, olive oil, tools to mix these things up with, containers to keep it in, palette knives to spread it with. It's a good thing I have been working at my kitchen island on this project, as I feel like a chef making this stuff. I played movies and music into the evening, tripping out to the rough shapes and reliefs of these two ladies I am sculpting. This one might take a week to finish, or maybe two years, but I like what I have and I've never really seen anything like it.

January 16 Sunday

With the exception of a jaunt over to see my niece and nephew this morning I stayed on the Twister relief. There is nothing like waking up at 6 am on a Sunday morning, springing out of bed and going right to the art with coffee in hand. I am usually up with or before the sun, always have been since college. A lot of my artist friends berated me early on for either working too hard or getting up too early, but I don't have many friends who are full-time professional artists twenty years later.

January 17 Monday

I returned to office duties, which I shuffle aside when I'm in the pocket of creativity. It is important for a working artist to check into the office element of his studio on a regular basis.

It's funny how people react to the art rap. I spoke recently with a new acquaintance who wondered aloud how I make art for a living. She floated the question several ways and I finally responded that I've sold roughly 1.5 million dollars in art to build my studios over the years, which stood her at attention. That's a small number for a lot of people, but it's enough for a non-creative to imagine surviving on.

The bottom line is that I really do this for a living. There is no secret fund keeping me alive. I eat what I kill, ever since college, every penny of the way. Whenever I remember this a smile rolls over my face and I know I can make it another month, another season, another year. Art survival 101.

January 18 Tuesday

Today I forced the call on a portrait that has been lingering in my studio for months which bore witness to my solitary journey on the easel during a tough passage. It's odd that a painting can grow roots to the point at which the artist does not want to let a painting go, but it happens. This is one of the hardest things to do, to release a work that is strong and has attached itself to the studio for one reason or another.

I am generally good at adhering to the rule of completing a commission on time, keeping the painting fluid, and getting it out of my world so it does not grow tentacles around my easel. They have to be right, but this is obvious as if they were not right for decades I would not have a collector base to begin with. If an artist ever forgets that the work needs to be right all the time he loses himself and becomes another thing, which happens out there in the creative wilderness.

January 19 Wednesday

I delivered the painting today and my new collector was very moved. There is nothing like a painting delivery. Lifetime trust is forged when the nail is hit on the head, when you see the surprise and warmth overcome a new acquaintance who has been wondering what you will be producing, nervously waiting, as commissioned art goes. The delivery is made, the painting is off the easel and into history, the artist's load lightened and inspired to climb the next mountain. Delivering work is always thrilling and brings with it a renewal of sorts.

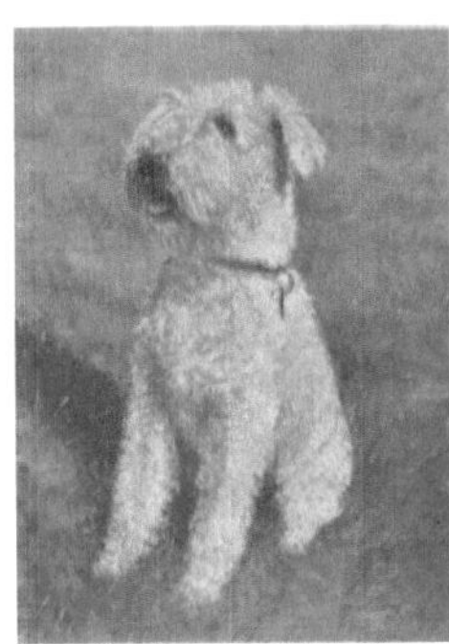

Zoe, oil on canvas, 24x18, 2011

January 20 Thursday

I got a call this morning from a new potential collector who made my day. Often times support for an artist comes out of the ether, when the work is right, when art has been delivered successfully, when the energy is right. This woman chanced upon a piece of art at a friend's home, then she spent an hour on my website. She wants to see more work, what inspires me, what makes me tick, so she is coming by my studio tomorrow.

There is something important about hanging around in one's profession long enough. Like my successful friend Alex says, half the deal is just showing up every day. You build your networks and they are overlapping circles over time. I never know who is on the other side of the phone when the calls come in out of the blue.

I remember when there were always cobwebs on my phone and crickets in the studio. The crickets and cobwebs come and go, but these days I also get calls out of nowhere from collectors I never knew I had who swoop in and buy work. Calls like this are reassuring to the creative survivalist.

January 21 Friday

My new collector Anne came by and bought a work I painted ten years ago, a painting that I have always enjoyed but that has not seen the light of day in many years. My inventory racks contain hundreds of paintings and sculptures, so it is hard to pull them all out in one studio visit. This is why I need to put that inventory book together.

I had no idea yesterday that I would make a new friend and collector today. I have to make a floater frame for this painting so I called my friend Steve with dimensions, who helps with frames and wood projects when I've got other things on my plate.

It's good to be an artist appreciated. We spend so many thankless moments, months, years in isolation, trying to solve the world's problems, often forgetting the teeming ocean of humanity around us in our deep meditation or survival phases.

January 22 Saturday

I am always prepared to hang a painting when delivering if a collector has a wall in mind. I always take a camera when delivering art, because installation photographs are valuable. I have sold over six hundred paintings in my career, very few of which I ever see after the fact. It is important for me to photograph every image that lives in my studio. If an artist does not photograph a painting or piece of art before it leaves his studio he is doing a disservice to his career.

January 23 Sunday

Every single one of the first 1000 paintings in my career has a catalogue number on the back of it. I built an inventory database that I update every season, or when a painting leaves the studio. I have a ritual when a painting completes itself. I take it down to my basement studio, photograph it on the shooting wall, then I wire it and catalogue it, entering this data into the database. I will color correct the photographic reference of the painting while it's in my studio, then I'll dump the image into my master archive in various formats. The archive is the link to an artist's past, present and future. If nobody is telling or selling his story it is up to the artist to record his own history until people start looking.

January 24 Monday

This morning I pulled off an acrylic still life based on a painting I made a long time ago. I have a photo reference of the painting so I made a softer version, which satisfied my creative juices while offering spec work for a gallerist who is trying to find the answer for the walls of a collector.

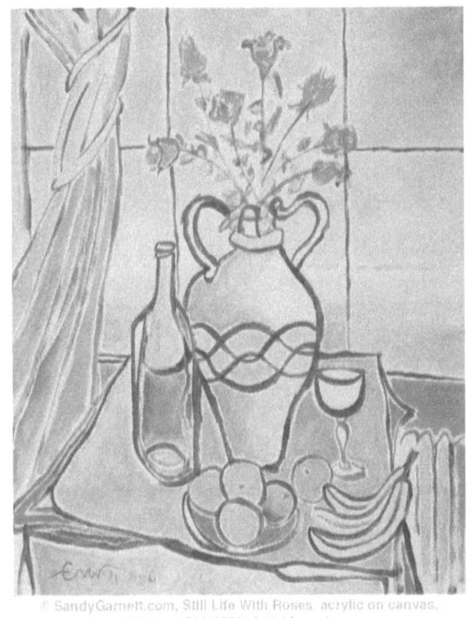
© SandyGarnett.com, Still Life With Roses, acrylic on canvas, 2011, cat 20111005, Artist Inventory.

In the afternoon I worked on my Twister relief, which is getting chunky and dimensional. Early evening my new collector called to tell me she read my book *Baloney Express* on the weekend and wants to give it to three people. She said that she could see my coming-of-age story from three perspectives, that the book is excellent and inspiring. My new collector Anne brightened my day as friends and collectors often do.

January 25 Tuesday

An artist's office is where his heartbeat lies; his collectors, his archive, his website, his contact with the outside world. A professional artist knows these things are all important to keep tabs on. A day spent clearing the office is a day well spent, worth it's weight in peace of mind. It's best for me to clear my office once a week. A clean office is always ready for a good workout, ready for any action or inspiration, ready to put out a fire or respond to a new opportunity.

January 26 Wednesday

I have two paintings in my sights that have been tempting me for 3 years and 1 year respectively, both with active buyers who want to see finished work. These are my insurance policies or maybe gateways into another way of seeing.

Cracking an abandoned, unfinished painting is a hard target. You hit it and you keep skipping off the surface, the painting telling you where else to place your energies. The experienced artist hones in, gives the painting respect, and the painting opens up for the artist again. This is a dance that can tango for months or years. I'm sitting with these two sweet pictures that need some love and I will bring it. I'd like to sign these paintings this week, but only if I find the right energy within.

When a painting opens up again, the sensation is like the opening of a flower, like a key is turned, walking through the door into a space that was left unfinished for the moment of re-entry. This sensation inspires not only the completion of the painting puzzle at hand but new projects, new paintings, new creative life.

January 27 Thursday

Time management is crucial to the professional fine artist. The solo artist, running his own studio, has to pick and choose his battles with a certain amount of caution and clarity. As the years add up, the inventory grows, the studio gets deeper, time management becomes all the more important. A fine art studio has many nooks and crannies to explore when one is not creating, spaces and ideas to hide in when weak or afraid, to bask in when successful. It is important to maintain a clean rudder and manage one's studio through the sea of time that one sails.

My goal this morning was to itemize bills and work on two canvases, but instead I built an obscure section of my website as I have a collector who might subsidize this work eventually. Sometimes I go with my gut feeling, forecasting correctly while taking my lumps in the present.

January 28 Friday

When I am in a head space, seeing and feeling a certain way, my inclination is to turn the tables. Part of this practice, let's say by moving between my Reconstruction paintings and traditional works, is to build bridges between these distinct ways of seeing while at the same time experiencing their unique emotive characteristics. Only by leaving one way of seeing or being do I fully appreciate the distinguishing features as I miss them, or as I find pieces and parts of them in another aesthetic field. This gets to the heart of my argument that I exist in the era of Reconstructionism (at least from an art historical perspective). This era is about building bridges between the genres, now that most of the artistic alphabet has been uncovered. Each genre is a letter that has been pulled from the sand on an archaeological dig. Now we have an alphabet. Artists combine letters to make words and stories, the strongest of which capture the zeitgeist of the era during which these art statements are created.

As art is about finding new ways to see I don't understand most creators in this Reconstructionist time who spend their lives in one way of seeing. There are exceptions, but I am not here on this planet to simply make a market as 'the guy who makes Fingerprint Portraits.' Building and reinforcing artist brands with repetition is one of the great paradoxes of the high art market structure, when the apex of creativity is to find new ways of seeing.

January 29 Saturday

Although two paintings were thumbing their noses at me, it was Saturday in New England and there was more snow than I can remember, so it was time to leave my hibernation lair and play with my nephew Jackson.

I got over there and we started piling a huge mound of snow. You start chipping away and in time you have a substantial piece of work. We ended up creating an igloo that was about 12 feet long. Jackson requested plumbing for the bathroom and a chimney for the fireplace we are to install tomorrow.

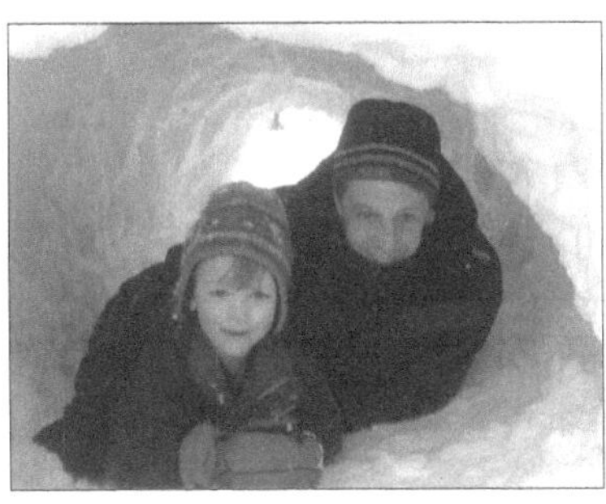

January 30 Sunday

When you go over a decent work with the wrong energy it can be like a yard sale when skiing, sliding down the slope fifty yards. You have to spend half an hour walking back up the slope, finding your crap and this can easily turn into days of work for the artist who wipes out on a painting.

Sometimes being a wise artist is about not doing anything. Today I left my ongoing work alone and did some sketchbook drawing, some writing, I slapped paint on a blank canvas, and I did not do any damage to existing projects.

January 31 Monday

I called my new collector Anne and told her I don't think

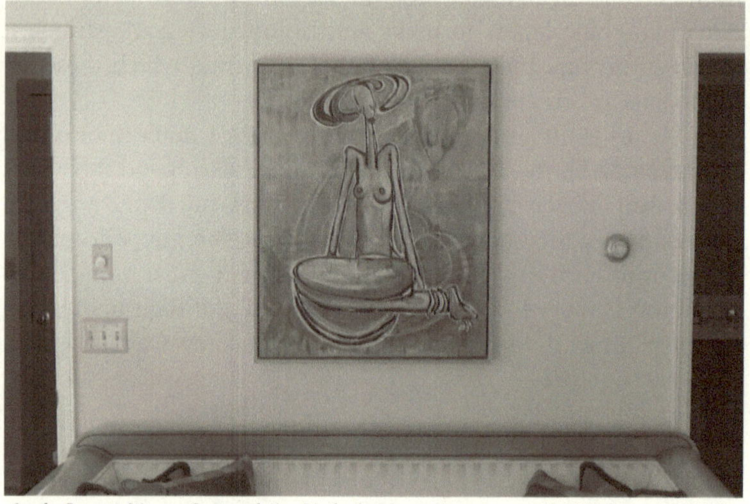

Sandy Garnett, Woman Contemplating Motherhood, acrylic on canvas, 36x30 inches, cat20000515.

her frame should be painted, that the raw wood looks nice. We set a time and I took the painting over. I'm glad I had not made more work for myself by painting the frame black, as the natural wood frame worked with the room, Anne was very happy and the delivery was successful.

When in doubt, or if I have a thought my collectors will appreciate, I reach out to them. If I'm not sure what they mean I will ask them to clarify exactly what it is they are trying to express. Sometimes their opinions change and they forget one opinion from the next, but as I am a detail-oriented fine artist and small business owner I usually attract like-minded people who elaborate until concepts, plans and projects are clear with both parties.

Miscommunication is the artist's enemy when working with collectors, or when working with anyone for that matter.

February 1 Tuesday

I saw music tonight, downtown energy of New York pulsing through, a city at the doorstep of my studio. I am usually in town (NYC) several times a month if not once a week, but the anemic economy has kept me more studio-bound lately. Sometimes I wonder what my life would be like had I moved into town straight from college.

My earliest memories are from my grandparents' apartment at 420 E. 79th. All of my maternal relatives grew up 10 blocks from one another. New York beats in my heart, and yet sometimes it feels far away, suggesting in me a competitive struggle during moments of weakness.

'Live simply and be prolific' is the mantra that has allowed me to live every day of my adult life as a professional fine artist. A wise old friend and collector told me years ago that I should drop everything and move into the city. Recently he altered his opinion, which surprised me, as insightful steadfastness is one of his strongest qualities.

My friend wrote, "You have designed a life that allows you to make what you want, you are self-sufficient, beholden to no one. Happy is the man who finds refuge in himself."

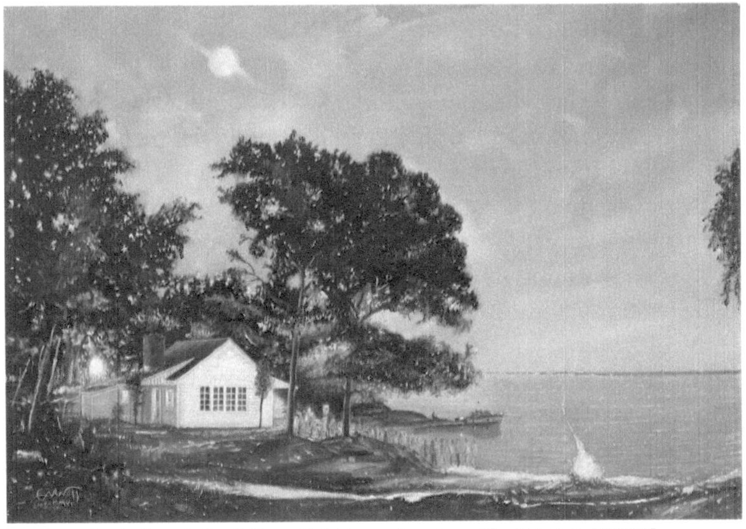

Sandy Garnett, Beach House Full Moon, oil on linen, 24 x 36 inches, 20080907.

February 2 Wednesday

I fell back into a painting that has been tempting me for several years. The painting laughed at me, I gave it respect, one tiny stroke, one sediment of paint and emotion at a time. It took the day, milling around in my studio, arguing with this painting, wondering why it was slow to open for me. But there it came. This is a traditional painting of sorts, a moody moonlight picture, a love letter to my youth. Part of the finish is letting it go, as the painting has been hanging around for a long time and successful enough to find a collector. I didn't want to finish this painting as I don't want the painting to leave my studio.

I put the canvas on the easel in the morning, made sense of the light, lines, color, vibration, my history of this old favorite haunt of mine, I gave some credence to the special place that I was painting, and hours turned morning into night.

February 3 Thursday

Getting back in shape is a good thing as paintings take physical energy from the creator. My body is thinner, leaner and wants to pick a fight with paintings that lie around the studio. I danced with a painting yesterday and it all worked out, other paintings perking up to vie for my attention. Unfinished paintings line my world, waiting their turn to light up the next week, the next month, the next inspiration.

February 4 Friday

I came very close to signing another painting that has been lying around the studio, which feels like setting the record straight with an old friend. At first the surface is glass and I have to chip away slowly, then the casing melts and I am back in, doing what I will with the space, the painting guiding the way.

The warming up and finishing of a painting is an acquired skill which propels the completion of other works in similar stages of incompletion, so these passages can be extremely productive. When this finishing energy visits I try to keep the top spinning as long as possible, as sometimes I sign five or ten paintings that have been waiting in the wings forever.

February 5 Saturday

The beauty of a properly designed, broken in studio is that it contains all of the work stations and tools I need as my creativity moves from one project to the next. I have four work stations in the upstairs loft, three on the ground floor and five in the basement space. It is good to have makeshift workspaces that can be moved on casters or put away as one's spatial requirements shift with each new piece of art. My family has always made fun of me for putting casters on all the furniture I design and construct, but it is very convenient to move my rolling kitchen island into the center of the loft space for a model to pose on for a new painting.

February 6 Sunday

This morning I sent out an email update and spent the rest of the day corresponding with my family, friends and collectors. This is a valuable way to stay in touch every month or two, it is cost effective, it leads people to the website, and reminds people about paintings or projects they have in mind. It is surprising how artists can let names, emails, phone numbers and opportunities go. I have always been very diligent about taking names, addresses, emails, before everyone had the luxury of social networks. Social networks are different from websites. A lot of artists do not tend to or grow their websites. This is bad business like not shooting one's art before it is sold is bad business.

For Americans it was the Super Bowl tonight, the apex of American Football. The Packers beat the Steelers convincingly.

February 7 Monday

I remember as a child always having this desire to make books. I would take construction paper or these glossy pages I had at my grandparents' apartment, fold them over and staple them together. Then I would figure out a theme and illustrate each page until my attention would drift into another project.

My mother was really good at keeping my childhood art and engaging the little artist in me. These old book samples come to mind as I hold my first hardcover book *Baloney Express* in my hands, which arrived today in the mail.

February 8 Tuesday

I solidified a Fingerprint Portrait commission in the city today. I will be painting seven Fingerprint Portraits on a two canvas diptych, four on one panel which represents the son's family and three on another panel which represents the daughter's family. The paintings will hang together until they move on to two households as individual pieces of work when that time comes. The commission will be a 70th birthday gift for the family's patriarch.

I have been in touch with the daughter and mother for several months about this project, who I met in Sari's midtown office today. They got my name and website from a fellow collector and designer who said this family might be calling. He mentioned this three years ago. Thank you Danny.

I've had people on my list for five years or longer before they were ready to collect. It is important to keep people updated passively, nurturing these relationships with respect, interesting updates and good humor.

One's contact list should be protected like the most important art object in the studio.

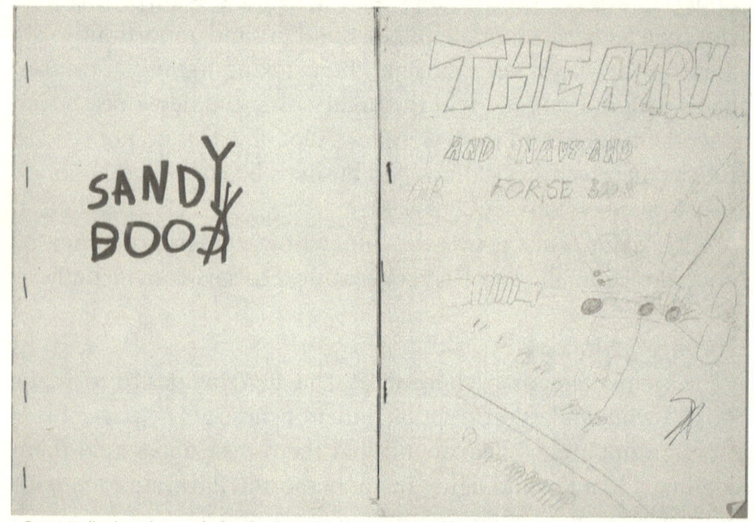

Garnett displayed an early fascination with the creation of books. © sandygarnett.com

February 9 Wednesday

I was in the city late last night with friends after meeting with my new collectors, so I am running on less than four hours of sleep, which is not optimal for the artist running his studio.

I am resuming racquetball with my brother Matthew, so I am readjusting to the 5 am schedule. This changes the rhythm of the studio, a healthy outlet in the dead of winter. I like to change up my schedule as it alters my creative patterns.

My art is most consistent and cleanest with a crisp mind, a healthy body, a rested spirit and a strong heart.

February 10 Thursday

It feels good to wake up at 5 am and smash the little blue ball around with my brother at 6 am.

Today I tinkered with the moonlight painting. I reached out to my interested collectors, who responded that they are traveling in California and will check in next week.

It is better to keep an oil painting open through the finish whenever possible. Wet paint is like keeping an idea fresh. When I have a good rap with a collector and receive a deposit I try to lay down paint immediately. If I hit the painting in flashes several times a day the work stays open and often finishes itself quickly, which offers a euphoric sensation that propels my studio.

When I chip away diligently at paintings, they feel like healthy daily hikes, at the end of which the mountain lays squarely under my feet. I have time to look out upon the surrounding vistas rather than scrambling up the last legs to make a frantic deadline.

Energy management is a skill and art form all its own.

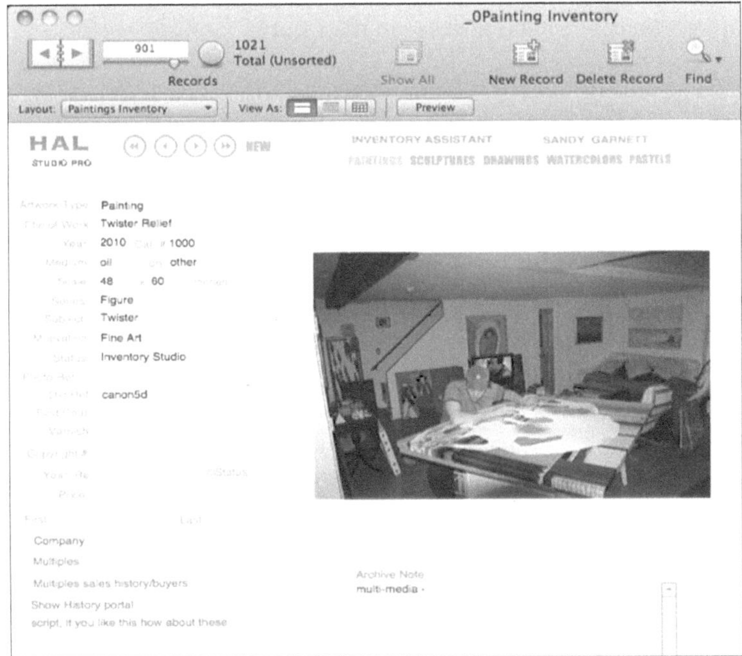

February 11 Friday

The best way that I have found to title a file of art for the archive is as follows: 20100949RAngelGirl10hRGB.tif.

This painting was made in 2010, it is catalogue number 0949 (career painting #), the R represents Reconstruction Series, Angel Girl is the title (or an abbreviation of title such that the artist can identify the image), 10 is the size of work (10 inches horizontal), RGB is the file type, tiff is the file extension type.

The beauty of this label system is that files fall chronologically into every 'body of work' folder. For a master archive each folder represents a painting, and within each painting folder are different file versions depending upon how that image might be used (print, web, etc).

This Garnett art catalogue system also works with press shots and just about anything that you are always looking for on your computer. For press shots of a recent show I will have a folder that is labeled 20090123PRSoloKRAll. This reads 2009, PR for press shot, Solo show, 0123 means 23 January, KR is my friend Kevin Robinson, who shot the folder of images, and All is an internal reference as I had several folders from that particular event.

We humans spend approximately 7 years of our lives looking for lost items. An image that is labeled properly right away will always be easy to find and use in the future.

February 12 Saturday

I was at an Oscar party last Saturday and bumped into my blue crayon drawing of Klimt with his cat, an oldie but a goodie that I had forgotten about. There is nothing like seeing my paintings and drawings on the walls that my friends live with. These moments remind me why there are so many good reasons to be an artist.

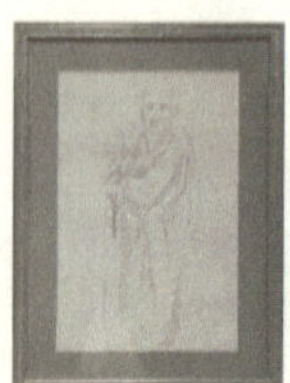

February13 Sunday

I spent ten hours on my inventory book today. I found some pictures I forgot I had made and I shot some paintings that I have never photographed, which is like revisiting old friends. When an artist's inventory is contextualized graphically the result can be very rewarding and good for business.

Archiving properly requires a lot of tools. I have a database program (Filemaker), Adobe Photoshop, a layout program (I use Adobe InDesign), lights and a camera. It takes awhile to learn how to shoot and color correct art the right way. When I started my career I spent a lot of money having work shot and color corrected. Now I can shoot my work, color correct, archive, and make prints in the comfort of my own studio, which took time to evolve but is smart in the long run.

February 14 Monday

Balance is the art of incorporating resistance or discordant energies into a realistic, sometimes harmonious, sustainable methodology. Happy Valentine's Day.

February 15 Tuesday

I received a deposit for the new Fingerprint Portrait commission. If I can sell another painting this week my heartbeat will return to peaceful meditation mode, where I am often at my best creatively.

Yesterday I finished the self-portraits and figures sections of my inventory book. Today I move on to the Reconstructions. Of the 247 Reconstruction Series paintings I have made, the database tells me I have 93 in my inventory, so this is a significant chunk of the 261 paintings currently in my inventory. Most of these paintings are shot, but I may have to shoot 25 or so today.

February 16 Wednesday

I have spent the past forty studio hours since Saturday shooting and cataloging inventory paintings. I am burning time up on this project but it's a big one to check off the list. I have two paintings to sign by Friday, so I am on edge, squeezing another thing in under the wire, which propels me to new levels. When I recognize this vibration I ramp up to meet the challenge, which is an important gear to have and hone, a thrill unto itself.

February 17 Thursday

Walter called last night to tell me that a friend we shark fish with died of a heroin overdose, a good guy with a wife and four kids between the ages of 12 and 1. Cam was the last guy on the planet I would have pegged for risky drugs.

This morning I'm messed up, angry, sad, and my heart is bleeding for Cam, his wife and kids, his world.

When I'm depressed because life smacks me in the head with a needless death I always return to the beauty of life, whatever the bad news. I am here for a short time and I might as well get the most out of it. Then I start thinking about how I have lived pretty much regret-free since freshman year of college, making art for myself and for my collectors ever since. It's odd how the death of a friend or acquaintance prompts one's own self-reflection about mortality, but I suppose this is the natural cycle.

I choose to live and rip the art up while my heart's beating.

February 18 Friday

I went over to support Danny, who was at the hospital with his best friend's wife when Cam passed away. I walked into Danny's fish store and he introduced me to Cam's brother Jack, who flew in from Indiana. Death was in Jack's eyes. I met his daughter, or I thought it was his daughter, but in fact it was Cam's daughter, this daughter who had lost her father, this daughter with a hole in her heart that will never be filled. I tried to cheer them up with silly humor, and eventually they moved on. I spent some time with Danny, then we went over to Walter's house for some old friend time.

I am awash in sadness for the family and friends of Cam. There is a service tomorrow so my weekend will be about mourning a senseless death that is devastating many people. I am only on the periphery but the shock waves are intense.

Only time, deep love, humor and a healthy outlook on the beauty of life begins to ice over the holes in one's heart, which are quick to open again at any moment the rest of one's life. Learning to live with deep wounds and scars, to live and to love despite the pain, this is graceful living. From grief can spring grace.

February 19 Saturday

Today was one of the saddest days I can remember. The service was in the form of a wake at a funeral home. Cam's wife and four children were there along with his parents, siblings, his mother-in-law, his wife's family, his friends, all pulverized by this shocking loss. I went over with Walter, and although he has been driving an ambulance as a paramedic for twenty years, he also said that it was one of the saddest days he had ever experienced.

After the service Walter and I paced around like angry lions, not knowing what to do with ourselves. In the evening we reconvened for dinner with our old group of friends, which was good for the spirit. There is nothing like close friends and family. I go into my cave and come out with new art, visit with people, mourn, laugh, dance around, shake it off, repeat the cycle.

February 20 Sunday

Tonight at a bar down the street I was talking to an artist who thinks Salvador Dali is a bad painter and not a Surrealist, which means that this guy is in some imaginary competition with Dali. The painter asked what I paint and I dodged the question, so he returned to his buzzed up trip about Dali, whose technical virtuosity is inescapable.

It's tricky to answer a broad question about what I paint because I explore a number of genres, forever resisting the notion that a painter should line up twenty ducks in a row that look like one another's inverted siblings.

Navigating a fine art career is a mirror game, but as my old friend wrote in a song that makes his band a bucket of money annuity, the heart brings you back. The heart is a moving target, so art for me is about capturing some essence of truth in an assortment of visual ways that will ring timelessly. I have been training my muscles to move fluidly between multiple genres as a matter of discipline and argument, so genres to me are like alphabet letters or tools or clothing, secondary to the heart and soul of the artist.

February 21 Monday

When the wolves come around in survival mode I eat sardines and crackers, I wake up early and work late, I restrict all spending and start to stretch, I tell anyone who asks that things are good while seeing as few people as possible who might sense my growing anxiety.

I need to sell a lot of art every month to make this career work, and sometimes people aren't buying. In these times I focus on good energy to combat the danger to my studio, I try to take it easy while reminding myself that it will all work out like it always has. It is confusing when I am doing some of my best work while riding the line, not knowing how I'm going to cover. The sensation is acute, painful and filled with adrenaline, the paradox stiff and unwavering to live with that rarely softens.

My general fortitude is challenged by Cam's death, so I have to stay healthy this week; early workouts, good sleep, light diet, positive energy. I need to do some nice things for people, which always feels good while perpetuating positive vibrations, and I get to finish two more paintings, one of which may have found a home with collectors next month in the spring thaw.

February 22 Tuesday

I split racquetball games with brother Matt at our 6 am slot, then I buzzed around my work stations into the evening with well applied intent that made for a productive day at the easel.

February 23 Wednesday

I had two studio visits from collectors this morning. One collector wants my inventory catalogue to give to his friend, who has a billion dollars and supports art that he believes in. This qualifies my inventory book and brought good energy into the studio.

Today I got into a May show with a 30 x 40 inch abstract landscape that vaguely resembles a color field painting. I painted this one several months ago out of nowhere and it has generated interest. I never know what will create the next wave of attraction, so I try not to pay attention to the fleeting fancies of passers-by.

© SandyGarnett.com, Landscape Study, oil on linen, 30 x 40 inches, 2010, Collection of the Artist.

February 24 Thursday

Reading and editing one's work requires time and patience like a lot of things. Editing is about drilling down to the core all the time. As a creative professional I am editing every single day, but the experience of editing a manuscript well and ruthlessly lives in a realm all its own.

February 25 Friday

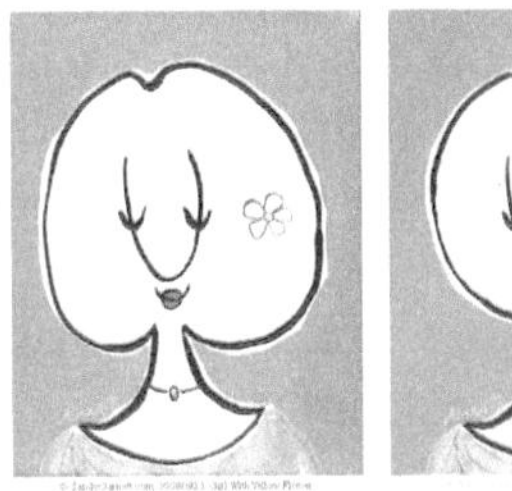

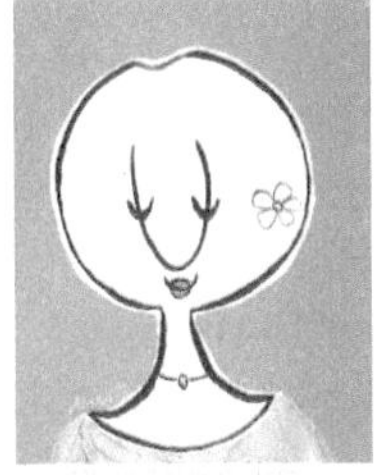

My friend came over to pick up a painting that I altered slightly as her house mate had recently opined that the subject's hairstyle looked 'like a penis,' which I found pretty hysterical.

February 26 Saturday

Artists feel like there is always time whereas non-artists feel like time is always escaping them. As a family member of athletes I appreciate this dichotomy. I enjoy running around after a ball; the rules, the time limits in some games, the boundaries, firm indicators of the 'reality' our society teaches us. Artists live half in time and half out of time, making work that does not tidily correspond with calendars, business or political systems, adrift and/or free from these anchors or anvils.

There are parallels and intersections between art and sports, so I use sports analogies all the time with my jockstrap friends, family members, and certainly when I am slacking off and need to pump myself up, put my game face on and get her done.

I played paddle tennis with a close friend today who runs money very well. He edged me out, although I didn't care as we were playing singles for the workout and we got a sweat in. We live on opposite sides of the career spectrum. His idea of success is running his fund, finding new takers, beating the index to achieve his goals while being a good father and husband along the way.

I am unmarried as I never wanted to expose another human being to this treacherous lifestyle early on, although I've fallen before and will fall again. My idea of success is the rush of a good picture, the flow of the hand meeting canvas, the generation from my soul of a spark that sends shivers down the spine of a painting, something that will move collectors long into the future.

February 27 Sunday

I stayed up too late, but sometimes in the night art abounds. I read part of a book, I watch a movie, listen to a song, I paint a picture and other things begin to emerge, things I have to put a highlighter on, things of relevance, not of me but of truth, things that will be here when I'm gone. When you chase ghosts like this you are a workhorse, a horse whisperer, you know your place and you are not looking for much else. Sure, larger success and an easier ride would be great, but who cares in the end? I am wary of glory like I am wary of fashion, things that come and go. How to be strong and record the time that I live in soulfully while spinning my brain on all the ways to make things that I have not yet seen before? For the art historical record this is not a bad play. I may get nipped in the short run but at least I'm playing the game of my own design, a game with heart, without big ego. Ego does not make a better man, although a little ego can help a humble man to survive in a pinch.

February 28 Monday

I pay for my independence by being under-known for two decades, which I second-guess when I am feeling weak. Half the galleries in New York City have shuttered since the market meltdown 3 years ago and I'm still here with 100 more paintings, a much stronger website, some published music, and newly published books to support the studio, so I don't have much to complain about.

March 1 Tuesday

I sat with my friend Ann last night who has an old soul. We talk about spiritual things interspersed with good humor and the time goes quickly. She prescribes to the notion that our souls are here this time around to learn something which requires our particular bodies, families, circumstances. I talked about the razor blade tightrope I walk on. Ann understood and said that you get so used to this edge that you start doing cartwheels on it, which is really true. Underneath my particular edge is a net of love and family that other people don't have, which makes it easier to dangle out there.

We traded thoughts, anecdotes, good books and films, laughter, these things which make long friendships, then I returned to my studio to finish an old painting. This painting has been hanging around my studio for some time now, so it was good to make a clean finish. I varnished the painting, shot, framed, wired the painting, then hung it over the couch where my collectors can see it when they visit. They've been asking about this one for a year. I will miss this painting but I will have prints. Prints are never the same thing as seeing the residue of energy on an original, but selling original paintings is how I make my way in the world, so prints are what I am left with when a painting finds its home.

March 2 Wednesday

After signing a canvas, the studio vibrates and is ready for another painting to finish. I tweaked a self-portrait and re-framed it before lunch. This one hung on my parents' living room wall with portraits of my two brothers until I got annoyed with a detail that did not bother my mother. I peeled it off their wall six months ago and fiddled around with a highlight in my eye.

In the fall my Mom was over and said, "What did you do to your lip in that painting? Something is wrong."

I had done nothing with my lip, but this is how painting changes go. I changed the highlight of my left eye and my Mom now doesn't like my lip, which I never touched. The painting was hanging peacefully for six years before I came along and made trouble. Anyway, today I went over there and luckily my Mom was out, so I slipped the painting back into place. Hopefully I won't hear anything more about how I stole their painting.

My family has seen this behavior before. I have given paintings to my brother Matthew as gifts, with a nice note on the back saying Happy Birthday I love you and all that stuff, only to steal the painting at a later date and paint over it or destroy it because the painting was bugging me. I've done the same with my brother Christian, giving him a painting then taking it back when he moved around from high school to college, out to L.A. and back. For an artist this is perfectly understandable, but imagine if my brother had given me a brand new television, then a year later he took it back and smashed it when I was on vacation because he didn't feel like that television was any good, then telling me that down the line he'd get me a better one. That's about the size of it.

There is a seascape on the den wall that I gave to my parents ten years ago. Awhile back a collector wanted something just like what I had signed over to my parents 'With All My Love' on the back of that painting. I went over for dinner and negotiated the painting back in order to sell.

"But I don't want another painting! I want that one right there!" my father said between bites of steak, pointing his fork with a potato stuck on it at the painting he had grown comfortable with, this seascape that was rightfully his.

"That thing?" I asked flippantly, motioning to the picture behind me as though it were a piece of rubbish, "That's nothing! I will paint you a better picture! Listen, I need three grand and I think I have a live one with John, who just bought those two prints."

My father considered, "Well, John's a good guy and he has one hell of a forehand... if you really have to sell that thing go ahead, but I love that painting."

My Mom enjoyed the negotiation because she didn't care. There was a boat in the middle ground of the painting that she didn't like as it was smack dab in the center of the canvas. I told her I'd fix it but I had never done so. Anyway, after dinner negotiations I took that painting away with me, but it came back when my collector bought something else.

Paintings come and go. All in the family.

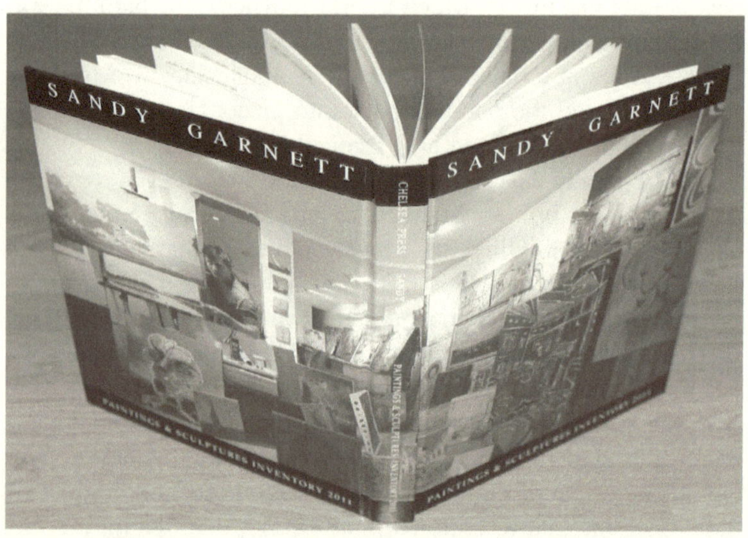

March 3 Thursday

Two weeks ago I sent out a PDF file and today I received my Inventory book in the mail, all 300 pages of full color, hardcover glory. For the first time in my career I have a book that displays the paintings and sculptures in my current inventory, another arrow in the art studio quiver. It feels good to hold a new book in my hands.

PJ dropped a check off for a CD design that I recently did which will be coming out next month. We talked about how an artist can't let his work go until it's good and done, like the painting I just finished after three years. He laughed and told me about a song on his new CD that took five years to make, which is right next to a song that took him five minutes to write and record. I know the way that goes.

March 4 Friday

I am in finishing mode, so I want to complete another painting today. I probably have 30 paintings in my studio that sit in various stages of incompletion. Finishing energy is strong and efficient when it comes, like a cook dicing vegetables pristinely at top speed for a gourmet meal. You have to fan the hot flame of finishing energy or that muse will disappear. Finishing energy warms the surfaces of unsigned canvases, so I get to dance with these paintings one last time again.

There are three major art fairs 45 minutes away in New York City this weekend and I remain on the outside of that equation. I could care less on the ego front but with a sliver of market share in auctions and the art fair circuit I'd probably be whistling Dixie and goin' to Vegas!

March 5 Saturday

Last night I went to the Bar Mitzvah of my friend Ingrid's son Mitch in town at Temple Emanu-El on 65th and 5th. My maternal family all attended St. James', six up and one over.

The Temple was beautiful, the service was spiritual, the party was festive, the dinner was delicious and very fun. We laughed and drank and danced and moved on to bars after the celebration. I gave Mitch an electric guitar that seemed to match his current aesthetic. You never know what people want in life, so you smile and do your best.

I was in town late, then drove a friend back to Hoboken for the evening. The next day we watched the St. Patrick's Day parade, which was surprisingly rowdy and cool. At ten in the morning people were walking to parties with 30-packs in each hand. My friend donated ten bucks to a firehouse charity and I got a navy baseball hat with a green 'New York' and four leaf clover stitched into the front. The view of Manhattan from the park was stunning on this day that wanted to be spring after an historic winter snowfall.

Getting out of Hoboken to the GW Bridge was a local crawl

through traffic lights with sporadic views of the West Side as the city lit up a cloudless March dusk. It seems the tunnel might have been better, then shoot up the West Side Highway, but that thought was refuted by locals, so I did what they told me to do.

I had dinner with friends in Greenwich and we wound up at a place on the top of the Avenue that had a DJ and fun, partying clientele. People were on the bar and beautiful girls danced provocatively with one another, interspersed amongst the tables throughout the candlelit place. A New Yorker friend was out for the night and said that you can't find a place like this in the city. Who knew one's heart's desire could be satiated at the top of Greenwich Avenue? I didn't, but the view was awfully nice.

March 6 Sunday

I worked on song lyrics, a small painting, and correspondence with several collectors this morning. I'm going for the finish on a painting that could sell next week if I get far enough out on that limb. Tomorrow I have a gravestone etching to do after 6 am racquetball, business taxes to organize, then I've got to set my studio up for a 5 pm meeting with a designer and her two friends.

Often there are gallerists, designers or consultants who want to work with me, which takes months or even years. This would probably be one of the largest advantages of going with a respected dealer in a major market, so long as they sold for me. I've heard good stories and bad stories. Answers are slow to emerge sometimes and I have found that it is often most efficient to exercise patience and prepare for when the right answers come to me, cross my path or fill in the correct philosophical blank, rather than chasing phantoms. The beguiling beauty of self-sufficiency remains her own ultimate seductress, particularly to those who serve her.

In the afternoon I went over to play with my nephew and hold the baby. Emma is starting to smile, laugh and coo when she is milk drunk, which is so good. I put together a variation of one of Jackson's railroad tracks on the basement carpet and I got some good pictures if I ever want to paint him at work with his trains. He is adjusting to having a sibling in his world.

March 7 Monday

Today I spoke with fellow creative Jerry, who is 85 and sharp as tacks, a real friend to talk to about making your own path. He has done a lot of things in his life as he works on his 7th studio album. He hosts a cable show that I have been on before. We lined up a television interview for April so I can plug my current projects.

Jerry moved to New York City after college and his first job was editing academic books. The first book to cross his new desk was the Philosophy book he had been tested on while at University that his college professor had written. In editing this text book that had been in print for twenty years Jerry found numerous errors and had to rewrite entire sections of the book.

This story reminds me of everyone who told me I needed a publisher who could provide an editor for the books I wanted to make, otherwise the book would never publish. It reminds me of everyone who told me I needed an MFA and a well respected gallerist or I would never make art for a living. It reminds me of people who told me I needed a record label to record my own songs, the first of which was published in an extreme skiing film. Sure, I look forward to working with gatekeepers in various industries, but they've got to decide to work with me first as I'm already doing my own thing.

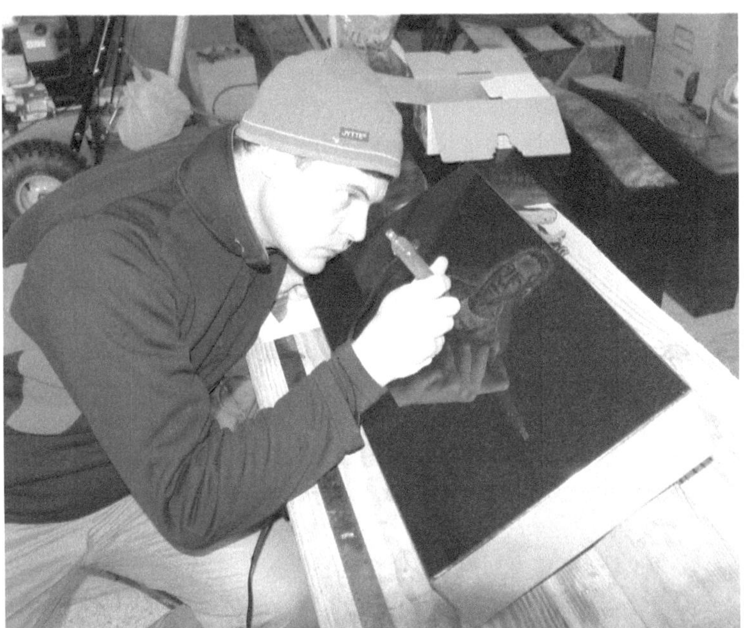

© SandyGarnett.com. Etching Forlivio Gravestone Portrait, 6 March 2011.

8 March Tuesday

An art consultant and her friends visited this morning from New York City. They are new to my career so they took my studios in while I entertained. I pulled a commission sale out of the meeting and future business with the consultant. They left at 11 am and the alleviation started to set in.

In the afternoon I etched a gravestone portrait. The etching took longer than expected but I got it done, the family was happy, and I had a chance to shoot the breeze with Don for awhile. Small business owners are their own breed; nobody understands us, and we don't understand anybody else for not running their own small businesses.

March 9 Wednesday

Achieving fluidity in an art form is a tall mountain. If one can ever get to that rarefied air the sights and sounds are mesmerizing. Making a living in one's art form is exponentially more challenging. When I started painting, making art was the hardest aspect of my art career. Now, art is the easiest thing about my profession. There are many moving parts to a working fine art studio that go into facilitating the easel time which I have designed my life around.

March 10 Thursday

I was up early to split games with Matt, then went right into the paint. Sometimes I spend a lot of time running the studio or working in other mediums and days go by without easel time. Getting back to the easel is like going to play with an old friend. I got paint on ten canvases today, which happens when I have been away from the easel.

A day at the easel is like a day at the beach, a day on vacation. People say that I should travel more and I tell them that they should subsidize my studies abroad. I have traveled a lot in the past but not lately. Creativity is like taking a trip. I mentioned recently to a friend who travels all the time for work that when I am making things, which is over half of every working day, it's like I go to Mars and come back for dinner. Art is my religion of sorts, a way of life, a way of thinking about the world, a way of commerce, a way of communing with others spiritually. People want the physical residue of an artist's meditation, and this arrangement keeps me in the paint. Art itself is the very best trip.

March 11 Friday

In the evening, to counterbalance ten hours of terribly boring Friday office work, I painted a life-size, beautiful woman with an hourglass figure and perfect, perky breasts (as my friend Janet teases), head tilted down, smiling peacefully. My contemplative nudes are some of my favorite subjects from imagination to paint and always bring lightness into the studio. I look forward to sculpting these pretty women into seven foot tall Garnett Figure bronzes with the proper patronage.

March 12 Saturday

Today I went hunting in Dover, NY, with Walter and Danny. There were only a few birds and swirling, cold winds. I didn't take a shot but I got in the spirit. I'm not much of a hunter but a lot of my friends are. When you are holding one of your best friend's guns in your hand walking through muddy fields you are not thinking about art. When you are laughing with Walter and Danny, in the backseat with hunting dogs muzzled in your lap for affection, you are not thinking about art. When you see the feathers suspended in the air of a bird falling out of the sky, you are not thinking about art. Or maybc it's all art.

Speaking of nature, I may see my friend Chris this week. He rescues exotic animals and has a facility in Stamford through his own company Animal Embassy. He's got a massive python, tarantulas, scorpions, huge turtles, chinchillas, a nasty old parrot that swears at you when you walk in the door, twenty snakes and twenty lizards, frogs. fish. That's a lot of chicken feed. He's doing a benefit for the wolf preserve in South Salem and asked me to join with my brother on Wednesday. Chris was driving around on speaker phone when he called with his new owl riding shotgun, peering out the window at other bewildered drivers. Cinematic.

March 13 Sunday

I swam with my brother and nephew this morning. Jackson is getting more aquatic, so I teach him swimming and he teaches me how to think with a new brain and a big heart.

As an artist I'm laying in wait for inspirational energies to move me into and out of projects that I keep open. Today I felt the flow of color field landscape so I plucked another painting out of the air quickly. I want surfaces around to make new work when

I am inspired, so after signing my new painting I went out and bought more canvases.

These abstracts will be a way for me to explore spatial, color field-related palettes while connecting with an audience that will support the work. Making new work is crucial, but art is voluminous and keeping one's inventory organized is like a game of chess or Tetris. If I'm not buying a canvas I'm stretching one, if a canvas is upstairs it's got to go downstairs, and if it's in my studio it's got to go to a collector's house. If I'm not making something I'm moving it around or trying to put it away. My space is good but if I really get on a ripper this year I will start to run out of room.

Sandy Garnett, Soft Landscape IV, oil on canvas, 24 x 48 inches, 2011, cat 20111016. © www.sandygarnett.com

March 14 Monday

I blasted out two more paintings today. It remains a strange concept that some paintings take ten minutes and some take five years to finish. When I have a strong painting day hope and faith in art are restored. I know I let myself go, I stepped out of the way, I got a lot of work down quickly and I'm not fussing with it. In between paintings I worked on an acoustic song to change up the vibrations. The answers have always been found in the art when I go to it properly. I serve it and it serves me.

Because my energy was strong today I am filled up, I will have a good creative week and I will attract the right answers. This is usually the hardest thing for artists to do, to forget the blinding pressure. The illusion comes and goes but the art continues to build and is a sturdy rock to stand on.

March 15 Tuesday

On my three easels I have two Fingerprint Portraits,

abstract landscapes and a Twister relief. This is a perfect example of the way I work in an assortment of genres simultaneously. In this Reconstructionist era genres and cultures are learning to communicate in ways that were heretofore unfathomable. One voice exploring so many ways of seeing invites abstract correlations. As I remain under the radar, my collectors have subsidized my wildly varying jaunts and cuts into polar opposite ways of seeing and making. A painting is a painting and the genre is secondary, as it has been in my studio for fifteen years. Where is the heartbeat in the painting? This is much more significant than the candy wrapper the painting comes in. I find it annoying that the twentieth century flattened so many powerful creators with silly rhetoric, arguments before paintings, genres before the spirit in a painting, deconstructing all art making elements out of painting just to see what else art could be. The warring of the genres was a component in arriving at our era, but this combative methodology has always struck me as archaic, juvenile, intellectual acrobatics conducted by non-artists pushing personal agendas. Artists who have fallen under the spell of mesmerizing art critics have made the cardinal mistake from the first step. The best art critics have always been artists who knew how to make things, or critics who try to follow with integrity and not lead with ego.

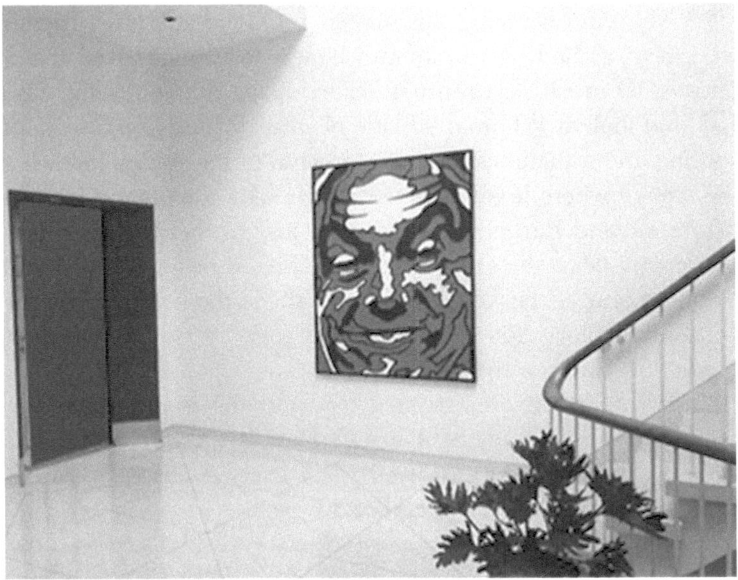

Sandy Garnett, Jack Nicholson, enamel on canvas, 66 x 54 inches, Private Collection.

March 16 Wednesday

I received an email from my friend Elaine, in town for a 90th birthday party with her husband, whose family is friends with the guest of honor. Coincidentally the guest of honor is a collector of my art. Mr. Kendall, retired CEO of Pepsico, who initiated their famous Sculpture Garden, bought two paintings at my first solo show, one of which hangs at Pepsico Headquarters in Purchase, New York. I have not seen this painting in 17 years. Elaine recognized the painting from college, took a picture and sent it with her email greeting, in which she asked to visit today.

Elaine brought her husband to visit, who was nice to give me a book of his accomplished architecture. We caught up quickly, I showed them my spaces, my art, we had some nostalgic laughter, and away they went. It's reassuring how many years can go by with some people and it's just like yesterday the rest of your lives.

March 17 Thursday

I was asked to speak on a panel in May for aspiring artists who are in high school and college. All I can think of is that I would not wish the curse of an art career on anyone, as much as I love it. I just saw a very cool documentary on Glenn Gould and one of his friends quoted Brahms as saying, "Unfortunately I am a bachelor thank God," or something like that.

My mind is racing this morning. One of my artist friends who has watched me curate and hang shows once joked that I have ADD or OCD. I think it's called being human. Some days I sit and look at Whitman's blade of grass for ten hours without moving and sometimes I am a whirlwind in the studio, following the energy where it will take me. Some days the energy is there before me and I articulate it precisely as I see fit and other days the energy beats the crap out of me. This is being plugged into the vibrations of the world, and artists spend their lives testing the winds like sailors. You can try to hold your course but you can't predict the water or the weather.

It's 3:30 pm on a school day and the loudspeakers are reminding me that it's St. Patrick's Day. People are going nuts already. You've got to love the Irish. I learned this early, as Bill O'Brien is my oldest best friend of 30 years.

March 18 Friday

My new friend Clyde came over as he needs me to alter

storyboards I made in December for a television pilot he has been working on. I used a famous actor's face in the storyboards and he wants the face to be more generic, as this script will go to a couple of stars and not just the actor whose face I used. Clyde suggested that I replace the actor's visage with an older version of my face. I've never done storyboards for anything so the experience with my new friend has been fun and engaged me with some new tools I will use in my future.

I remember spending the most boring day of my life as an

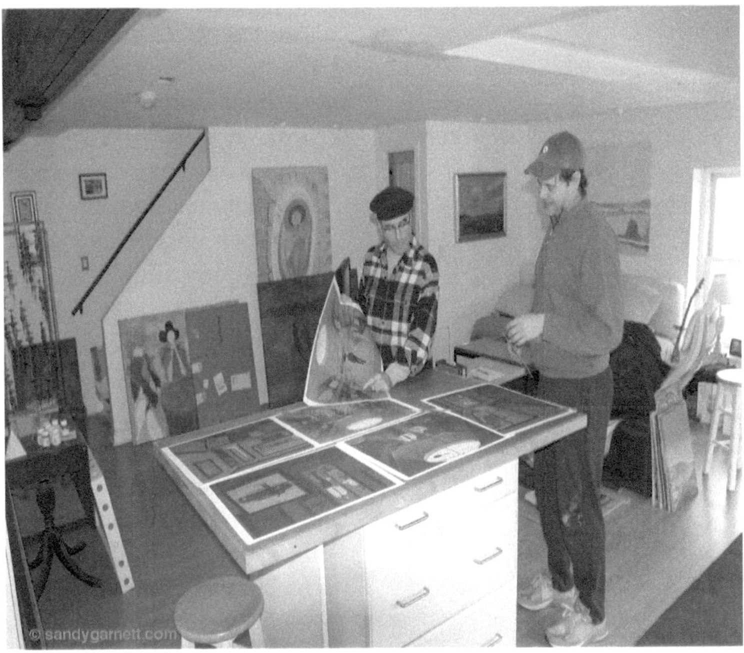

extra in a Woody Allen film. My shoes made the final edit. I was paired up with a pretty girl and we rode the escalator down in the shot right behind Bette Midler and Woody Allen stand-ins while production set the shot up all day. The last run when the cameras were actually rolling we didn't even know that Midler and Allen had stepped in. At least I got a date with a pretty girl out of that one day I will ever be an extra.

March 19 Saturday

I had a studio visit and lunch today with my new friends Rob and Mary, who went to art school but don't make art for a living. Mary said that I am fearless to try anything, how refreshing that is for her to see in a professional painter. This made my day, coming from an MFA.

I went to St. Lawrence University (not an art school), where I made many lifetime friends, almost none of whom are creative professionals.

In college I made art for bands that were blowing up at the time, which was very hard to get into and all consuming, so I figured my own world out pretty quickly without the aid or affliction of an art school environment. Now my collectors are my lifeline, hundreds of good, intelligent people who tap me through various aspects of my art catalogue. After college I never chased the New York art scene because every minute of schmoozing ephemera is a minute away from my easel, for better and for worse.

People ask how I make it all work. It remains a mystery to me. I have to be okay with never knowing what's going to happen next yet somehow trusting my intuition, my energy, or the grand scheme of things. The more I step out of my own way and ask the universe for help something usually comes in. I can't explain it. It's been happening the whole journey, often at critical junctures. Things sort themselves out with the right energy or art or meditation. I try not to ask too many questions.

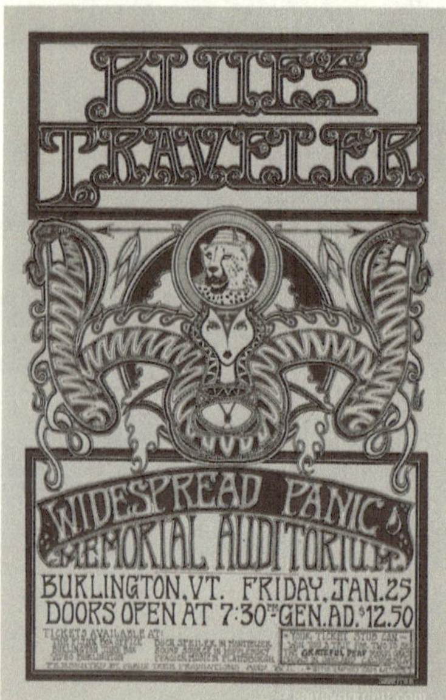

Original ink poster ©sandygarnettt.com

Rob asked me if I have highs and lows that I have to monitor or medicate in my twenty year art career. He was a musician for awhile, he's sober for decades and takes antidepressants, which prompted the question. Sure, there are highs and lows, but not an imbalance in the art system brain. I'm in gladiator territory, a solitary game I play and could not do with drugs. I'll have a glass of wine but I don't like anything else. I need to feel all of life coming through me, I need to feel the rhythms of energies in order to intuit and survive. If I'm not happy then I am sucking for some reason so I have to locate the issue and adjust the mechanism. The death of family and friends is as bad as the pain gets, and then there is lost love, which really stings too, but I haven't been in love for awhile so this is not on the radar.

Early evening my old friend Ed called and might commission a marble Fingerprint Totem, then another collector checked in about a 1996 painting from my inventory that he wants. These calls came out of nowhere.

March 20 Sunday

Genres are like clothing. In the end people don't care what you are wearing if you come with a good heart filled with stories. The genre is secondary in this era but nobody knows it yet.

When I am in the desert, starting to hallucinate, running on fumes, and stumble upon the next watering hole, relief is one of the best things about my job. My years of Sisyphean rock rolling have been supported again and I am rejuvenated. I have to be strong this week, work out well, eat healthy and get good sleep. The art animal, living off the land, hungry and lean, eating what I kill, this is no joke, this is art survival without a net every day. A Sunday of R & R.

March 21 Monday

I just achieved a patent for my Revolutionary Family Totems.

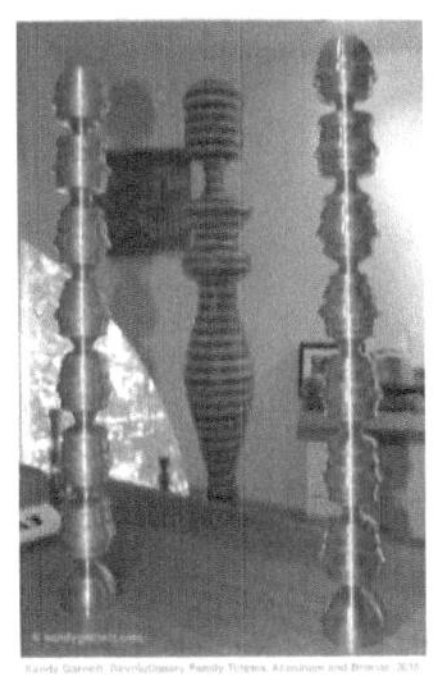

It only took three years arguing with a woman in the patent department whose third language is English. She misinterpreted our argument all this time due to a language barrier, but the peer review appeal finally went through. Apparently there is a correlation between patent examiner talent and the economy. Good job patent department. My intellectual property lawyer and good friend Tom felt that this was a victory, as it is apparently difficult to patent art-related items.

March 22 Tuesday

I landed the marble Fingerprint Totem. I have to send eight fingerprints kits out to Ed and his siblings across the U.S. so they can make fingerprints to send back to me. In the meantime I have to design the sculpture dimensions so I can place the marble order, which will take a month or two. Then I have to design a pedestal, but that will come later.

March 23 Wednesday

I sold another painting that I have to deliver to Jamaica next month. My collector Nevada wants 'Mother and Child,' a 1996 oil on canvas that was a study for 'The Mourning,' one of my best paintings of that time.

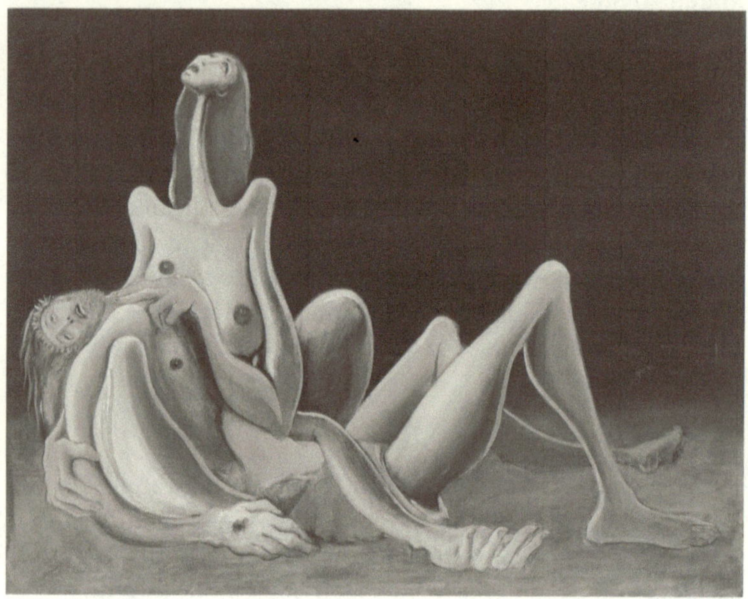

Mother and Child, oil on canvas, 22 x 30 inches, cat 19960213, © Sandy Garnett.

March 24 Thursday

6 am racquetball is a great way to wake up into the day. I split sets with Matt again this morning.

Studio rhythm takes days or weeks to achieve. When I'm humming my work and mind are clear and penetrating. When the studio is light with work I find myself dancing on the backs of turtles with alligators in the midst, so I am trying to find my groove and settle down with this influx of new studio energy.

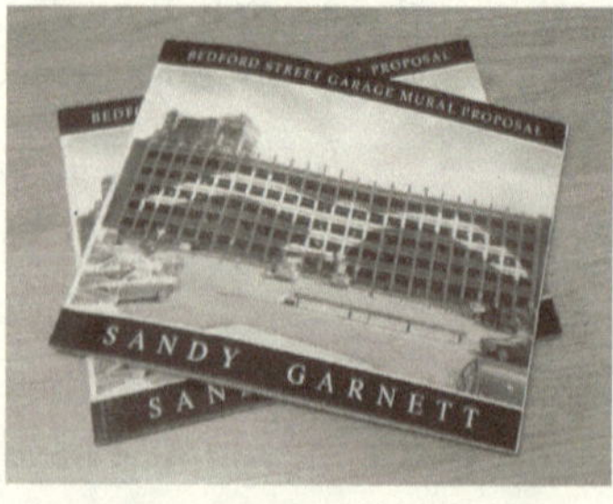

I received eight copies of the mural proposal book I sent out for last week, which will impress Committee members. Artists forget how productive they have been until they see or hear something they made before, which reminds them that a lot of energy went into that thing.

March 25 Friday

I got a call from my old friend Andy for a music poster. I spent college on the drawing table, so doing a concert poster for friends a couple times a year is a way of staying in touch with my roots.

I sketched out the poster concept for Melvin Seals & JGB Band. This is a timely week to sketch out a music poster because I saw the band Furthur at Radio City tonight with Bob Weir and Phil Lesh of the Grateful Dead. They sounded great. I don't get to concerts a lot after having spent a number of years working in the music industry, but my fraternity brother Mike flew in and had a ticket for me, which was very nice of him. Last year I did a poster for his birthday that our mutual friend Andy commissioned and made into shirts for the party, so I think taking me to the concert was Mike's way of thanking me for my art energy. Life is short, friends and concerts are good.

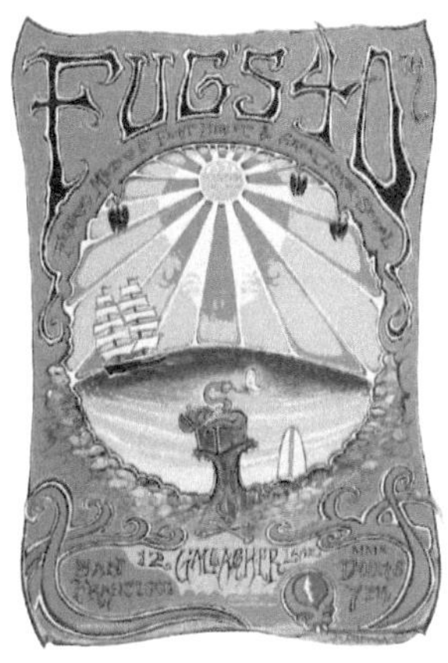

March 26 Saturday

I completed the Inventory book edits, altered the cover, registered the ISBN and prepared PDF files to send off. Producing a book is a process that requires attention to detail, not only in the writing and editing of a book but also in the publication of that book. There are overlapping data sets which need to be applied to different aspects of a single project, kind of like one of those origami flowers that when properly designed collapses perfectly into itself. When a piece of data is off the whole thing gets screwed up, so it's all about layers of edits over time.

My paintings and sculptures subsidize my book projects, which are hours away from the easel. I should have delivered two paintings last week, but I had to make another mural proposal book, which is a long term game of hopscotch that keeps the studio moving forward with calculated risks.

March 27 Sunday

I shot photographs of myself in order to overlay an older version of my portrait into storyboard edits for my friend Clyde. It was amusing and efficient to use my own visage and make myself older. I am working with my new Wacom tablet, which gives me a digital pen to draw directly into Photoshop. Like my friend Phil has said, I should have bought one of these years ago as it is a great tool that I will use all the time.

March 28 Monday

I designed and ordered the marble for my new Fingerprint Totem, and I started to design seven Fingerprint Portraits that I will paint on canvas later in the week.

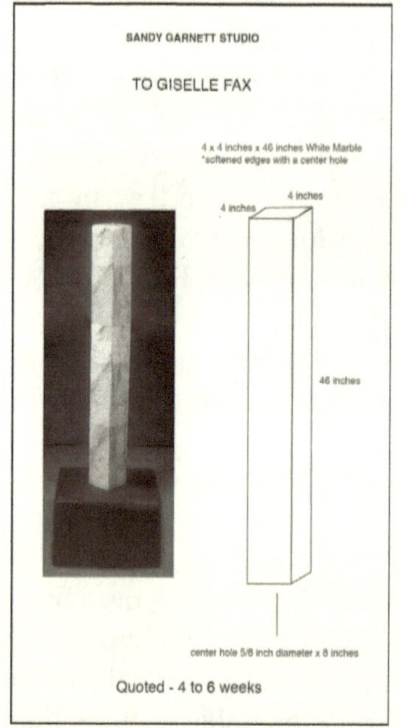

March 29 Tuesday

In the afternoon I picked my father up from the airport. He brought back a scrapbook of his father's athletic achievements that my Aunt Sally gave to my father on his visit. My grandfather pitched a no-hitter lefty in high school, was captain of squash and tennis at Choate and played at the U.S. Open, right-handed that is. He was a great golfer righty as well. I bat lefty, shoot a lacrosse ball and hockey puck lefty, golf lefty, but I throw righty, write and paint righty. That's some strange ambidextrous stuff.

March 30 Wednesday

The heat is on but I'm in the pocket, feeling the edges of my spirit brush along the tunnel at a quick pace on a good track. Sometimes I am a mole digging aimlessly for magic or safety and other times like now I'm on a fast rail, trying to stay out of my own way so I don't steer off an embankment into the forest. The time passes, the days go by and I feel the blur of creativity, a cocoon of sorts, my way of communing with the world when I'm in this place, good energy pulsing through my studio, coming from old friends and collectors. There is a certain truth to building something strong over the years that people continue to support.

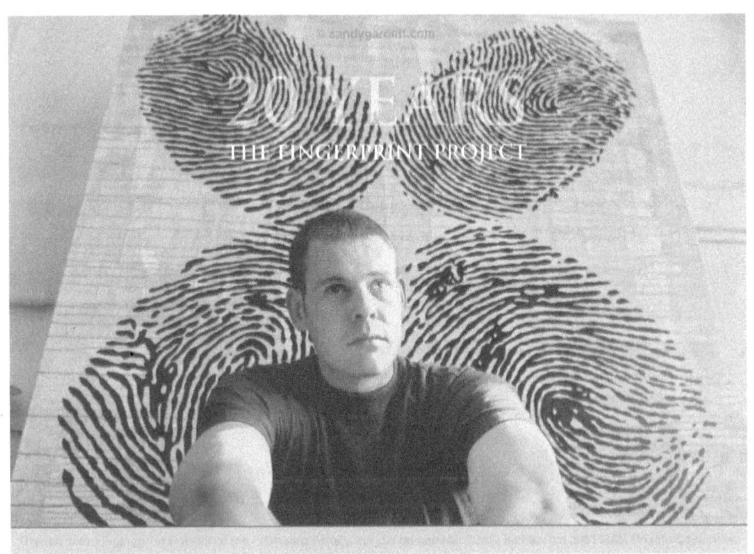

March 31 Thursday

I edged out my brother 16-14 in two long games. I win then I feel bad for him. He beats me like yesterday and I am pissed for losing but proud of my brother. We go back and forth so this is the best way to have a long-term exercise partner.

Andy was very happy with the concert art so I sent that in for posters and shirts.

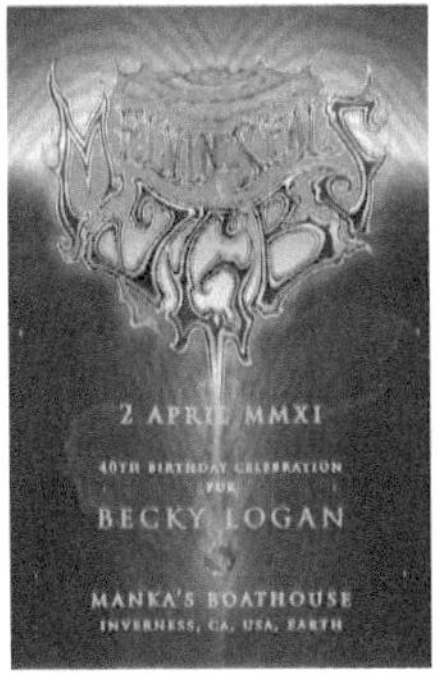

I painted the off-white backgrounds on two Fingerprint Portrait canvases, then I mixed a modified burnt umber I will be using for the fingerprints. I need to paint seven fingerprints in a very symmetrical composition freehand, so consistency of paint is important. As I will only be using one color, I mixed a large batch of this color so that my creative flow will not be interrupted mid-painting tomorrow by running out of paint.

In the past I have screwed up in all the wrong ways on the easel and in the studio. A wise craftsman addresses each project properly to avoid having to repeat the process, lose time and money, frustrate a collector, frustrate himself. A lot of paintings are not like this but these two paintings are all about technical precision on a tight time frame, so they have to be done right the first time.

April 1 Friday

Today I painted for thirteen hours. The work was very detailed, so it was slow going, methodical. Rushing this sort of painting creates liabilities, and as the surface is so sensitive, mistakes cannot be made or the painting will spin out. I dropped my brush once, but thankfully the brush fell away from the canvas without the bristles striking and corrupting the painting. Had the brush dragged down the canvas it could have been like taking a thick black marker and dragging it across a pen and ink maze on paper, potentially ruining the entire thing.

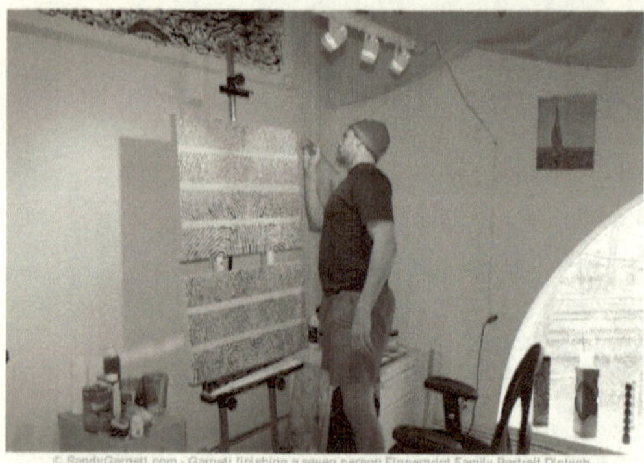

© SandyGarnett.com - Garnett finishing a seven person Fingerprint Family Portrait Diptych, oil on canvas, 20x30/15x30 inches, 2011.

As I painted I listened to 'Searching for Bobby Fischer,' a great movie about a child chess prodigy that illuminates lifestyles and training styles as contrasting colors on a chess board, the monochromatic filtering into the positives and negatives of my Fingerprint Portraits. I listened to 'The Shawshank Redemption,' my favorite film, perhaps because one's dreams take many years to achieve, like the characters who evolve in the film, like the paintings that I slowly chipped away at the way Andy Dufresne does with his little rock hammer. These analogies may seem silly but I use stories and tricks to keep me at the easel, sewing my lines away, off in fictional worlds of film and music, combining and recombining themes, circles and mazes and chess boards and narratives, until by the end of the evening I had two signed paintings, spanking fresh and waiting to dry so they can soon hang on the walls of my new collectors.

April 2 Saturday

Today I added vocal tracks and some backing tracks to my song 'Sylvie.' Soon I will post a video teaser for the 5 song EP I would like to release this year. My first single 'Busted Wing,' which made it into an extreme skiing film, surprised friends and collectors, who didn't know that I have been a closet songwriter since college. 'Busted Wing' is an angry breakup song whereas 'Sylvie' is a sweet, romantic kind of love song.

I spent the afternoon into evening tinkering with music, which offers counterpoints to painting, the way writing a book does. The juxtaposition of mediums is a constant charge.

April 3 Sunday

Designing a crate to transport paintings with wet sidewalls is an example of paying for procrastination, although the crate made me look very professional.

The stakes were high, not in a way that made my heart beat faster, but everything had to fall into place or I would miss my meeting. While shooting the work for my archive I was afraid one of the canvases might fall off the wall, which would have smudged the fingerprints and ruin a painting. Wet fingerprints are very finicky. Wet canvases want to be left alone, and they get ornery when you start messing around with them while they are drying.

I made the box carefully and slowly. I drilled eight 1 inch holes in the plywood wall for my fingers to find purchase so I could screw into the back corners of each canvas stretcher. This allowed the paintings to 'float' inside the box without touching anything as they dried. I mounted the cover on the crate, screwed two large black aluminum handles on the box, and carried the crate by its new handles out to my car.

I left at 5:20 pm and got to Houston Street by 6:00 pm. The drive was fluid, it was a sunny afternoon in early April so I was in jogging shorts all day and for the delivery. I enjoy driving into town, particularly when the traffic is not a nightmare and I'm not in a rush. I have driven in a thousand times and I know every turn, every nuance in the road, the stupid S-turns of I-95 where all the accidents happen, the best views to see the water and the city. It is forever strange to pop up on the Bruckner before the bridges and see my beautiful New York, twin towerlessly haunting a decade later.

I was almost out of gas, which was stupid. Nothing like pushing your luck flying down the FDR... 60's, 50's... come on, I think I can make it to the Houston Street gas station. My collectors are on Bleecker so I found an easy parking spot and had time to get a coffee. I dated a girl who lived around here a while back and love this area... charming, quaint, low slung buildings, a little hip but not too bustling, a great location.

I pulled the crate from my car and walked with this heavy, unwieldy box a couple blocks to the building. I went up to the fourth floor, walked into Sari's loft, met their cute son and did my art delivery song and dance. Sari is receiving the painting for her mother Suzan as this is a surprise birthday present for her father. Since her parents share an email account Sari has been my contact, as surprise art gifts often go.

I unscrewed the six cap screws that held the top on the crate. Sari, her husband and son were very happy, there was a conversation about each fingerprint out of the seven, I screwed the cap back on the crate, shook hands with my collectors and was on my way. I walked out into the street buoyant, as successful deliveries always make me feel.

I crossed the street, passing the subway stairs, and there was my truck, with the front door wide open. I had been on the delivery for 20 minutes while all of New York City wandered by, leaving the door as it was, not touching a thing. My drill was on the front seat, my ipod, loose change, clothes, books, my sunglasses, a bunch of other crap was just sitting there for anyone to take. When I got back in my car several passers-by wondered with concerned expressions if it was in fact my car or I might be a thief. Good old New York.

April 4 Monday

I am going to Augusta with my Dad and my brother Matt tomorrow. I haven't been on a vacation since I was on Walter's boat in the Canyon and we caught that 308 lb. swordfish last September.

Famous architect Frank Gehry said recently, "The best advice I've received is to be yourself. The best artists do that. People look over their shoulders too much. I tell kids that come to Yale, where I've taught every other year since 1978, to find your own way because then you're the only expert. Some people might not like what you do, but still, you're the only expert." (Wall Street Journal, 2 April 2011-Edited from an interview by Jackie Cooperman).

The above quote encapsulates my career. I learned to not care what other people think, which is a really hard thing to do. Show me an artist who can do what I can do and we'll make lifetime friends. In the meantime I sold ten grand in art this month and I'm onto career painting number 1023.

April 5 Tuesday

Brother Christian drove Dad, Matt and me to the airport for our 6 am flight. We took a puddle jumper to Augusta and my cousin in-law Chuck was on that flight. Chuck picked up a rental car and drove us over to the two houses he had booked for the week of the Masters Golf Tournament, something he has done with clients and friends for years. In the afternoon we walked the course, which is very hilly, something that does not read on a television screen.

We returned at the end of the day and had dinner with Chuck's fellow guests. There were two father and son groups. Fathers and sons belong together for excursions like this. Camaraderie was in the air. We ended the evening with a little family poker before turning in.

It is good to be away from my studio for a moment. My father has dreamed about going to Augusta his whole life, so it was special to watch my father take this place in with the same boyish enthusiasm that he has taught me to have for my art and many other things in life.

April 6 Wednesday

We were up early and I made breakfast for the crew. We got to the course after rush hour and followed the par 3 tournament.

Golf courses were not originally designed like amphitheaters for spectators, so it is interesting to see where the crowds gather. There are different styles of golf spectating. There are the people who travel with a group or player, there are people who set up in one spot that offers a good vantage point for several holes, there are people who hang out around the clubhouse and the press tents, angling to catch a glimpse of a famous player. We had clubhouse passes so we sat at the outdoor tables for lunch. A number of famous players and media people were in the vicinity. One of Chuck's friends is a well known golfer and he came over for introductions. Everyone was very cordial in that Southern way. There are plenty of friendly people in the Northeast, but starchy reserve is part of New England's social architecture. No wonder my paternal ancestry is rooted in the South.

After golf eight of us went out to a family restaurant. Tomorrow the tournament begins so the vibrations in town are filled with excitement and celebration. We returned to our house and resumed poker until very late, which gave me a chance to win back the money I lost last night. I watched my father all day into the evening and tried to capture these moments of him in his element for when I am an old man remembering good things about family and life.

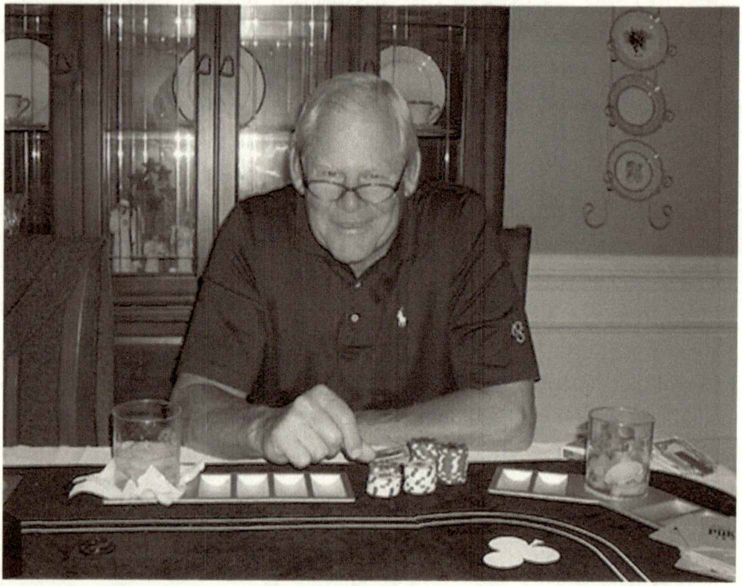

April 7 Thursday

This morning we took it easy, packed and got to the course at 10 am. We sat in several key locations to watch the golfers come and go. The crowds were bigger and getting boisterous on this first day of the tournament. We wandered today, getting a feel for the atmosphere, taking in the players and how they operate at this level of excellence year round. The weather was perfect again and I got a mild sunburn, which I like at the beginning of a new season to remind the studio artist in me that I am a biological creature genetically predisposed to walk in nature and sunlight for health and a change of scenery.

Our flight was at 5:30 pm so we left the course on time and went into travel mode. Two airplanes later we landed in New York and my brother Christian picked us up. I got home at midnight. This was one of the best vacations I can recall, a quick step away to Augusta with my brother Matthew and my dear old Dad. I hope to return with them again.

April 8 Friday

While I was away my friend Jen, who writes and edits professionally, ran through *Baloney Express* and created a detailed list of edits. I spent the first half of the day making these corrections, grateful for Jen's good energy, then I resubmitted files to my on-line printing and distribution source. This means that I will not be able to get books in time for a signing at my upcoming Open House, so I had no choice but to push that back by two weeks. I sent an email update with the corrected dates to my list, which precipitated email dialogue with thirty friends, family members and collectors through the end of the day.

In the early evening I recorded chorus tracks for 'Sylvie,' aligned it to a slide-show and uploaded the video so people can listen to the song while looking at my paintings.

My old friend David owns a Frank Lloyd Wright-designed home in Connecticut for weekends when he wants to get out of the city. We have been talking about an outdoor sculpture since last summer, when I delivered his bronze Revolutionary Family Totem sculpture to him.

I have this idea of stones spilling from the sky and formalizing themselves into a New England rock wall, sort of like visualizing a stone wall shooting up out of the ground totemically. I've never seen a stone wall shoot straight up in the air. Tomorrow I am going up to a film festival in his neck of the woods. He edited a short film and was involved in producing a feature for this film festival, so I will get to see some of his work and we can talk about art. Before bed I did some spec work on several ideas that would work on his property.

April 9 Saturday

I arrived at the festival for a 10 am block of short films. That was over at 11 am so I said hello to my friend David, his parents and other friends who had been involved in the production of the films. I reluctantly agreed to go back to his place for lunch, feeling the pull of studio work. Lunch turned into an afternoon of movie talk with people who appreciate film like I do. I spoke with David about the sculpture and this inspired new thoughts.

The afternoon spilled into evening, so we drove back into town again for the film festival awards. I was going to head out after the awards but returned to the house for swimming and dinner. I was with four writer/directors and three other creative folks who make a living in film. I don't spend a lot of time with fellow full-time creative professionals so this was refreshing. I enjoy making amusing parallels between painting and moving pictures or music, and it seems that creative people in other mediums like to play that game as well. Someone said that everyone at the table was playing hooky from a project, as a creative professional's work is never done.

April 10 Sunday

It was my turn to sit for the afternoon at the Loft Artist Gallery that I have belonged to for many years and have curated shows at.

My friend and fellow artist Catherine came into the gallery on the way to her adjacent art studio and asked if I would like to jury a show at another regional Gallery Association, so I will meet that Committee next week.

At 5 pm I went over to brother Matt's house to play with my nephew and hold baby Emma. Matt, Jess and Jackson are adjusting to the fourth member of their family.

Before turning in I received an email from my new collector who surprised her husband with the Fingerprint Family Portrait diptych for his 70th birthday present. She sent photographs and was very appreciative, reporting that all in attendance loved the paintings, several of whom would like to visit my studio.

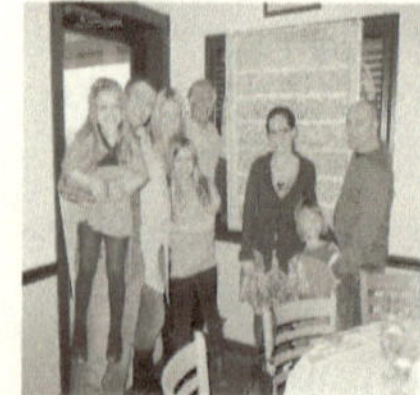

April 11 Monday

My body thanked me for 6 am racquetball after a week of debaucherous food and drink. As an artist it is good to have discipline in body and spirit on the one hand, with the ability to loosen the reins and let it all hang out on the other. Changing frequencies seems to stimulate my creative receptors, which keeps life and my artistic process fresh and intriguing.

I am a Guild Member at Silvermine in New Canaan, CT, one of the oldest guilds in America, so I reported for my quarterly four hour shift to prepare for a new show. I am very fast at hanging art so they put me to work on this task that a lot of people are slow at. I used to measure everything but now I am much faster eying out walls. I don't like to waste time in millimeters before seeing work on the wall, so I get the work up and adjust from there.

After an afternoon of painting I attended a Condo Board meeting at 7 pm. I am one of the only owners who works from home and the only professional artist here, I like to know what's going on, so I have been on the Board for years. I try to provide comedic relief because so many of the issues we have to deal with are silly bureaucratic things, as life goes. Owning two properties and understanding the dynamics of Condo Board ownership provides transparency that helps me to see my surroundings clearly. When renting a studio, there is no clarity.

April 12 Tuesday

There is often a convergence of art and commerce when the art is from the right spiritual place; like the way dowsing rods detect water. I need to drive the bus to find an oasis, or more likely the bus drives me, in what direction I'm never sure. What is the right work, the right direction? I have to follow my heart, which usually starts at the easel.

I have not been on the easel every day this winter, a place I have spent so many years at that it has long been my real home. When I get in the cockpit and take her for a ride I feel the wind in my hair, I start flying, I feel free and often answers come in. A good painting day is what I live for.

April 13 Wednesday

I approved *Baloney Express* for publishing and ordered sixty hardcover books. It is difficult to believe that *Baloney* is completed after having traveled with me half of my life in notebook form. The sensation is ecstatic relief.

April 14 Thursday

Today I met with my aunt and my father to discuss a pictorial history book of our family. We waded through images that go back to the first cameras, so this will be a challenging project to produce. I talked to my father and my aunt about scanning in all the photos they want to use. They need to scan their images, then I will edit and design the project. They are hoping that we can disperse hardcover books to the family in September during my cousin Reyn's wedding weekend in Vermont. This will be a tall order but I accepted the responsibility.

My acoustic guitar is buzzing, which is untimely as I am working on recording a song that requires me to strum two strings softly at the same time. It just so happens that the two strings I need to strum softly at the same time are the only ones that are buzzing. It may be a change in the weather. Musical instruments are fussy bitches, unlike power tools, which when inoperable just tell you to go screw yourself all up front and loud-like.

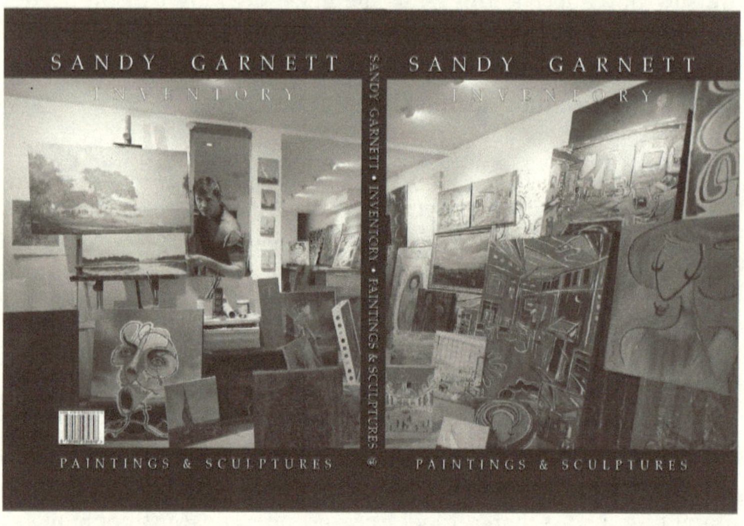

April 15 Friday

I spent 12 hours color correcting the next proof of my Inventory book. Color correcting images for print and other forms of publishing is critical technical work for an artist to learn about and get fluid with.

At the end of the day I received a call from the mural committee I recently submitted a proposal book for. There were 20 submissions and I have been selected as one of two finalists. I will meet with the Committee in ten days for a final presentation. This was a very good way to end the week, but now my mind is flooded with budgets and technical issues, contemplating a mural on the façade of a five-story garage that is 70 feet tall and 125 feet long.

April 16 Saturday

I generally like to keep a clean house, but down time is good to exercise my mastery of puttering, a method of cleaning the studio peacefully, like raking a rock garden. Assorted lyrics, to-do lists, sculpture concepts, business cards, napkin doodles, tear sheets, references that litter my floor, coat my kitchen island, line my staircase, all must be filed away to cleanse the palette.

An artist's space is everything; an anchor point, a home, a refuge, a space ship, a lover's nest, a think tank, a wailing wall, a drawing board, a watering hole, a presentation tablet, a gallery. There is chaos out there in the world, but there can be peace of mind inside the walls of an art studio.

Most artists rent out of necessity, and their first bosses are their landlords. As art is a game of space, living in space that an artist has purchased can be a great relief. It has allowed for deep meditation that dulled the edge of exposure I grew so used to when I spent the first decade after college living like a ghost ninja in a commercial space that I was not allowed to live in.

April 17 Sunday

Last night I drove to a dinner party in the pouring rain, deep into the country bowels of Westport, where the horse manure is palpable through the running of my primitive automobile engine. I was greeted by my friend Rob, who had an umbrella to take guests into the attractive, contemporary home set back into the landscape, surrounded by a pretty pond. Inside I met my hosts and eight other very nice, interesting people. We laughed by the fire, splintering off into various conversations as dinner parties go, then we sat for dinner in a warm dining room at a narrow, long table which held ten places. The host's brother had whipped up a delicious beef bourguignon that the guests enjoyed after Rob gave a very nice introduction to each person at the table. The music danced, the candle light flickered, and our conversations flew all over the place. I sharpened my self-effacing humor on several people and juxtaposed my solitary artist process with the architect across from me, who works with 1000 people over a decade to design and erect a skyscraper. When he flies into a city he sees his skyscraper, but ironically the security guards for the building he designed, who were hired away from the local strip club, don't believe the architect and won't let him in to see his own building. Artists understand this concept deeply, so I laughed with my new friend and we look forward to respective studio visits. There were two internationally recognized musicians at the table, two architects, two city planners, two commercial realtors, a branding professional and the token visual artist.

I wondered while driving home through the cats-and-dogs rain why intimate dinner parties are not always on my calendar. The dinner inspired me, so I returned home to write thank you notes and emails to everyone who had been there before bed.

April 18 Monday

I barely edged my brother out two racquetball games to one, dusting the weekend cobwebs off.

This morning I spent half an hour explaining to my father how to make folders on his computer over the phone, which was like doing a jigsaw puzzle blindfolded.

Before lunch I recorded my song 'Northern Lights,' the best two track recording I have done. One track covered my acoustic and vocal and a second was a drum track. It is good to hear a nice version of this old song whose melody and lyrics are campfire friendly and timeless.

I painted a treasure map for Jackson's Birthday Backyard Pirate Hunt. I cut some canvas off an old roll, primed and painted it tan like the color of parchment, then painted a map that he can roll up and tie off with a red band.

Jackson was very happy with the map and a bunch of small presents I gave him to unwrap that I also wanted to play with. I got him a parachute guy, some balsa airplanes, some darts with soft tips to throw off the deck, a bubble maker so he can blow bubbles, some toy cars for his tracks, which we set up for jumps inside when it's raining.

April 19 Tuesday

I spent the day pricing the materials and equipment I will need to produce the massive mural I am a finalist for. The fee must be contingent upon the complexity of the painting, but there is likely a set budget and I don't know which one of my designs the Committee likes yet. I can't give two months of my life away for a loss. If I win, this public art project should help my studio and not hurt me. I have to proceed with no expectations, which are hard to suppress.

April 20 Wednesday

I went over to my friend Bill's for his technical advice on the stone sculpture sketch that might be 15 feet tall. Bill is an engineer, architect, wine expert, historian on mechanical music machines, he has a great family and the most impressive home workshop that I have ever seen. Compression versus tension was the dialogue, along with ten other factors, in realizing this sculpture which my friend David might subsidize into being. A vertical stone wall that curves like a waterfall is great in the imagination and even on paper, but bringing that into reality will be a lot of math, steel, stone and light.

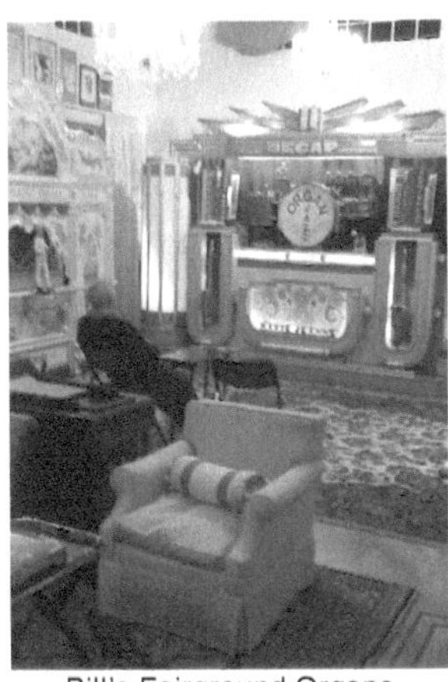

Bill's Fairground Organs

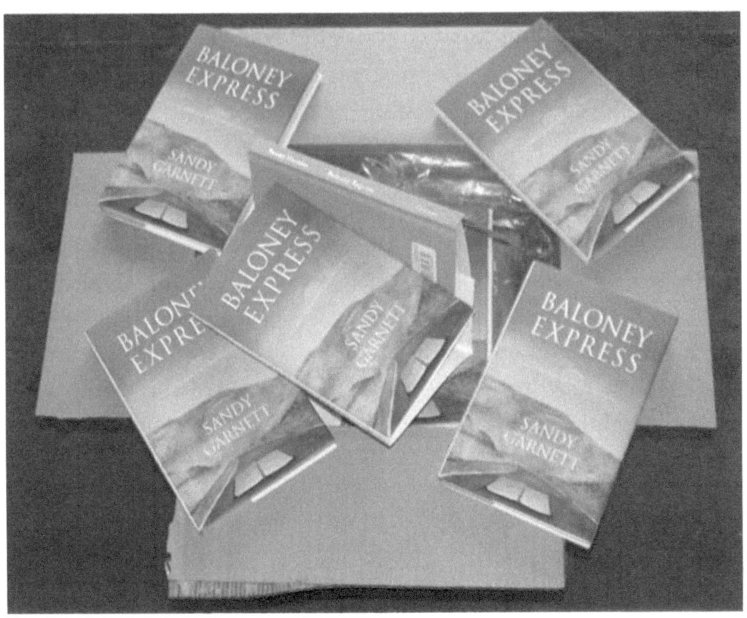

April 21 Thursday

My first *Baloney Express* book shipment, the first book of

my career, came in today. It was an unheralded affair like most of my milestones are. It felt good to open the box and sit there with hardcovers in my hand, pondering this never-ending project that has reached it's formalized conclusion. When you spend half of your life with a thorn in your side about a project that never made it, and then you finally get the project out of you, it's surreal. There was so much psychic energy tied up in the fact that my old book had never seen the light of day. The release is a slow waterfall that will keep giving back to my spirit. The sense of accomplishment is large.

I have presold 50 copies of *Baloney* so I spent the day filling orders, migrating in the evening to flesh out a song that has been rattling around in my head like ball bearings for years.

April 22 Friday

I feel the wolves starting to circle and I need someone to cover soon. I spent the day organizing my office, which was long overdue and felt right. I faced off with my mountain of bills, kicking and screaming, punching at phantoms, roundhouse blows to the cranium, chiseling away, robbing Peter to pay Paul. Sometimes, like today, the damage is not as bad as you thought it was. I never know where the next support is coming from so I try not to think too much about the ledge that gets narrower as I casually peer over my boot tips into the abyss.

April 23 Saturday

I did a backstage pass for a friend's birthday party today, which was quick and fun. I Photoshopped hip sunglasses that hung from the v-neck of his shirt in the childhood photo I was sent. I whipped up some rock and roll typesetting on the backside of the laminate design as this guy is well known for his life's work in the music industry. I enjoy making art for my musician friends once in a while, remembering my college days as a full-time artist for the music industry.

April 24 Sunday

My art has been spread into new mediums that are maintaining my spirit, but the easel is starting to do her pole dance again, that sexy cobra number which stops me in my tracks and beckons my return. There is a painting that has been teasing me for 9 months and holds a riddle I want to unlock. It just sits there tempting me like an insolent bitch... come play with me... what, you don't have time? Poor you. My Twister reliefs are doing the same thing again. Sometimes I feel like I should be farther ahead on some work, but if an artist achieves excellence and originality with one work of art, he does not have to make a career out of that series. At least I don't. A painting can emerge over time, and when I nail one way of seeing I reflexively skate in the opposite direction. This way of making never gets old and fills my spirit. I will circle back in time and a series will grow in my studio over the years, mulling through a number of genres, percolating like the slow maturation of an old, sturdy tree. This might sound flowery but it's accurate. If one paints in a number of ways it takes years for bodies of work to gain heft and cohesion, with historical glue in between.

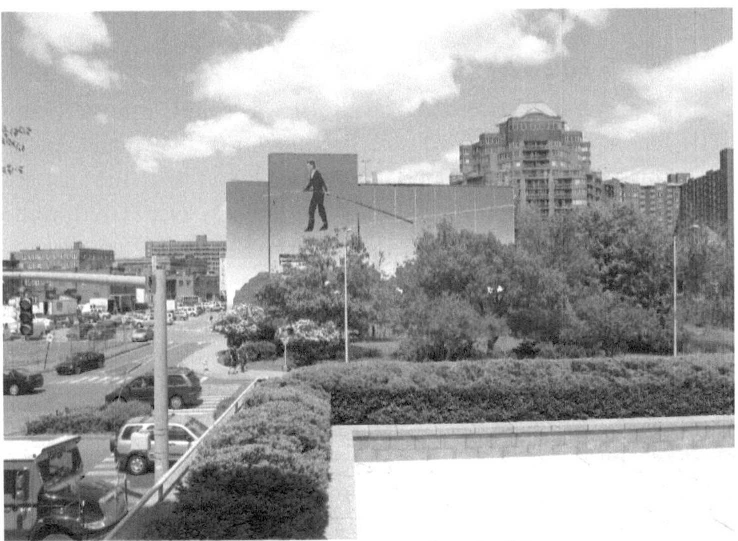

'Tightrope Walker' concept for Stamford Garage

April 25 Monday

I spent the day on another spec design for the mural presentation and I researched lighting, paint, man hours, airless spray guns, methods of proper spraying patterns on large buildings, lifts, time frames, public art payment schedules.

A lot goes into proposals, and there are no sure things. I don't have public art projects under my belt yet, so I am the underdog going up against artists with more public art experience. I went for this one because I know the building, the Committee knows my work, and I figured I might as well give it a shot. Ten years ago I was told that I had won a public art commission in the same city, but that went quietly to someone else who made what looks like a utility pole with a hundred thousand dollar budget. The current proposal is the first I have made in a decade, so at least it's good to be a finalist.

April 26 Tuesday

I received one of the only gorilla hand prints and fingerprints in existence this afternoon. The foundation that contacted me likes the idea of The Fingerprint Portraitist making a New York City art show of gorilla fingerprints and hand prints. Sure, no problem, find me a gallery because this is strange enough to be very interesting. Apparently there are only 700 gorillas in existence today, which seems like an alarmingly low global population.

April 27 Wednesday

At the mural meeting I sat down with the Committee and things changed quickly. Two walls became one wall, which became a portion of one wall, which became maybe a vinyl enlargement of a painting. The 'unofficial budget' that was never stated in the RFP (Request For Proposal) was reduced to a sliver of it's original 'suggestion.' New information aside, the meeting went well and I might have a shot at the reduced commission.

Usually RFP's include a stated goal, budget and timeline, so I will exercise caution the next time a budget is not clearly listed. The key thing is to incorporate this experience into future proposals and projects moving forward.

April 28 Thursday

Last night I watched and recorded my second appearance on Jerry Laird's half hour interview television program. He likes the fact that I survive by my art and that I explore painting, sculpture, writing, music, design, multimedia. In 85 years Jerry has had a number of careers, he has a young spirit, and he supports regional people with his long-running public access 'Carousel' show. I did pretty well. If I relax I know how to amuse and communicate effectively when I do the occasional media spot.

April 29 Friday

I sent an Open House reminder email to my list and spent

the rest of the day painting and doing correspondence, as email blasts go. I spoke with a new collector about a Fingerprint Project she wants to pursue, friends in North Carolina, Seattle, LA., Chicago, Florida received my signed books and thanked me.

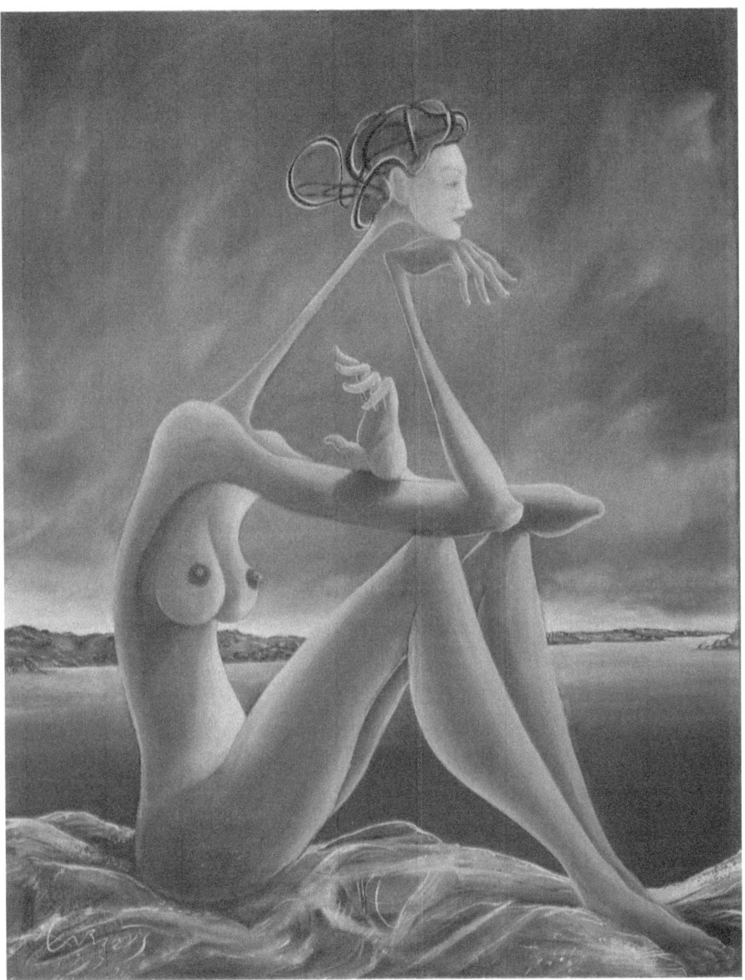

Sandy Garnett, Contemplating Woman on Rocks, oil on canvas, 30 x 24 inches, 1999.

April 30 Saturday

I had zero visitors from noon to 4 pm, at which point fifteen people piled into my studio as if they'd all popped out of a clown car together. I signed 15 *Baloney* books and started a fun dialogue with a nice couple who visited last year. I pulled my Musicians painting out again, which they want but which is 8 x 7 feet tall, too big for their practical minds. They settled for 'Contemplating Woman on Rocks,' a 12 year-old gem.

I moved into my place seven years ago and this painting has hung in the same spot ever since. She has been one of my closest studio friends for her peaceful beauty. The sale is bittersweet, unlike most other painting placements, but the number was right so I had to let her go.

When I go from not being able to pay the bills to covering an instant later I am grateful and sometimes frustrated at the same time. Why do I spend my life playing chicken in fast traffic? Why am I not more successful so that I do not have to live this feast or famine lifestyle all artists know? And then in the same breath I qualify why I live on a roller-coaster.

"It has to be this way for you to stay brutally honest."

May 1 Sunday

Today I had twice as many visitors, sold 20 books, met some new potential collectors, and picked up a commission. At the end of the day, after an hour of wine laughter, seven people became three, so I walked down the street with Kim and Patrick for appetizers. They are amongst my best collectors and have become family friends. Collectors who return, collectors who want to continue a dialogue because they care to stay in touch, collectors who are friends are the best.

After dinner I got a call from my old pal Phil. He was in the mood to talk and I was in the mood to entertain him with my silly stories. At one point during our meandering conversation he took another call, then clicked back.

"They got Osama Bin Laden, talk tomorrow."

I turned on the news and watched President Obama (a guy with almost the same name) report on the death of our nation's latest greatest villain. I never believed that he was the height of evil given his chummy resume with high and mighty flourishes, but who cares what I think. One less asshole in the world who propagated the buzzword 'terror,' not unlike our media or elected officials who carpet bomb us for their corporate-coffered, politically correct corruption. Karma is lifetimes.

May 2 Monday

The day after a show or Open Studio is always tricky. There is thrill or disappointment, so I counterbalance whatever extreme is pumping through my veins, monitoring the erratic spirit of my heartbeat. I think that stage actors and touring musicians have to work with this energy constantly, professional athletes certainly, armed forces. The 'post-show blues' poetically describes the human condition and its preceding counterpoint, whatever performance that happened to be.

I took it easy today, working half speed, a momentary respite this busy spring. I recorded a song, watched a movie or two, chipped away at my website, posting 5 strong new reviews of *Baloney*. These reviews confirm I have a writing voice that people want to support, which is one of the best feelings I've ever experienced in my art career.

I ordered frames for four landscapes that I will be showing on Thursday. If I'm lucky I will sell some work. Art is a poker game, and you are sitting at the table wondering if you have the best hand. Your collectors are at the table playing with you. You do a conversational dance, measuring one another out. Your job is never to flinch, to hold on for dear life while you are falling out of an airplane at 15,000 feet with nothing beneath you. This is a thrill ride sure, it creates the ebb and flow of an artist's existence, his studio, his lifeblood, his inspiration, his output. I've earned every inch of this turf by the blood trail that has brought me into this unique space.

I remember listening to Arthur Danto's pompous, bullshit talk at the Whitney in 1997, as he explained to me that art had ended, that 'art' since 1963 was not 'art' but 'post-historical character.' There were a bunch of artists and collectors sitting there, nodding, laughing politely, applauding these intellectual acrobatics. Art is an institution and will never end, it is a language, a way of life that people live, who are on a path to originality, a singularity and universality that can be held in the palm of the same hand. I've seen that place and I live it, so Arthur Danto and other failed creatives who spend their cynical lives kneecapping or beekeeping artists with their poisonous pens can kiss off.

May 3 Tuesday

I saw my mother's singing group today and they were radiant. My mom was beautiful and I was proud to be her son. Their songs soared and enlightened the people in the audience, most of whom have seen younger days. I felt compassionate for the older people who had trouble getting around. They had once skipped and played and excelled at sports and were captains of industry and made big bubbling families and are in this place now, slowly fading away from view. The elderly who were decent in life should be carried around on bronze shields to teach us all.

May 4 Wednesday

I sat with an old friend in the afternoon who was in emotional trouble, trying to keep his family intact. His anguish was vocal and palpable. He shared on account of my witnessing news he was receiving as we sat there for lunch. He did not intend to share with me but there I was and I was a good listener. I stayed with him until his family could relieve me. I saw him at one of his darkest hours. I am not his best friend but I will be his confidant for life. Nothing is more important.

Honor is a strong thing to live in. Honor is quiet and foreboding but there is grace in honor. Most people don't think about this. Information slips from the mouths of people all the time, a sign of weakness really. I hear an admission from a friend and that friend is the only one who holds the key... if he does not bring the key to jog my memory that information is lost. This is the only way to be a confidant. A confidant holds power that he or she did not ask for but treasures and forgets. By listening and being compassionate one human being can be of deep assistance to a fellow stranger in need. Sometimes people in their moments of weakness must share the circle of life that perpetuates the best of humanity.

May 5 Thursday

Art is humanity in motion; compassion, grace, deadly precision, soft and hard at the same time, a lover and a killer all rolled into one.

I have to choose my friends and inner council members wisely or I will be shelling out energy that I can't afford to give. A lot of people get wrapped up in strange vibrations, then spend their lives chasing the bouncing echoes of their energy draining behavior, unawares, one step behind.

It is terrifying to walk on the edge and find one's own voice, one's own truth, the most difficult thing I've ever had to do. It's hard to find others out there with their own voices but they are sprinkled around, blossoming leaves on the tree of life.

May 6 Friday

I had lunch with Alan and Jeanne, married 50 years, two of my favorite people. I worked with them on a project they brought to me 13 years ago, illustrating and publishing *101 Uses For a Long Schlong*, one of the funniest cartoon books I have ever seen that should be in every single bathroom all over the world for its humor. Alan shopped it to publishers, it went right to the top of every publishing house, and the rejection letters were impressive, but nobody would touch the project. Alan Abel is our nation's most famous hoaxer, whose dossier and hysterical storytelling are remarkable. Our friendship has remained mutually inspiring over years of many brainstorming lunches about the arts in general.

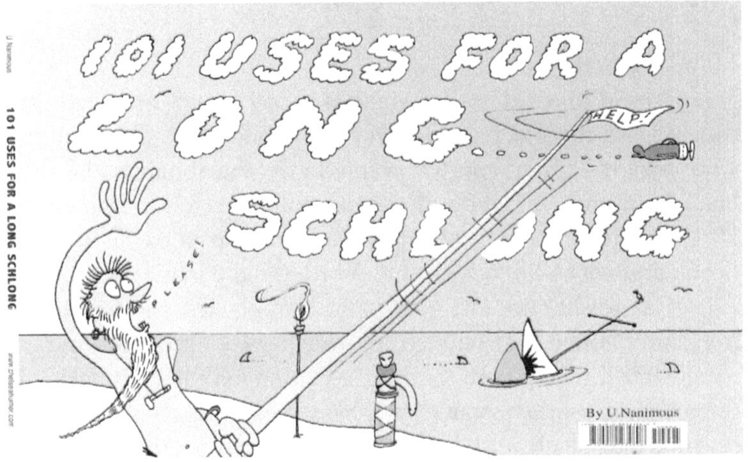

May 7 Saturday

I went 2 games to my brother's 1 this morning, edging him out this week.

I emailed my Dad that I will be etching a NY Rangers logo on a gravestone. When the Rangers won the Stanley Cup my father bought 30 highlight movies of their season to distribute to all his friends. His enthusiasm has always been infectious, even for the prospect of his son etching a Rangers logo on a granite gravestone.

"Great news!" he emailed back. I often juxtapose my father's boundless enthusiasm with my mother's New Yorker deadpan wit and gallows humor, a balance that makes perfect sense to me at least... maybe because I am the blend.

May 8 Sunday

Art surrounds and enriches me, but paradoxically I cannot afford to purchase this art; I can only afford to make it with my own hands.

May 9 Monday

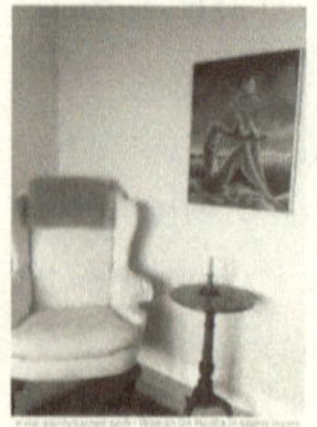

My friends who bought 'Contemplating Woman on the Rocks' sent a photograph of her hanging in their Maine house, which made me miss my painting. The answer to every feeling is to paint, so I went to the easel with post-racquetball coffee in hand and started painting another Garnett figure.

May 10 Tuesday

I went to a car wash, which is a real luxury as usually the rain washes my old beaters. The blue-uniformed, abrasive dick who 'took my order' sported pointed gray facial hair and a dyed black buzz cut with white tube socks pulled up to his long shorts. He seemed like the type of guy who would start a bar fight or get drunk and knock his kids around. I ordered the manager's special.

Car washes are fast food joints for vehicles. Inside, I drank free shitty coffee that scalded my tongue. I picked up some car swag while listening to the blaring television infomercials, taking in the array of synthetic car scents, heavily wafting cheap perfume, ceramic tile bleach, and the greasy spoon order for the entire shop that came in as my hot wheels popped out of auto-cycle.

They finished my car with that cheesy tire polish I dislike. There was a cop waiting for his car. An illegal alien drove the cop car out of the car wash and started drying it. He understood no English. I wondered why the cops would have an account with this place if one of the head guys was a dick. I saw the fire chief pull in as well. When my car was done I struggled to get a new steering wheel cover on. The fire chief signaled to me, probably in Morse code, and I opened the squeaky door.

"It might take you awhile to get that thing on yourself. Here, let me help." He put his weight into it and we got her done. I shook his hand, thanked him and was out of that car wash for good.

May 11 Wednesday

As kind of a washed up athlete who wandered into the wild

lands of art, bringing with me a jockstrap mentality, I liken art to sports all the time because my family is filled with athletes and this is how we communicate.

Athletes have a work ethic around their minds and bodies that artists don't necessarily think about. I apply these principles to art survival and it helps. I am used to getting abused and beaten up in this game, another thing that athletes are good at. They get beaten down, they get back up and keep coming at you. They take abuse with a longer eye on ultimate victory. They sacrifice their bodies for the sake of their team. They are team players. They know how to get along with other people, how to go through good times and bad with their teammates, how to rise to the occasion, how to win, how to have honor, how to get better. Artists don't operate in these parameters. A lot of artists are non-athletes with sometimes weird vibrations. They are not all easy to get along with. They are territorial and defensive often in ways that would seem petty to the athlete. Athletes know the rules and it's all out in the open. If you can do this you are the best man. There is none of that in art. In art the goal line is always changing, depending upon who has the power, holds the key, is in the right club, throws out the most intellectual acrobatics, angles for the strongest strategic position.

A lot of art people make fun of athletes because athletes can be dumb jocks, and artistic kids get worked over because art people are different and sometimes they suck at sports. This divide happens early. You can see it on the playground like a National Geographic special. Neither way of seeing is incorrect. Both ways of life perpetuate the fabric of humanity as we are all united, even if this is hard to see. One can be a great athlete, artistic, intelligent and decent. Artists can be athletic, intelligent and decent as well. Usually the extremes dominate and stereotypes get all the headlines, as stereotypes go, as media goes.

May 12 Thursday

The captain's seat on my jeep broke so my brother Christian picked me up at Vinnie's, who is the family mechanic. Years ago I explained Vinnie to my mother in New Yorker.

"Mom, I walk in and say, "Hey Vinnie." He turns around and says, "Hey, what?""

The next day my mother took her car to Vinnie and so it has been ever since with all the cars. Vinnie is the honest mechanic who tells you not to waste your money on stupid repairs. I don't waste money on cars, but I'd like to think that I've outgrown that decade-long phase of unreliable shit boxes I burned through to get my fancy pants to this point, driving an old green Grand Cherokee Limited with 180,000 miles on it. Oh yeah.

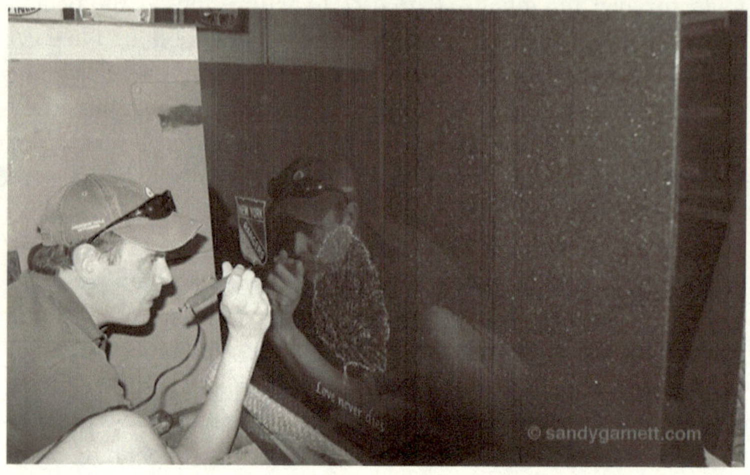

May 13 Friday

I went over to the monument shop and spent four hours etching a New York Rangers logo, an oak tree, and in cursive 'love never dies' below the tree. I always feel like I'm doing something nice for families when I do a gravestone etching. Gravestone etching is a great way to break up painting sessions on either side of the day. Easel > gravestone > easel = creative day well spent.

May 14 Saturday

I swapped my van for my car at Vinnie's so he could work on a few things. My friend Danny, who owns Fishtales Seafood Company in New Canaan, gave me this great van with low mileage when he bought a new one a couple years back. I did his website and I do art stuff for him when he needs it. We were out on Walter's Canyon Lady, cutting through fog and looking out for floating lumber on the way to Montauk when it came up.

"I'm going to get rid of my Astro," Danny said.

"I used to have a white Astro and loved that van."

"You want an Astro? This one's blue. Low mileage. Great van to go to the markets in Boston and New York. It's so reliable that I sold it five years ago and bought it back again when my friend stopped using it."

He certainly did. When I went to pick it up Danny emerged from behind the glass case of fresh fish and took me out front. The van was all dinged up, and when he opened the side door I almost fainted when I caught a whiff inside. Years of baking sun crusted the fish sauce soup glaze all over the carpet, rusting out the rear bed. Danny waved his arms around like he was revealing a beautiful blonde after having sawed her in half during a magic show, as if to gesture 'Ta-Dah!'

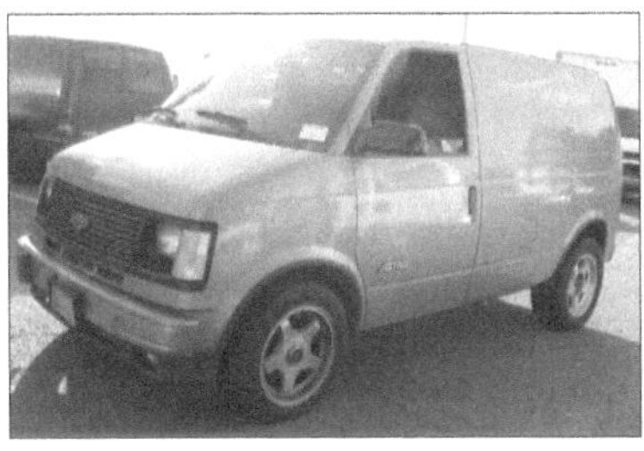

"Danny, she's a real beauty. Thanks so much."

I cut away the wet fish-smelling carpet, I peeled the mats out, I ground away the floor rust, I sprayed the bumpers matte black, the rusty hubs silver, spot-sprayed blue lightly inside and out, and I sprayed a textured black paint in the back bed. I aired the van out and over time the fish smell drifted away. Voila is right. New van.

Artists are always moving stuff around so small vans are great. Every time you need a van for five minutes it's a pain in the ass rental, so why not pick up a used van if you have a couple bucks and the space to park it? You use it once a month and everyone wants to borrow it as well, which is fine with me.

May 15 Sunday

I received an email from a collector who wondered if I remembered her. Do I remember her. My mother brought her and her pretty friend three years ago. I thought it would be a quick spin but they were serious and inspired me to pull out my entire inventory over the course of a five hour studio visit. Beth wanted one of my best paintings then and I delivered 'Contemplating Woman in Red' a week later. She is interested in another painting so

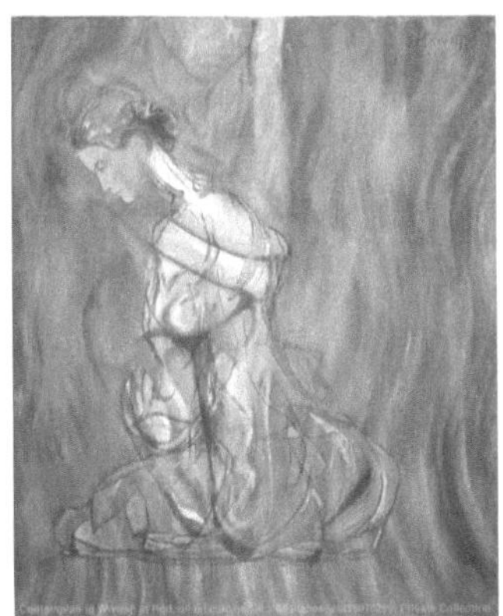

we started talking about it via email today. Thanks to my catalogue system I quickly identified the image and hopefully have found a home for this recent painting.

Collectors help me live my dream so they are very important people to me, always appreciated and never forgotten.

People know you for the few moments they scrape into your energy. As a working artist who covers a lot of aesthetic ground I have many people who only know me for one or two works they might have seen in passing. I find it interesting when an old friend discovers that I have another body of work they've never seen before. It is the long string of one's experience that often makes the most interesting story, like the arc of an arrow in flight from quiver to target. The breadth of one's life or career can be illuminated with diligent archiving and balanced, artful documentary.

May 16 Monday

In the bloody art game you learn to trust only your own shadow. Maybe this is the place you need to arrive at in order to survive by your creative talents alone. Your hunting instruments are sharp, your senses are on another plane, you live in a spirit world and can make fire to feed yourself for the next day. This is not for the faint of heart. It's for the lion heart. It is a rare space and it is isolating. The isolation is a necessity and a curse at once. Sometimes you wonder if you will ever feel the sense of community again that is life, love, family.

I am on the cliff so long that I am rusty and numb. I have to be reeled back in from the brink. Here is love and friendship. I have been to this edge, I have seen this flame, I hold it with me and I can talk about it, I can make with it, it is clay in my hands. It will take me down or I will bring it back to my village, where it can be shared or ignored. This sense of community is something I long for sometimes, my illusion of less struggle perhaps. In togetherness humans can achieve a different sort of magic. This balance, this moderation, this meditation, this concentration makes me wake up and want to do it all over again.

May 17 Tuesday

This morning I crushed my brother 3 games to 0. He owes me after he stomped on my head all last week.

It was pouring when we left the gym at 6:50 am. I was drenched with sweat so I couldn't feel the cold, sideways rain slashing my face. I hopped over huge puddles and watched the rivers of water stream into the gutters at stop lights on the way back to the studio. Paper art and books don't like the rain. Stone and oil on canvas don't give a crap, like the marble pillar they just cut for me in Vermont.

I always felt like I died in a puddle on some stormy battlefield in another lifetime, so I don't like the rain. Other people can't wait get out there, prance around and do Broadway numbers when it starts spritzing. I don't understand this sentiment, although the net result of an early season rain is green bloom; everything plump, ripe, all the leaves filled in, juicy, ready for action, ready to inspire the mind.

This reminds me of my friend's son Gerald, who woke up his father to report that Riley was dancing. My friend rolled over and Riley, a female lab, was going nuts on her dog bed, just humping the hell out of it. Later that morning Gerald got on all fours and imitated Riley's dance to his mother and sisters. Time for some puppies and fluffy, green leaves of spring. Plus the stripers are running in Long Island Sound.

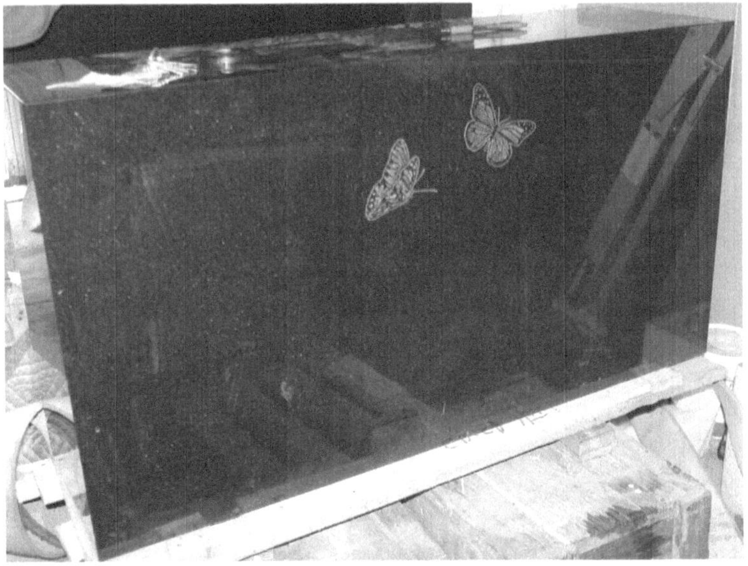

May 19 Thursday

I etched two monarch butterflies on a massive slab of black granite today, then I etched a chainsaw on another stone. While I etch my mind drifts from current projects to life and death to thoughts about karma to thoughts about the rhythms of the diamond-tipped buzzing needle skipping across the surface of the stone, my hand on the cold surface to steady the instrument. Sometimes a spirit will come in as I am giving my energy out, trying to do something nice to help the grieving family along. I'm never sad when I do an etching. Sometimes a story is sad but I'm there to do nice things for the living and the dead, so I feel peaceful and protected in some way.

May 20 Friday

After painting all day into the evening I went to Walter's for an old friend function, a special generational place that has been the site of some of my best memories and friendships. Places hold a key to the heart as humans move through time. I remember being in Mykonos, Greece, feeling like a spec of dust in the wind, like I belonged there, like I could die there, the Mediterranean blues lulling me into a deep sense of peace and soulful slumber. I'm feistier, so the Mediterranean is nice to visit but I'm afraid I would not get much done in a beautiful place like that if I lived there. The New England seasons have a haunting nature all their own, a constant cycle as people move through their lives. This place represents spring, summer and fall in New England, on Long Island Sound, breathing in the saltwater smell fused with fire and music and laughter and decades of friendship, gathering, celebrating life and love and sadness over the years. It is spring and spring feels good.

May 21 Saturday

Today I worked with an old friend, bringing him up to speed on a sculpture project I will be pitching. My friend can go into your house and fix everything, rework anything, or turn your house inside out if you ask him to. He is strong, fast, reliable, professional, smart, technical, with attention to minute detail, in appreciation of how people process aesthetics, how they think, he knows how to communicate with people who have a lot of stuff. He deconstructed a project or two for me, going right to the source of some of the questions I had for him.

I have learned that if I don't know something I will ask someone who knows more than I do about the subject. When I get the more astute opinion of someone I respect I will apply it quickly. I have built a solid network of problem solvers to help me run my fine art studio. This takes time and relationship building, a little humility, humor, patience, a knack for finding and nurturing talent.

May 22 Sunday

After a day of family time and art making I went to the bar down the street for a drink with the bound copy of this document to read and make notes on. There was a group to my left which including a drunken brunette, who sauntered over, swinging her beer around like a lady of the night, real sexy-like.

"What the fuck are you doing writing on that book?"

"I wrote this book and I'm taking notes for editing."

"You didn't write that, Mr. Smartypants!"

She swiped the book out of my hands and I pointed at the photograph of me on the back of the mock book cover. She still didn't believe me.

"Well I think this book is a piece of crap and I think I'll just shove it up my cooter!" she warned, as she tossed the book on the bar and leaned back into her smirking friends, who seemed amused to take in the show. I had another drink and left the bar when the pouring rain let up.

"I think your book is retarded!" the sloppy-cocked woman mustered as I left my barstool.

"Thanks very much for that!" I said, on the way out the door, which got a laugh out of this bitch's friends.

I wondered what this person was missing in life to go after mine, not out of compassion, but as she might make a good fictional character. I started writing her background on the two minute walk home through the midnight mist, but her character was only about two minutes long and not worthy of much else.

May 23 Monday

My car is falling apart. The A/C vent leaks water onto my foot every time I take a corner, so my car smells like a putrid sauna. The center console top I rest my arm on broke so that falls off while I'm driving all the time. There is a rattle where the catalytic converter is busted, the ignition sticks, I've got an old crappy stereo, my way back is destroyed because of the battery I let sit there for months. The exterior is fine, scraped up a little, the rear bumper is a little pinged, the antenna is bent. The four-wheel drive is iffy and the transmission sometimes doesn't kick into gear, which makes me nervous around railroad tracks. The left front light has a loose wire so I have to remember to tap it until the beam starts shining. My door squeaks loud enough that Walter, who likes his new cars, laughs every time he hears that piece of shit door close. When I start the car up with the A/C on the whole neighborhood can hear my fan belt. I've got a steel squeak in the wheels as they roll that just gets louder. The tires need a changing. Maybe I could trade a painting for another car one of these days.

May 24 Tuesday

This evening I sat on an art panel designed to encourage parents to support creativity in their high school students. There was a professional actress, two high school musicians who have performed professionally and a high school ballerina who has also been accepted and is taking classes at Julliard.

The MC was a talented music teacher and speaker who warmed the room up. The high school students on the panel spoke about their semi-professional experiences maturely, the actress was animated and informative, then I read from a script I had written about my experience as a student artist and how I migrated to a fine art career. I am better off the cuff than reading from a script.

Teenagers are trying to be adults, and the adults around teenagers are trying to allow them to maintain the beauty of their optimistic youth. During the panel I tempered my perspective about entering a career in the arts. When I started off on the art career I had very little skepticism. It's like walking into a paper shredder. Have fun! You'll shine like a diamond! Laughter. Applause.

May 25 Wednesday

I sailed tonight with Captain Al, Pete, and Phil on Al's 33-foot Far. I have been in the bow for three years. This is a work horse position as I am changing and setting the jib and spinnaker, that big puffy sail for downwind legs that makes for nice photographs. Long Island Sound sailing is its own animal. I started racing five years ago. The first year I was ballast, the second year I was learning the bow, the third year and last year I was in the bow earning my keep.

The sun was shining and the wind cooperated with us until the last downward leg, when the wind died and the smaller boats caught up to us. The boats in our fleet are handicapped as they are all different designs, sizes and shapes, which is frustrating because each boat performs differently depending upon the nature of the wind and water during a given race.

I am happy to be back on the boat for another season and leave shore behind with friends, working together, sharing stories, laughing, competing weekly with some beer can racing.

May 26 Thursday

The climate in our time is so different than the vibrations that abounded before the market fell apart, and this was three years ago, not yesterday. People were consumed with objects and expansion and home equity lines and material things. A lot of this language, this perspective, this need for physical objects has been replaced by a growing humility that I am not used to seeing. I never had very far to fall financially, so when people with a lot of material wealth started talking about losing their stuff and how they no longer had the money they used to have, I was not really in the same boat. I mean, my boat has always been the same one.

May 27 Friday

I finished and archived the little portrait of Alex for her sister Vicki this morning. She was coming from Vermont into Brooklyn for her sister's birthday tonight. I asked my brother to give her the painting today while I was in Long Island selling art.

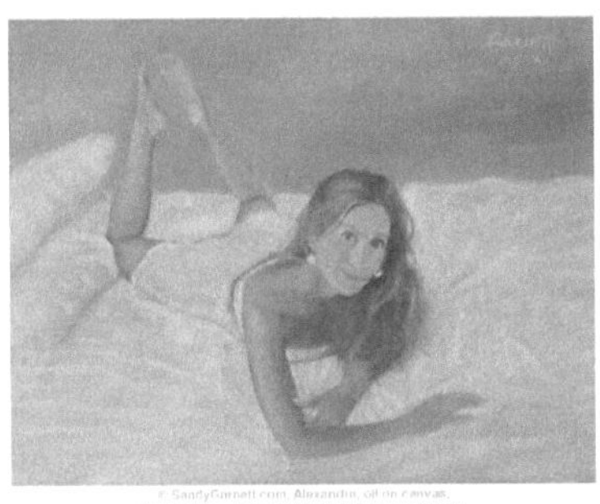

Ferry culture is a well-oiled machine, the perfect mix of organization and relaxation. You have to pack and plan to be there on time, but then you get on the boat and you kick back with other like-minded people, drawn to ferries, to islands, to moving from one place to feel another way for a weekend. The flip flops come out, the mellow family communing, the tables of storytelling simmer, people talk about old memories, different places, all the while on board a large ferry that tucks in 100 cars and 500 passengers, traveling on Long Island Sound at 18 knots. Island culture, vacation culture, boat culture, seasonal culture. It is good to get out and enjoy the turning of the seasons along with everyone else who appreciates the brightness of

New England when the cold goes away and summer comes again.

May 28 Saturday

Gallerists and consultants note that my prices are too low, which I agree with. Most of my sales are direct, I have built my name organically over time, and I am self-sufficient, which is valuable. I walk in no man's land to a certain extent. Collectors and gallerists ask me why I am not yet represented, wondering if there is something wrong with me, if I am tricky to work with. The answer is no, I am easy to work with and I have been asked to sign with gallerists in the past, but I like the freedom to make whatever I want, which does not easily fit into the architecture of the contemporary high art market. In order to cast my broad net and make my case I needed to paint the first 1000 paintings and 50 sculptures in the hinterlands, outside the overbearing influence of any market regulation that might narrow my focus into a 'name brand' worth looking at by the standard conventions of New York City. Now that I have a foundation built on my own? I look forward to finding the right gallerist(s) when the time comes.

May 29 Sunday

Artists are project people, with projects lying around from various periods of their lives that can always be picked up and worked on again. Some projects are fire hose blasts, completed quickly, others develop incrementally over time, some take decades to reveal. I played around with my new Twister painting this morning and I scraped the glaze off a song that needs help. I have too many songs inside of me for this visual artist to get out, so I might as well make a couple of good ones.

Songs are different creatures than paintings. In a painting all of the information is presented to you in one image, whereas with a song or film the audience must absorb the work in time-space. Writing and reading seem to fall in between somehow. Paintings will simply project themselves at you like songs do, so you have to close your ears or look away if you don't like what you see or hear. A book sits there silently on the table and can be a doorstop or start a revolution. Strange, interesting business, juxtaposing mediums.

May 30 Monday

Memorial Day. Respect to all who have served.

Last night I went to the beach for a Memorial Day barbecue

with friends from the fire house that best friend Bill's family has always belonged to, so it was nice to see everyone. I've done tee shirt design for their fundraiser every year for twenty years, and although I am retired from this type of work I will always do their tee shirt designs if they want me to. Firefighters are good people who work hard and have nice families. There is no pretense, they work together, their hearts are in the right place, they get an adrenalin buzz from the equipment and machinery of their business, there is camaraderie that is a lifetime of depth in these institutions, all with the overarching goal to put out fires, save lives, keep their hometowns safe and peaceful.

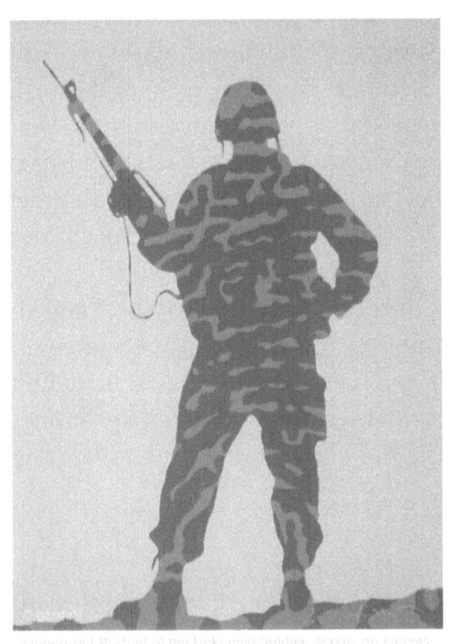
Fingerprint Portrait of the Unknown Soldier, acrylic on canvas

Thirty kids were running around on the beach. The older kids, the young men, who are now firefighters as well, sat with their fathers around the grills, generations slowly bleeding into one another, blending with one another, bonding with one another. This continuity is important for communities but is often lost on many people who feel disconnected by contemporary society. Uproot, move to a new place, make new friends, have a transient job, eschew tradition, make your own self up as you go, give yourself a face-lift every decade. In the loss of community the spirit is at sea, free yet without safe harbor often. There can be safe harbor for deep thinkers, daily meditators, focused spiritualists who see beyond this planet, this time, into other worlds I suppose, but nothing replaces community, a sense of tradition, friendship and family.

May 31 Tuesday

Artists are twenty-four hours a day, but it's good to check your artist at the door sometimes, enter into different worlds where art doesn't matter. When you dive in the pool and your nephew is jumping on your head, art just does not matter at all. When you are laughing with your family members about an event in the past, art does not matter at all. When you sit in a line with your Dad and two brothers watching the NCAA Lacrosse Championships and you see Virginia beat Maryland 9-6, you remember that art does not matter at all in this world... the world of lacrosse. Yes, lacrosse is its own art form, and yes, art can be found in any of these activities, but a painting or a sculpture have no bearings in these places. The important thing to remember in the spaceship of art is that I am also along for the ride to be a participating family member; useful to society in that way, not just as a grommet art rogue rolling the rock up the hill in my studio yet another day of torture and glory.

June 1 Wednesday

Art is the pearl in the oyster. You dive down, hold your breath long enough, get comfortable in that underwater space, avoid the dangers of self-sabotage, pull up the oysters and start prying them open. A pearl can be found on every afternoon diving off the bow of your little boat if you get used to it and the water gets used to you. You learn to stay respectful, healthy, keep your head on straight, take what nature gives you, exercise gratitude, peaceful living, perpetuate the good juju so you can wake up and do it all over again.

June 2 Thursday

The Mural Committee loved my new concept of a tightrope walker that would have a kinetic component to it. I brought all of my art books, which the Committee poured over enthusiastically during the meeting. On the way out a Committee member asked if I would make a smaller version of a painting she had seen in one of my books, a still life Reconstruction from 1997.

I returned home a little confused by my good luck. If I get this project it's fanfare, some meal tickets, art studio fuel, and it will qualify me for other public art projects of this scale.

June 3 Friday

When I stumble upon an incomplete picture, my job is to inform the painting, to sit inside it, to bounce light around like a flashlight, to play with the palette, to get micro and macro with the space, to build the painting into a meaty, breathing experience that no longer requires me.

I walk amongst these things that are cast about my life, lying around to goad me and tempt me at every turn, every corner of my existence in this space I have built, this temple of contemplation for lack of a better term. I find kindling to light a fire that will see me through to the next day. I live with the stories that make me who I am and will move along the winds of time to other places and other people. The residue of my paint brush will emote long after my heart is beating. In the best cases these parts of me will inspire the next crop of human beings in their quiet moments when they sit with my canvas or sculpture to contemplate the things I once thought and felt and made for the ages, if only for a moment.

June 4 Saturday

It's strange to live timelessly, but there are rewards. The faces grow older around me but the ideas remain fresh and fleeting, shimmering in the sea of humanity from where they are caught and placed in glass to reflect upon. I am a fisherman to this extent, or an excavator, a historian of sorts as I walk along the lines of this earth in my particular time. My time will pass but the passage that I speak of is the passage of all living, thinking, breathing creatures to a lessor or greater degree. To know that one is walking this way is powerful, strangely, and often is the only vibration necessary to propel the next adventure. People say I should travel, which I do. From any one of the easel chairs in my studio I visit lands that are foreign to me and there is a thrill in every experience, a bright burn that can never be recounted, although the remnants of my journey can be found on these shreds of canvas I have informed all my life.

5 June Sunday

Last night Walter called and we grilled on his deck. We watched the Bruins lose to Vancouver in the second game of the Stanley Cup, 3-2 in a 14 second overtime. We talked about life, music, friends, fishing, all the things that best friends talk about. It was late enough and he told me to sleep on the couch.

I woke up, had a bagel with the kids, cracked them up a little bit, juggled the soccer ball with them, then drove home to watch Federer play against Nadal in the French Open finals. I called my sailing captain Alex, whose son is ranked in Connecticut tennis, because I wanted to watch tennis with someone who gets it. He told me to come over. Walter called and told me to go to the beach in the afternoon as he was taking his kids there. I watched tennis with Alex, then beach. A lot of old friends were there, laughter and a good time. My friend Caroline ordered 15 *Baloney* books for her book club, so this was a good way to cap the weekend.

June 6 Monday

Back on the court at 6 am, we split games 16-14, 14-16. The competition was tight and we both held steady. I don't mind an even match, a great way to start any week.

Morning was spent on inventory book color corrections and sketching out the poster for Walter's party. Afternoon into evening I hit the easel hard and got some focused painting in.

June 7 Tuesday

My studio was a mess so I cleaned it up all day. I designed my studio so that it is always dynamic, never boring, warm yet utilitarian, a space that can look very clean, orderly and professional for meetings and studio visits without too much effort.

June 8 Wednesday

Three Mural Committee members visited my studio at 11 am. After pleasantries, they sat on my couch in a row and informed me that I have won the public art mural commission. They want the runner-up to do another wall in town, effectively trying to get two art projects for one budget, so they asked if I could think about doing the tightrope walker mural project for 'half price.' I was gracious and thanked the Committee members for their time and energy, the rest of the day tortured about how to manage a severely reduced budget.

My sailing team got off the starting line okay, but the wind died and we were drifting, getting sucked out to sea by the emptying Long Island Sound tide. There was no sailing to do, so before they called the race I presented the mural prospect to my three finance-oriented teammates. They all concurred that I have to take the mural project, that the exposure is worth its weight.

June 9 Thursday

Sometimes sleep is a clarifying agent. The sensation of

winning this public art commission, shaded by healthy skepticism, sunk in today and energized my spirit.

The economy is flagging, people are out of work, hungry, beaten, tired, changing careers to make ends meet, their retirements gone, their house values drawn and quartered, the carnage long and wide, and I just won my largest art gig ever.

I painted in the morning before going to curate and install a show with my friend Lina at the Loft Gallery in Stamford. Hanging shows with Lina is fast, sharp fun. After we haggle amusingly over placement and lean the art against the walls, I hold the work up, Lina directs the up and down and left and right, then we both look and adjust. I moved one painting seven times to get it right while she was labeling the work at the end of our session. She does her thing while I fuss about inches and shadows. Composition of a show, a painting one inch left or right, can make a huge difference. Lina gets this too but she enjoys watching me labor over the tiniest details. It amuses her.

After the show was squared away we stepped outside into the steady rain. Artists forget weather. I am painting and not in the weather for days, then I go on an errand and realize there is a change in the temperature, or it is raining, or it is sunny. We drove over to a Greek restaurant for dinner with Lina's husband Larry and our friends Patrick and Kim. We talked and laughed and ate excellent food. Kim and Patrick had recently been to Charleston and had taken a day drive to see Pearl Fryar's world famous garden, something I discovered and passed along to Patrick after seeing a film titled 'A Man Named Pearl.' I'm happy my old friends took the time to visit, enjoying a personal tour from Pearl himself.

June 10 Friday

My inner council aligns with me, adjusts as the information seeps in, encourages me, supports me, gives good energy. I give it back when I am called upon. Trust and love. Selecting the best people to grace one's inner council is a lifetime, and the seats must shift as people come and go, as people die or change and are reborn elsewhere.

I spun by the art opening I installed with Lina then I stopped by Walter's to watch the Bruins lose to Vancouver. He talked about the shark fishing schedule and field clearing machinery, which he has been investigating. I told him that Matt and Phil think I should drive a hard bargain about the mural, while Bill and others have told me I can't pass it up. Walter said that usually I would have to pay a lot of money for a billboard promoting myself. This is the best argument for doing the mural that I have heard all week.

June 11 Saturday

I picked up a commission to paint a smaller rendition of my 256th painting, a still life with roses and oranges I created 14 years ago. This was the first painting I made with Phil. He got a vase, roses, oranges, wine, a wine glass, we set up our easels and painted for three or four hours, then we played chess and talked about girls when not talking about art. This was the beginning of a big creative time, the year I really started making some ambitious original work, after a year of heartache. The woman I had lived with for three years and her son had moved to LA and I had broken it off after my aunt had died of cancer. I felt a vacuum, no support on the lover front, so I fell out of love and let the girl go. The hardest part was letting the boy go, who I thankfully remain in touch with. This was a triple dose of sadness at the same time my creativity was blossoming, so I always look at this first still life nostalgically. Paintings are markers in time like photographs in family albums. It will be nice to reprise that painting with a lighter heart and a more fluent paintbrush, 750 paintings down the road.

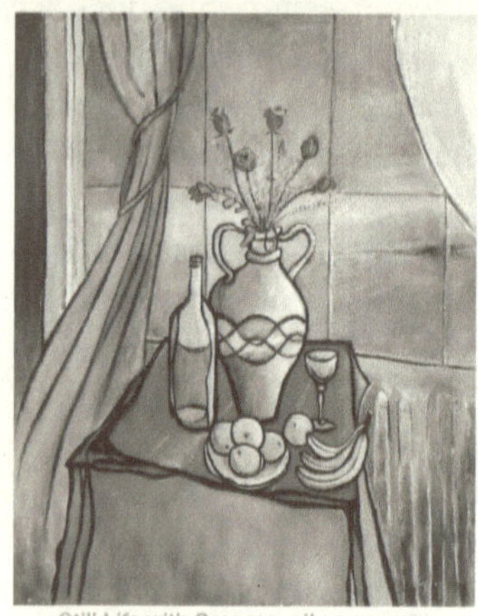
Still Life with Oranges, oil on canvas, 48 x 40 inches, 1997, © Sandy Garnett

June 12 Sunday

Last night I went over to Walter's house for dinner and drew with his kids. I showed his daughter a music making program that will complement her video editing inclinations. After dinner I was going to a party my brother Christian's friend was throwing and Walter wanted to come along. Bella didn't mind so off we went.

The party was fun. There were good people and pretty girls. A new friend wants me to meet her friend, whose wife is a highly regarded gallerist. My friend's only condition is that I will give a painting to her if I get picked up by the gallery. No problem. I have had this offer on the table years now for anyone who will help me find the right long term gallery relationship.

I have been independent for twenty years, I have painted 1025 paintings, my art has bought me my home, my studio, all of my stuff; my cars, the clothes on my back, the food that I eat, the music equipment that I play with, the couch that I designed and built, the dates I go out on sparingly. If I had a couple big guys in my corner my prices would not double, they would shoot up five or ten times. I could put braces on my future children's teeth, outfit them for sports, take them to all the museums and some fun shows, send them on summer vacations, and put them through college. Maybe this is wishful thinking, or maybe this is my future. I just have to keep slinging the paint and we'll see which way the wind blows, as my mother might say with a cute smile.

It has been suggested that the mural might occur next year as opposed to now. It seems that some people are working on details to help me as an artist, which is rare and welcomed. Sometimes it makes me feel not so alone when I have a little support. When I use the word 'alone' I mean in the context of fear that nobody will support my art career, which all artists understand. This solitude is deep and dark and dangerous, a game of chicken with the soul. You have to hold, hold, hold out, not flinch while the terror starts to consume you, the thought that you might not pull it off, that you can't cover, that you are underwater too deep. I never gave myself a choice, a back door, I never fled to another career, I never went away from the center, the art center. The art was always the answer, always the key, so in times of desperation I must lose my inhibitions, shelve the fear and frolic in the pure joy of art making. In this space, flirting with oblivion, the true self emerges, and this energy somehow resonates, perpetuates, rings into the souls of others who hear my call and come in to support me. This is an unspoken thing so perhaps it's not for telling but it is my truth as a professional artist for twenty years. I don't ask questions. I just try to live simply and be prolific, I try to live in the solution. Love perpetuates love.

June 13 Monday

Last night after dinner I was walking to the car when a bug flew directly into my left eyeball. My eyelids reacted immediately by closing and crushing the insect into parts that got lost in my eyelids, which staggered me back and confused my brain all night and this morning. I just found another piece of the bug and used a cue tip to extract it from my lower eyelid. It will come out in the wash. It's good to have two working eyes whenever possible as a visual artist.

6 am racquetball. My brother took me 16-14 and I got him 15-8 in a strategic, well fought battle. I made a bunch of errors but I am reducing the frustration, letting that dissipate. Hanging onto frustration is like crying over spilt milk, and you can't afford even several seconds between points to do this because it will hurt your mental fortitude.

I went over to visit my father, who sat with my aunt Sally, up from Florida, to work on the family pictorial history book. I was their tech geek for an hour, showing them easier ways to manipulate, organize, lay out photos for the book, make captions, copy and paste things, do screen shots, label images, transfer files from CD's to the hard drive. This is all cursory stuff but I've been doing it for a long time. I commended my father and my aunt for working together to make this family photo book. Everyone will be really happy to see it, and only five of us know anything about it, so the surprise should be really special.

June 14 Tuesday

We split games again this morning. Chasing after a ball for a team athlete is so much more fun than running. I am a better artist than I am a runner. The best runners blank out, space out, let time sift by, which I do when I am in the Zen zone of art. But when I run I start creating, then I get antsy to make art with my hands after three miles. Running is not half the fun of smashing a racquetball at your brother every morning, playing the angles, a couple of thrilling points, a smile and handshake after some stiff competition at 6 am on a school day.

I started the still life commission and memories flooded my mind of the night the original was painted. I remember that Phil was frustrated because I was painting in my early Reconstructionist style and he wanted to watch me paint traditionally, which I had been doing all that particular day on another canvas. No, I said I was working on blending different styles and genres, just to stoke the flames and laugh with him a little. These thoughts and other paintings from around this time emerged from memory with paintbrush in hand today, recreating an old image... pure joy.

June 15 Wednesday

I started hand lettering the poster on my drawing table, I sketched Bob Marley on aluminum as a birthday present for Walter, and I worked on the still life into evening. I moved from easel to drawing table to recording studio to office computer, letting the work do what it would with me. These are my favorite creative days, and often feel like full day meditations.

June 16 Thursday

The management company of the building one of my art organizations is in, which gave out short term 'licenses' and not leases when we were kicked out of the old building, wants to tack on an electric surcharge that will increase the rents of 40 artists by 33% next month. The fallout from this 33% increase in rent for my forty artist friends is big. Essentially the message is 'find another building because we don't want you here any longer.' I lived that feeling every day for ten years and it really sucks, as most artists can attest to.

This is a typical situation that artists have to endure when renting. They move into a delapidated area, they exist like cockroaches for decades, they beautify the place and bring a lot of people into the adventure of living on the edge, some people get it, buy the properties surrounding the artists, gentrify the place then toss the artists out.

Artists are treated like crap, looked down upon, beaten up for their originality. This was clear to me early on. People would look right through me when I said that I was an artist, or they simply would not believe that art is how I sustained myself. I used my stubborn nature to become self-sufficient, something that most artists can never achieve for one reason or a million reasons. After twelve years of post-college struggle I bought and renovated my two FU spaces. Now when I hear stories about artists getting eaten alive I am happy that I never have to put up with that bullshit again. When someone owns your space as an artist? They own your ass. Figure out your FU space, something that nobody can ever take away from you, or you will be paying dearly for that insecurity your entire life.

June 17 Friday

My South Norwalk loft is in a charming, three story, sixteen-unit, red brick Industrial Revolution-era building, a stone's throw from both highways that run through Southwestern Connecticut, here in the suburbs of New York City. I like my building because it's quiet, at least on paper. I have the top corner loft facing the Danbury train spur, so ten trains pass by lazily at 15 miles an hour every day, something I find more interesting than annoying, and a crowd pleaser for studio visitors and dates. I overlook trees whose leaves I can touch out of my half moon window, which makes my space feel like a tree fort 9 months a year, a feature I really like for its privacy and allusion to childhood wonder, an indispensable tool for timeless creativity.

I left a loud building, chaotic inside and out, unbearably so. The week after I moved into my first real estate purchase here in South Norwalk, developers broke ground in the parking lot across the railroad tracks directly in my view of the Norwalk River, which feeds boats and rowers into Long Island Sound. They brought this massive machine in that pounds I-beams into the earth and started on their 18 month project to erect three large, fairly attractive buildings, two for lease and one for purchase. Out of the noise frying pan and into the fire.

I have been wearing jack hammer headphones for years now. They are part of my daily meditation. I have a set in my loft, on the kitchen floor, in my basement inventory space and in my car. There is nothing worse than starting on an intricate gravestone etching right when my friend fires up the sandblasting mechanism in the next room. One false move and that 1000 pound piece of polished granite is screwed by my skipping hand, sitting in stone dust, trying to etch a delicate portrait.

Quiet is easier for writing, thinking, designing, painting. This week sound has been on the offensive. On Tuesday utility trucks were rolling on the railroad tracks trimming back overhanging limbs. Right around the apex of my creativity the chainsaw guy in the bucket outside my window might as well have been cutting wood at my easel it was so loud. On Wednesday there were diggers in the parking lot across from me all day, droning on, moving pavement. On Thursday the lawn guys were running leaf blowers and lawn mowers all afternoon. Today the diggers are back and they started roofing a nearby building. Tear, staple, repeat.

Some weeks noise is hard to silence, even in this studio I selected in large part due to the fact that it was one of the quietest, most peaceful spaces I have ever found.

June 18 Saturday

I hopped in the car with Matt, my nephew Jackson, Chris, his son Garrett and off we went to the Irish Festival. I drained all my cash at the gate, buying food tickets and ride bracelets for the kids. There were a bunch of bouncy rides, slides and obstacle courses filled with air, so the kids had exhausting fun while the adults hung around and drank some beer.

I bumped into my friend Mike as we stood there watching kids do the obstacle course. I haven't seen Mike in a year or two, but it doesn't matter with some people. You just drop right back into good conversation, picking up and tying all the loose ends that bind your histories together, bringing your respective narratives up to speed over a couple of jokes. I fed his three kids food tickets as he'd run out and I had bought too many.

After eating good food and more rides we returned to Matt's, where I ran around with Garrett and Jackson for another hour in the backyard, playing a monster who was chasing after them, beating them up a little, letting them beat me up a little. Kids practice all this and sometimes get too aggressive, hitting you with lacrosse sticks or hard objects. So you have to ping them back just hard enough for them to understand what hurts and what is acceptable when roughhousing. I said goodbye to them and Chris said I was awesome with the kids on the way out, which felt good.

I drove to Walter's and we talked fishing on the back deck, as I am off sharking with him on Thursday. Two of his three kids were home, Abbs being away at a sleepover. We had food on the grill while the kids tried to find entertainment. Finally it was resolved that we would watch the movie 'Rocky,' which they kicked and screamed about, but settled into quickly. They were hanging off my neck and climbing on me for parts of the flick, or they were draped over me like lazy puppies. Kids are love, and they came to love Rocky.

June 19 Sunday

I've got an old computer I like for it's screen. I've been using old programs on it, using too many programs at once, recording audio on it, doing too much with an outdated studio brain. After a bunch of computer freezes you start to wonder about the health of your digital world, then you start to wonder if you can save all your stuff, then you wonder why you waited so long to get a new computer in the first place.

I bought a new computer and got it going while cleaning out the old one. It's good to migrate computers with life left in the old one before you lose all your data. Once I lost two computers at the same time, including a 300 page manuscript (the original draft of *Baloney*), so I try to have quarterly backup drives in 2-3 locations. This is tedious but worth the effort to preserve my studio history.

June 20 Monday

A friend checked in who has moved back to the area, someone I always wondered about after we had enjoyed an evening together many years ago. I will see her tonight and I have nervous energy that I do not know what to do with.

June 21 Tuesday

Tebre came over last night. I am romantically taken, booked by this person for as long as the engagement lasts.

It's hard to find someone you care about who does not mind the artist in you all the way down to your core. Everyone likes the idea for five minutes, but it's not that simple.

In Tebre there seems to be mutual attraction, respect, old friendship. I am having trouble thinking about anything else today, the warming of my heart. It has been years since I have come close to admitting this.

June 22 Wednesday

Today was a good painting day. I let the paint take me where it wanted me to go, which is peaceful art making.

I am getting on a boat tomorrow morning for the annual shark tournament off Montauk at the end of Long Island in New York. I will be working with my eyes throughout the trip, Thursday through Sunday, taking it all in as I ramble off on another fishing adventure, this thing that breaks my years up, a weekend or two a year over the course of my adulthood. Often I return depleted in some ways and inspired in more ways, appreciating the insight that I gained by spending half a week on the boat with a rotating cast of old and new, trusted friends.

June 23 Thursday

I got to the dock at 9 am, which is a leisurely time to start off on a boat. The Canyon Lady's generator was malfunctioning, so we had to wait for a specialist to come check it out. The generator on the boat will have to come out to be repaired, which Walter was hoping to avoid. For the trip we got a gas-powered inverter to provide electricity when we turn the engines off, lay out a chum slick and drift all day fishing for sharks.

We left the dock at 11 am and cruised up Long Island Sound, stopping at Plum Gut to fish for blues, which are good shark bait. We caught one but it was too big to use as live bait. We pulled our lines and made our way to Montauk Point, where we picked up three bluefish that were the perfect size for our purposes. There was a heavy weather cell that socked us as we started in, with some sizable rollers, very little visibility and a lot of electric going off all over the place. This was a hectic half hour ride, but jokes were being thrown around as we powered through it and into the harbor. The storm left some rain as we found our slip and washed down the 35 foot Carolina Classic Canyon Lady.

Once the boat was squared away Nathan went in and registered us for the tournament. We walked over to the tent in the parking lot where the Montauk Marine Basin was hosting the start of the weekend event. Familiar faces and spirits stretched out around the tables, eating barbecue and downing the beer flowing out of kegs in the corner of the tent. The blood runs fast so you and your crew have a lot of nervous energy, bumping into other old friends and strangers who are all gathered there with the same anticipation for good things to come... or bad things, or no things. This feeling crosses all boundaries of sports, whether on the pitcher's mound, the lacrosse field, the ice... doesn't matter. This feeling is the buzz, the reason we were all here, gathered under this tent, vibing off the pulse of the communal energy, making the energy bigger than each and every one of us.

Walter and Nathan got in line for the calcuttas, which are side bets that can pay off handsomely if you pull in the right shark. Marcus and Trevor were hungry, so they convinced me to take a piece of chicken at the buffet. Carl, the owner of Montauk Marine Basin, got on the microphone and ran the Captain's meeting, going over the rules and regulations of the tournament.

West Lake Marina is a seven minute walk but we take cabs back and forth from there all weekend as we are tired and don't want to walk on the side of the pitch dark road, dodging drunk drivers and crazy cabbies. Everyone ordered and we sat there looking at old black and white movies of tuna and shark fishing. The food came and we ate quietly, laughing occasionally, focused on the meal, sleep, an early rise and adventure. Dinner ended and I went to the hotel room with Trevor while the rest of the crew returned to sleep on the boat.

There is a rash of bedbug activity blossoming in New York City. Two of my friends have picked up bedbugs in their hotel travels, and I'm starting to date a girl, so I don't need any trouble in that department. I brought a self-inflatable roll-up camping 'mattress,' I put on workout gear head-to-toe and slept on the floor. Trevor found this amusing as he peeled back the covers on one of the two queens. The last image in my head was watching Trevor's favorite show, 'The Deadliest Catch,' when a captain yells at his crew to get down on deck before a rogue wave crushes his boat in the Bering Straits.

June 24 Friday

At 1:30 am there was a pounding at our door. I opened the latch and the owner of the hotel came in, angry that people were in this room, 10 drunken college kids behind him, waiting to come on in and abuse the shit out of his place. Trevor explained that the maid had given us this room when the owner was out. We said the room was under Walter's name. Walter had called ahead like he has done for the past 15 years and spoke to the owner, so the owner backed down. No problem. I went back to sleep immediately but Trevor told me he tossed and turned. I don't blame him. This hotel is alright but the action never ends.

I was down at 11 pm and up at 3:59 am. Our boat is a three minute walk away, so this is convenient. At 4:10 am we walked down to the boat, past a dozen people who were still up raging, drinking, banging down butts out on the long stretch of porch, saying hi along the way.

On the boat we roused Walter, Nathan and Marcus, who were out down below. They came up one by one and we started making ourselves useful. The captain needs to make a call on where to fish by talking to a few trusted friends, reading the charts and doing his captain's intuition. You need to get your bait in line, your chum buckets, and tons of ice. The marina bustles at 5 am. You want to make friends with the dock hands and grease them with nice tips so they remember to come back and take care of you... the next day, the next tournament, the next year, the next decade.

This trip is different because the other boat, Fish Pig, that we usually have dinner and party with during tournaments is out of the water. Nathan, the captain of Fish Pig, is fishing with Walter this summer. Walter brought his first mate he lobsters with, Trevor, and Nathan brought Marcus, his old friend he's been fishing with since childhood. Marcus's father and Nathan's father have been on hundreds of hunting and fishing adventures together, so this makes sense. I'm the happy fifth wheel, the least experienced fisherman on a very experienced crew perhaps, but I know Walter like nobody else, I've been on the boat for the 15 years of tournaments and on Walter's boats for 25 years. I've pulled in a bunch of sharks and tuna on the reel and on the rail, but I don't need to hold the rod. I try to get on one tournament a year. Shark tournaments are cost prohibitive, but I think about them all winter long. These weekends forge strong bonds and memories with people who are attracted to this passion, pastime, profession, humor, way of seeing. The guys on the boat live for big fishing and it's always a buzz to be riding with them. I take orders, keep them laughing and try to be a voice of reason whenever opinions are asked of me. There is always value in a strong back, an easy demeanor, good humor, a steady head, no sea sickness, Canyon fishing experience, dogged loyalty, and some art skills in my case.

We motored out of the harbor, idling along with 25 other boats in our time slot, waiting for the 6 am start. This is one of my favorite parts of shark tournaments. You're bobbing there in morning mist, checking the weather, the current, your body temperature, your excitement about catching a big fish, the camaraderie with your team, looking out at a field of competitors. These guys don't fuck around. There are a lot of strong teams in this fleet, guys who have pulled in big sharks for decades, guys who know their boats, their crews, their favorite fishing spots, how to win, how to take down a shark that places in one of these tournaments. So you are standing there looking at half the fleet, the 6 am radio start comes in and all these guys gun the engines, all this testosterone swirling in the air, massive machinery cranking up, boat bows piercing the sky, huge wakes behind these shark chasers, shooting through the chop, saying, "What do you want from me?" to each other, each crew plotting their victory dance. This is our weekend, this is our time, we need to keep the good juju in the boat.

We rounded Montauk Point, the lighthouse beautiful and gray in the morning light, and fired off southwest. I like to stand on the port side, next to Walter's right console, braced by the tower, looking at the oncoming sea, feeling the rush of the engines underneath me, the boat cutting through the water, bouncing, pounding at the legs. We usually go south 25 to 50 miles, so the commute is part of the reflective element in fishing. My mind is a constant circle of art survival so it's good to unplug and charge up with deep friendships in a completely different world, a totally foreign arena I like to visit. High stakes shark fishing is the answer for me once a summer, then a tuna trip in the fall. If I had some dough and could afford a little more leisure time I'd get on the boat more often into Walter's lifeblood.

We idled down and checked the drift, Walter and Nathan analyzing the temperature, the Continental shelf we would be drifting over, how the 2 foot rollers might send us and our chum slick through the course of 9 hours, how this spot felt to them. There was concern, they wanted to make the right decision for the boat, but as another captain said last night, this is shark fishing, so you just have to start with some bait in the water. The boat lined up, Trevor and Marcus started prepping the rods and the bait. Nathan was line master so he is doing the rigging and baits this weekend. The first piece of mackerel went in the water and was hit instantly.

Nathan turned a weary eye and said to nobody in particular, "It's going to be a long day."

A long day it was. We caught 21 blue sharks between 8 am and 4 pm, which is constant work for the whole crew. Nathan baited rods nonstop, Trevor was on the deck backing Walter and in the tower looking for big fish, Marcus and I were reeling, wiring sharks and giving them love taps when we clipped the lines, hoping that they wouldn't be coming back to the boat. Blue sharks take the baits of the makos and threshers so they are a pain in the ass because they just keep circling and will hit lines repeatedly. The water was teeming with them. Midday we threw back a 50 lb. mako, so this was a good sign, but no big fish. We burned through tons of bait, most of the handmade leaders and the rubber, squid-like, brightly colored skirts that cover the hooks and attract sharks. Those things are a couple bucks each, but every time we wired a shark Walter would get into the act.

"I want that fucking skirt! Do not clip the line without that skirt! I don't want to lose all our skirts on the first day!"

We always try to get the skirt, which is often one or two

inches from the gnashing, bloody teeth of the hooked blue shark, flipping around, freaking out, all his friends below him right there, dorsal fins breaking the water, one foot deep, one yard deep, eyes and heads and teeth and fins everywhere, a sharkaleidoscope off our transom all day long. When you are clipping a wired shark you are leaned over the transom, your hands right at the water level, trying to do your work but avoid being bitten, a great place for an artist's painting hand to be.

At 4:30 pm we pulled in our lines, put the rocker stompers away, which steady a drifting boat, pulled the chum buckets, the albacore heads dangling off the transom, which one blue shark hit earlier in the afternoon. The ride back was quiet, we were a little beaten up, disappointed that we hadn't caught a fish we could weigh. We did pull the last blue shark we caught into the cockpit of the boat, his jaws chomping away, pissed off and confused, out of water for the first time in the prehistoric existence of his DNA. But his length did not qualify him for the tournament so we set him back in the water. He was only 7 feet long and therefore under the 200 lbs. we needed him to be to compete with. Sharks that are just on the cusp don't make it, but you never know. Nathan won $73,000 last year with a 67 lb. yellowfin tuna in a different tournament... dat'sa niice.

On the way in, around Montauk Point, the blues were running, hitting the bunker that broiled on the surface of the water. Trevor and Marcus pulled out the umbrella rigs, which have a number of lures on each, and dropped them in the water as we started trolling alongside 10 other boats that were looking for trophies, dinner or baitfish. A minute after the lines went in the water both rods went off. Trevor pulled in four blues on his umbrella and Marcus pulled in three. We peeled the fish off their hooks and dumped them in the live bait well, which cycles clean water to keep the fish alive. I reeled in another rig with four blues on it. We repeated the process for ten minutes and caught twenty blue fish, most of which went on ice as the live bait well was filled.

We got back to our slip on the dock, cleaned the boat down and started shooting shit with the other fishermen. There are some good sharks on the board, a 255 lb. thresher in the lead. We packed the boat up and went for a late dinner to West Lake. We were all a little tired and wanted to get some sleep, so we turned in right after dinner and some fishing stories that laughed us off to bed.

June 25 Saturday

We were up at 4 am again, this time for the 5 am time slot. The fleet of 50 boats goes in two waves, 25 boats at 5 am and 25 boats at 6 am, so the start is less of a dangerous shit show. We stayed in closer than usual, set up by 7 am and started picking up some blue sharks quickly, but this morning felt different. The fishing weather was perfect. There were 2 foot rollers, which kept the chum slick moving with our drift. When the sea is flat the chum sinks quickly so a slick is hard to make, the slick being the miles long trail of fish blood and guts that sharks move on up through, attracted by the smell of easy prey, dead or injured fish, dead or injured humans. Nathan laid out three lines off starboard at different depths and a live bluefish on a kite off the port side. This was a very experienced, well organized crew; two captains with styles that contrasted and meshed in just the right ways, lots of humor, lots of good energy moving around the boat. Nathan's measured, analytical nature is something I understand, so I figured out how to make myself useful as he prepared the lines. I dressed the leaders with skirts and I prepped the weights with rubber bands, along with a bunch of other organizational details the boat should employ in the future to save time.

We hit four or five blue sharks, which started coming in, but the load was lighter, the baits sat a little longer in the water so they could do their job.

I was down below making sandwiches for the guys when Walter yelled, "Sandman, get up here!"

Around the port side they pointed at a dorsal fin cutting through the water at a nice clip, ten feet off the transom. Mako. Big enough to place.

Nathan said, "Let's all calm the fuck down, everyone should shut the fuck up and listen to me." Everyone shut up while we all tracked the mako, waiting in anticipation. Then Nathan spoke again.

"Where's my fucking bonito! Give me a goddamn piece of bonito! Motherfucker!" Marcus dug a bonito out of the bottom of the cooler, carved off a fillet and gave it to Nathan. The shark circled around the bow to starboard, back towards the cockpit. There were six or seven blue sharks underneath the transom and Nathan didn't want the blues picking off his bait, so his bait had to be tossed the right way, leading the mako. The bait sunk for five seconds and the reel shot off. Nathan picked the reel up and we all wondered out loud if this was the mako or the 7 foot blue shark that had been cruising around underneath.

Trevor, observing from the tower, and Nathan sounded in unison, "It's our mako."

Walter started the boat and I cleared all the lines; the rods, the rocker stompers, the chum buckets, the fish heads. It is easy for lines to get tangled when you have a good one on, so you have to clear the deck to minimize errors. Walter started leading the boat with the shark.

Nathan said,"He doesn't know he's hooked. We don't want to piss him off. We just want to gently bring him to the back of the boat."

The shark never really ran or freaked out because he wasn't sure what was going on. Nathan's reel was off the port side and Marcus prepared the gaffs.

Marcus told me, "I'm going to put a gaff in the tail, then I want you to feed me the next gaff and we'll get one in the head."

The mako came up alongside the Canyon Lady and Marcus gaffed him pretty well in the tail, pulling the shaft off the gaff, which was roped to the boat. The mako didn't like that, being dragged backwards, hooked and gaffed in the tail. We brought him up again and Marcus got him in the side of the head, then we tail wrapped him and I cut the line to the rod.

As the shark lay backwards and upside down in the water, wired by three lines and helpless to escape, we discussed the mako's size. Walter brought out the length to weight chart. Marcus asked me how long it looked. I spend my life calculating length from various viewpoints but I didn't want to speak too soon.

"You have a tape measure in here?" I asked. I took the tape from the v in the shark's tail (the fork length) to the front of the dorsal fin as the tape was not long enough.

"This is 48 inches Marcus, he's got to be seven-ish. Can you pull him to the boat so I can get the other piece?" Marcus and Nathan pulled the shark's tail and the gaffed head to the boat and I leaned over the transom, trying to get as close to the shark as possible, taking note of the black eye of death peering out at me. I was pretty accurate, calculating 34.

"I'd say the shark is approximately 83 inches," I said.

"How long is that?" someone asked.

"That's seven feet minus one inch."

As we dragged the shark backwards, a pod of 20 black dolphins came up on our transom. Some of the dolphins were going after the head of the mako as makos have been known to prey upon black dolphins.

"We have to get him in the boat or these dolphins are going to mutilate the mako's head," Walter said to Nathan.

Mutilated sharks are disqualified from the tournament, so we opened the transom door and started dragging the bad boy in halfway. Now the shark's head was sticking out of the transom so close to the back of the boat that the dolphins left him alone.

"He's still very alive and very pissed. We don't want a pissed off mako busting up the cockpit," Nathan said.

"Look, we get him in the boat and rope his ass down so he doesn't go anywhere," Walter threw back at him. A conversation between the two captains ensued and they decided to bring the shark in.

We took our time, but we got him through the transom door, roped him down and covered him in white plastic to keep as much of his weight on him as possible for the trip back. The mako didn't know what was going on so he didn't really put up a fight, which in unusual. Makos are ferocious fighters when they get pissed. They'll jump out of the water, over the boat, at the boat sometimes, twisting, turning, breaking lines, fucking your shit up, flying into the cockpit, biting and injuring crew members. This mako came in mellow, lulled into the boat; luck, preparation, a clicking crew, experienced guy on the reel, the stars aligning.

It was only 11:30 am, but we weren't going to beat this shark, the limit being one shark per boat per day, so we headed back in. We were ecstatic but nervous because this shark was just on the edge of making money. The chart said 239 lbs. but Nathan thought our shark was wide, maybe 255 or 260. The ride in was clean as the water had laid down, which was good news for us. Flat water means that it's hard to get a slick going and would make fishing harder for our competition in the afternoon.

We pulled into Montauk Marine Basin and backed the boat up to the guy who spends two days standing on a platform in order to operate the winch that hauls the chained sharks out of the cockpits of every boat that comes in to weigh. There was a small crowd hanging around, and there were some sharks lying on the dock being measured and analyzed by a fishery that uses the weekend to collect data about sharks. The curmudgeon on the platform had seen it all, and if there is a dig to be had he makes it to keep all the fishermen at bay. I'm not sure what drives this sort of character but it's amusing to be around once every year or so. Our crew tried to wrap a chain around the tail of the mako and the platform guy kept shaking his head. Third time was the charm, we wrapped the tail correctly and platform guy got the winch rolling. The mako was pulled slowly out of the cockpit and around us we could hear murmurs talking about our nice mako. The weight was 249 lbs., which put us in third overall place behind a 252 lb. blue shark and a 255 lb. thresher. We had entered a number of different competitions within the tournament so I didn't ask questions. Nathan looked depressed and Walter was happy. Nathan didn't like the nail biter and said that he had thought our mako might have been another 10 lbs., which would have put us in the solid lead. We cleaned our boat and gear with toothbrushes, twiddling our thumbs as other boats started rolling on in to weigh their sharks.

None of us liked the idea of sitting around on the dock as the crowd swelled into the afternoon to watch as 15 more sharks after ours were weighed. Between 1:30 pm and 6 pm there were seven sharks that weighed in between 229 and 245 lbs., so the competition was pretty razor thin. We just stood there listening for hours to the 'Jaws' soundtrack as it pumped through the speakers and into the growing audience. Anticipation rose every time a boat pulled up with excited, expectant crew members. The clock struck 6 pm and Canyon Lady was declared the third place winner. What a rush.

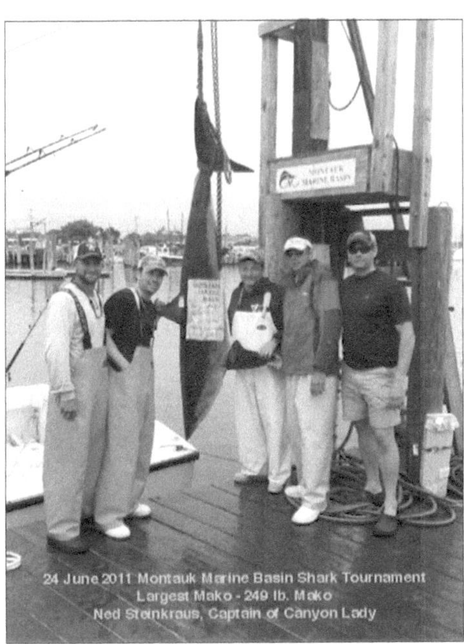

249 lb. mako, Montauk Marine Basin, NY, 2011.

The awards dinner was a quick walk from the boat, where

the captain's meeting had been held, under the massive parking lot tent, spilling out with buzzed up fishermen. The mood was festive for some and tortured for others, as these high stakes tournaments go. After all the prizes and applause, bellies full of food from the dinner tickets that were part of our captain's bag, we adjourned to the Canyon Lady. Nathan and the crew wanted to go out but Walter wanted to protect his winnings, positions hardening as the booze flowed over the crew and partying visitors on board. Eventually I went out with Nathan and Marcus, we saw some pretty girls, had a couple drinks and returned to Walter, fast asleep, smiling with another winning notch on his belt.

June 26 Sunday

We hit the rack at an unusually reasonable Saturday night hour for winners and got up before 7 am. We cleaned the boat up and went to breakfast. Nathan had along with him an overnight bag with our $63,000 in prize money tucked under his arm, which we referred to as 'the football' instead of referring to it in public as 'the bag of cash.' The crew was ear-to-ear grins, glowing from our score yesterday, basking in victory.

After a big sit down breakfast we returned to the boat and cast off, but the port shaft was not functioning correctly so we checked back to the dock for several hours of troubleshooting. It was resolved that we would take The Canyon Lady back on one engine, which increased our commute from 2.5 hours to 10 hours. We got out of the harbor and after twenty minutes of puttering Walter and Nathan decided that we ought to turn around, leave the boat to be repaired at the marina and find a way home. I suggested the cabbie Lorraine, who had taken us around a couple times in her taxi over the weekend. They liked it. I called in and haggled with Brian at the front desk. We agreed on $520. plus tolls (and tip) to get us back home in a taxi van. Deal.

The boat secured back at the dock, we had to cut 200 pounds of mako shark into smaller pieces so the meat would fit into conventional coolers the Marina sold for a million dollars. We ran this exercise efficiently, with Marcus cutting the fish up and me packing the shark into two new coolers on ice. We unloaded the rest of our gear from the Canyon Lady and the full-sized van pulled up. We agreed not to talk about the football of cash as there was no need to bring other people into that conversation.

The ride was four hours of shitty traffic on a Sunday

afternoon, but we got her done. For a while we were driving alongside polo ponies. I didn't understand why they would face horses towards lanes of opposing traffic as it seems this would spook them more. Someone suggested that they were facing the driver side and I accepted that for the moment, but it still didn't make a lot of sense to me.

We got home, had one more laugh about our win and we were all off, back into our separate worlds and lives, the way teams come together, get something done and leave with unified memories that never quite seem to fade. I was on the fence about doing this trip like I was on the fence about last September's trip during which we pulled in a 308 lb. swordfish. That one struck at 2:47am and Walter fought the fish for 4 hours with 6 foot rollers until we were able to bring the sword alongside, get gaffs in and tail wrap on. The moral of the story is that sometimes you just have to say yes and throw caution to the wind. I'm good at this in my art career but I'm a little conservative with my energies outside the studio. Maybe I should relax a little more on my tightrope walk of life.

June 27 Monday

I went over to Fishtales Seafood in New Canaan and checked in with Danny. Walter had dropped 190 lbs. of mako off to cut up into steaks. Danny asked me what I wanted.

"My share," meaning 1/6 of the mako... a cut goes to the store for the trouble of cutting nice steaks. We had a beer and I made Danny laugh with weekend stories of our mako triumph.

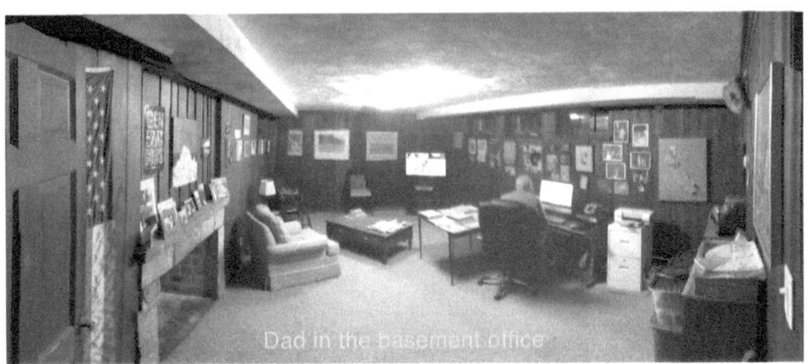

Dad in the basement office

June 28 Tuesday

In the morning I got lost in the still life painting on my easel.

Revisiting old paintings is like hanging out with old friends, and as long as my brush is moving around with the rhythm of the canvas, time releases itself and I fall into the Zen-zone of art making.

I went over to my father's basement office and checked out the family photo book that he and my aunt have been working on. The basement was our paradise as kids when we moved into this house, so it always stirs warm memories. There were mountains of family photographs that Dad has been scanning and laying out for a hundred hours. I love going down there and seeing him at work on a family project. It will be my job to formalize these files into a professional book by Labor Day.

My friend Lina is putting together a book for an artist who passed away named Larry Lewis with Larry's niece Sharyn. I will be designing and producing the book. The gig will pay alright and is good energy to help my friends and expose an unknown artist whose work might see the light of day.

June 29 Wednesday

At noon I met with a regional art center as I have been asked to jury a show for their 300 members. I sat with my friend Catherine, who recommended me, and two of the Board members who help run things over there. We talked art for awhile, they seemed to like me, so I will be judging an abstract show in the first week of August. This will be my first time jurying, so I appreciate the opportunity.

In the past 3 years or 50 races I've missed only one sailing race due to injury, so I'm old reliable in the bow, which is why my old friends picked me in the first place. Matt's birthday mako steaks took precedence this evening, so we went over for a nice dinner on his deck. My family likes anything that involves projectiles, targets, scores, winners and losers, so my brother was happy to play the corn hole game I took over for him. The mako steak dinner came with my unwinding story about catching the money fish, and the family recounted old funny stories about Matthew in family lore.

June 30 Thursday

My Dad has completed his portion of the family picture book. His computer is acting up so I told him it's time to get another one. At lunch we went over to the computer place.

I knew the computer I wanted, the same thing that I had just bought for myself, but the salesman wanted to sell us anyway.

When I know what I want, I don't want a sales guy to rip that object out of my hands and ask me if I'm sure I know what I'm looking for.

"I'm looking for the object that you just took out of my hands."

"Well, let me be a source of information for you. You are all business. I want to see your human side."

The salesman wanted to see my human side while telling my father how he (the salesman) had arrived at this computer store after two decades of a career in acting, explaining that he is currently involved in putting on a production of Oliver Twist. My Dad took the bait.

"My son is nice to talk to when he's not this busy. He's a professional artist. Sandy, put up your website." I put up my website on the floor model computer, capitulating slightly. A video with my recorded song came up. My father got excited.

"Look, he wrote a book and he makes songs too. Here, turn up the volume." My song 'Busted Wing' started cranking in the store. I turned the music way down, pointing at the slide show. This annoyed my father.

"Now we can't hear your song!"

"Listen Jordan," I said, reading the guy's name tag, "I'm not a dick. We just have a lot to do today. I've done the research. I've had 15 of these computers before. I bought the same one last week for my studio that I want again today. Can I please just buy this?"

Disappointed, Jordan moped along through the sales process. I patted him on the shoulder, I told him that I appreciated his time and patience, and then we scrammed out of there, my father gimping behind me because he was sore from spinning at 6 am with all the pretty girls at the YMCA.

"Sorry Dad, I didn't mean to be a dick but I don't want to hear about that guy's acting career right now. Clearly he's a nice guy but I'm up to my neck over here," I swept my hand across my neck as we got in the car. My father waved my thought away to explain that he understood, although he thought I had been a little bit of a dick. I was just all business and didn't have time to play patty cake with a computer guy who wanted to talk about his acting career under the auspices of finding the humanity in me.

July 1 Friday

The apex of the artist and collector relationship, for me

anyway, is when I sell paintings and sculptures that are in my inventory (because I made them for myself). There are many degrees of fine artist. Since the market fell apart I have lived light and shifted with the tectonic plates that keep crushing people who fall through the cracks. I have survived in no small part due to my low overhead, creative range, and a solid collector base that has developed over many years. Creative range allows me to take commissions in almost every aesthetic field, like the painting commission that came in today from a long lost friend who found me online. You never know where your next gig is going to come from, and you never know what that gig might be, so it is good to keep the body rested, the mind open, and the tools sharpened.

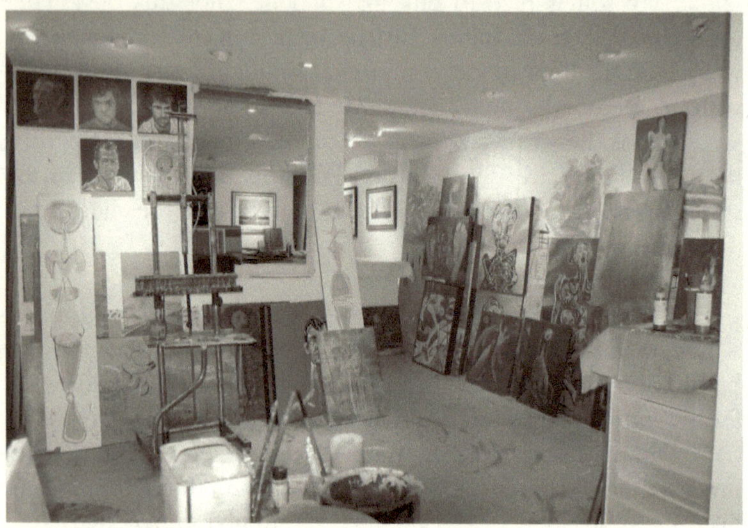

Saturday 2 July

I took Tebre with Walter, his wife Bella and three kids to fireworks at the beach. This is a short life so it's important to do things like watch a fireworks show with a best friends' kids, lighting sparklers so they can run up and down the beach, buzzing along while the boats line up out on the water behind the barge as the sun sets and the flare goes out to signal the start of the show. I sat there with this woman who just returned home, holding her hand, looking at the fireworks, Walter's kids draped on top of him, the shimmering reflection off the water, the fireworks dust raining gently down on enthralled showgoers, the booms in the sky, the flickering lights, the lazy wind, a perfect evening. I'm not used to feeling this full.

July 3 Sunday

Walter called to tell me there is room on the boat for the Tri-State Shootout on Block Island in August. My share of the mako winnings will cover the next tournament so I'm in.

July 4 Monday

Happy 4th of July.

I finished the poster, then sent it off to Walter and two fulfillment places that will print posters and tee shirts.

July 5 Tuesday

Having a lot of art projects is much better than cobwebs on my phone and crickets in the studio.

July 6 Wednesday

Sailing was fun but we were slow off the line and this year we are competing against boats with wildly varying handicaps, which can be frustrating. We thought there would be no wind but the wind picked up. As we were light on crew, as the tide was just so, and as the wind made a racetrack, we didn't bother with the spinnaker. This makes my job in the bow infinitely easier so I was not complaining. The humor was good, the sun was out and the mission of escaping shore again with my old friends was achieved.

After sailing I cleaned up and walked over to see my friend Annie, who was out from NYC to watch her professional trumpet player boyfriend Bill. The band was something else, and there were old friends I had not seen in years.

A working musician and a working visual artist lead completely different lives, but often creative blood is thicker than water. I sat with Bill and the keyboard player Neil between sets and we juxtaposed music making and visual art, which is a fun game I've been playing with Annie the actor for many years. In the second set she got up and sang a song, the band backing her up, talent sparked the place down, a nice venue with a friendly, captivated audience to inspire my midnight walk home.

July 7 Thursday

My friend Frank came by with his two kids today. I showed him my studio, the working projects, I gave his son Mace some

Rainbow Riders books to read. Frank asked me technical questions about my operation like the financial analyst that he was before going the teaching route. He asked me what percentage of my income was commissioned work. I haven't thought about that in awhile, but maybe 70% of the paintings in my career just had to come out of me before I found buyers for them.

I talked shop with Frank until his kids got bored, then I showed them the glass floor I built into my loft upstairs that allows the skylight to illuminate the kitchen below. I showed Frank how I renovated my space, then I showed him how I make my songs, how the timeline on each track goes. I showed him this book, how I am writing it in a layout program so that I can fire it off to a printer whenever I want a galley sample. Like his business models, these projects have patterns and templates that can be recycled for ensuing projects which share similar structural properties.

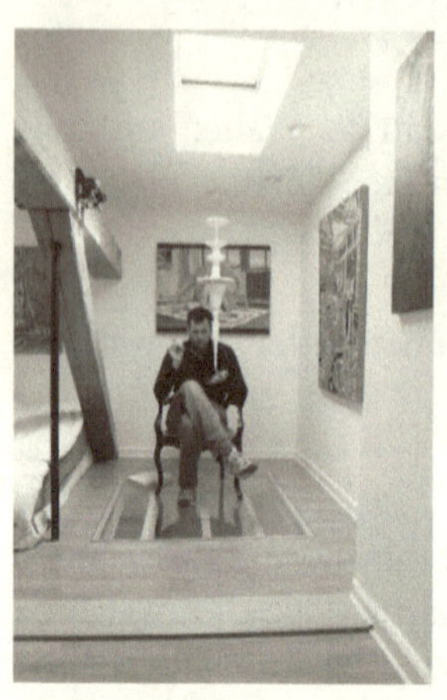

Visitors to the studio often ask questions whose answers elucidate new insights, which often inform or inspire new art.

July 8 Friday

An artist has to be protective of his time as time is all we have to make things. People often ask of an artist without understanding how much time and energy they are really asking for.

When screwed for time, just send an email update to your list of 2090 people. 100 people went right to my website, I got fifty emails back from friends checking in, I sold 5 books and might have sold a painting out of the email blast. My intellectual property lawyer clarified that the patent I received is a utility patent and not a design patent. You always get something wrong however hard you try, so you just have to learn while letting the small stuff go.

My network is my lifeline and I have never forgotten this.

July 9 Saturday

Sometimes I look outside my window at an earthly object like a tree and spirits speak back. This is a hard point to arrive at as a human being, but it happens to me with accruing frequency. Maybe this is because I meditate so much of my art in the spirit world. The brain is like the bottom of the ocean, its topography unmapped and mysterious. I spend my living days demystifying processes that at first I can't figure out. This is part of the beauty of art making, being okay swimming in the mystery of life. The voyage, the adventure of discovery is what life is all about so we can take our wisdom to the next spiritual level or realm when our time is done here.

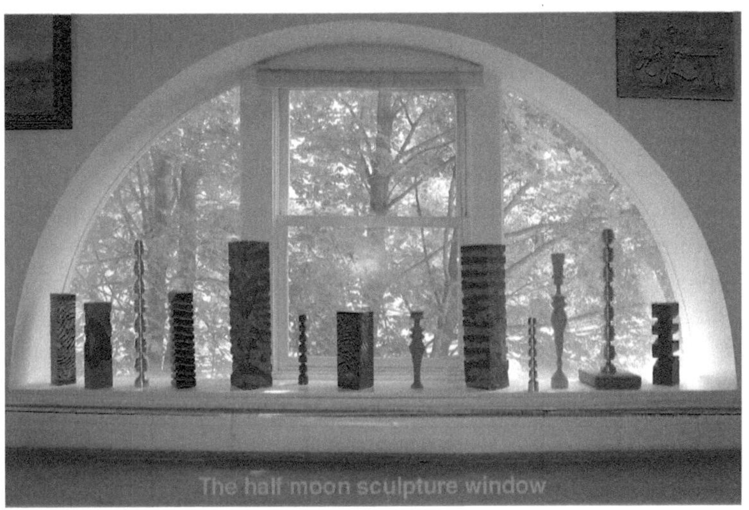
The half moon sculpture window

July 10 Sunday

Yesterday Derek Jeter of the New York Yankees picked up his 3000th hit with a home run. What a talent. Apparently the guy who recovered the baseball on a bounce in the stands is from St. Lawrence University, my Alma Mater. He told the media that the ball belonged to Jeter, so the Yankees organization gave him box seats for the year and heaped a bunch of Yankees swag on him. My friend Pete at the beach tonight said that the best thing would have been if the guy had told Jeter that all he wanted was for Jeter to throw the wiffle ball at his kids for an hour one summer day. You know Jeter would have done that.

July 11 Monday

I am trying to solve the dilemma of that massive mural. Hand painting or airless painting is cost prohibitive. Building wraps are printed mesh vinyl pieces that are grommeted onto the sides of buildings and have a decent lifespan. I could get this done for half the budget, but it feels like a cop-out, more of a commercial billboard than a fine art installation.

The budget will still be very tight if I try to make the 25 ft. tall tightrope walker out of aluminum, hand paint and mount that 40 feet in the air.

July 12 Tuesday

I went into town tonight to meet Tebre, her mother and her aunt as our families are checking us out. The city was a hot 93 degrees and I wore a button down shirt that felt like 220 grit sandpaper. I parked my jeep close by our meeting spot. After a pleasant dinner I air conditioned the car and picked the ladies up outside the restaurant. I drove Tebre's aunt up Park Avenue to her place, then we flew out and up off the East River Drive, over the Triborough, Bruckner, 95. It was smooth sailing until two motorcyclists criss-crossed in front of my car at 90 miles an hour. One of them dumped up the road and traffic came to a grinding halt an exit before ours, so we got off early and drove locally. I dropped Tebre's mother at the station where she had parked her car, then we went home for a nightcap.

July 13 Wednesday

The more random the art project the less likely I am to photograph it. Note to artists - photograph everything you make and label it so you can find it in the future. You never know who will ask for what, and if you have made something like a new collector's request, you should have proof in the form of an acceptable portfolio shot. Sometimes the smallest portfolio piece can lead to the greatest success. I once had a colletor who wanted a painting for $1000, but ended up buying 7 paintings for $45,000, one of my largest sales to date. The reason? I had a portfolio sample of a small painting I had sold that this new collector liked. You just never know, so I do my best to be prepared for any artistic situation that might come my way.

July 14 Thursday

My father and I went up to see my cousin in-law Chuck in Westchester to deliver a hunting sign I painted for his cabin. Dad said he'd show me the back way. Instead of turning left on Lake we kept going in a circle that brought us back to Lake again 11 minutes later. I recorded the dialogue, hamming it up a little with Dad, who started getting really pissed off at himself for being lost. Family members can be the greatest source of humor, most often when they are not trying to be funny.

I saw my cousin Lisa and their new Burmese Murphy, then we followed Chuck over to his hunting club, which I had never been to. The clubhouse is classically understated, the rustic main room sporting mounts of every game animal in the United States. We had lunch in the friendly, bustling dining room, then drove to Chuck's cabin, wound up on a jeep-worthy ridge. We found a spot, hung the cabin sign, and Chuck was very happy, a gift to him for our invitation to Augusta.

On the way back I played the audio recording of me working my father over while we were lost. My father and I laughed our asses off the whole ride home.

July 15 Friday

I had a fluid day moving around the studio, cruising from work station to work station, project to project in the creative pocket that I have built brick by brick over two decades. When you build things with solid foundations the wind might shake them but they will stand firm. This is how the construction of an art project is. If a painting is approached, designed, planned and executed the right way then the painting is strong throughout and will have a nice timelessness to it. I don't just mean the painted image, but the materials; the canvas, the stretcher, the cornering, the paint used, the layers of sittings, washes that need to be built up the right way, in the right order, so that every move is a solid improvement over the last. Not all paintings work this way, but a lot of them benefit from a methodology and process.

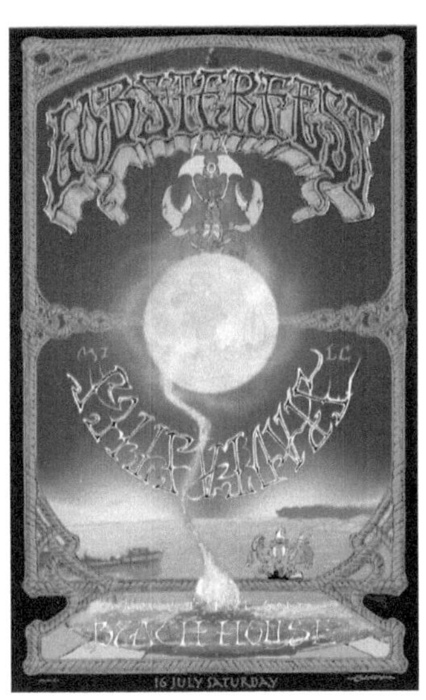

I went over to see my old friends who are playing in the band to listen to them practice the evening before Walter's party. People were setting up Danny's catering while the band took a break and laughed with Walter. I walked up, said hi to everyone and showed them the posters. Posters make bands feel good for any gig. We all signed the posters with silver markers that I had brought along; one for each band member, one for Walter, one for Danny, one for my archives.

July 16 Saturday

Tebre told me I had to put last night's story in this book because it was so good, although I was not planning on it, protective as I am. She was entertaining very close friends who were in town and it got late. She missed the 12:23 out of Grand Central so she got on the 1:04, arriving around 2:00 am. Before the train spun out of there I told her not to fall asleep and she said no problem, that she's never missed a stop as a result of sleeping on a train. At 1:45 am I called to confirm her train station. I didn't hear back. I left a message suggesting that she was probably asleep and wondering aloud what I should do. Time was short so I drove over to the closest train station in an effort to play defense. I parked, walked into the station, climbed the stairs onto the platform and was surprised to see 100 people waiting for a train to take them north from South Norwalk. I continued calling but Tebre was clearly asleep.

The train was coming so I put my game face on. This was going to be a tough one, because when Tebre falls asleep a stick of dynamite will not wake her up, I've come to learn. The train pulled in fast and I started scoping out the cars. As the train came to a stop the doors opened and I ran against traffic towards the back of the train, looking in all the windows as fast as I could. The conductor turned a wary eye.

"Look, my girlfriend is on this train and if I don't find her this will be bad."

"Oh yeah? What does she look like," the conductor said flatly, looking at his watch.

"She's about this tall, pretty with dark long hair, most likely sleeping," I said as I craned my neck and danced around the conductor, looking into the next car.

A group of women who had gotten off the train had taken an interest. One of them pointed fifteen feet away and asked excitedly, "Is that her?" I ran over. Tebre was out like a light with her legs up against the back of the seat in front of her.

"That's her! Thank you!" I gestured to the pleased-as-punch

solid citizen who had spotted Tebre. The conductor shrugged as I ran past him onto the train.

I could not wake Tebre up. I tried everything. The conductor and passengers were getting very restless and a little nervous as well, wondering if there was some sort of medical emergency. I put her bag on my shoulder, picked her up and Clark Kented her out of the train, thanking the startled conductor along the way. Some people clapped as I took a seat on the bench outside, all wired up, not believing that I had found her and saved us both from a very shitty long night if I had not been so lucky and heroic frankly. People on the platform were around and couldn't believe what they had seen. Tebre continued to not wake up. The doors began to close and a cell phone shot out of the train, skipped on the platform and landed a yard from my feet.

"Thank you!" I waved at the conductor, whose visage dissolved in reflective glass as the train pulled north into the 2:05 am full moon. This event actually had bystanders, gawkers, fans. If someone had shot a video I would be a momentary internet sensation.

Tebre came to in my arms and I got her walking. She has not been sleeping much at all, she'd had some drinks, she was out late and when she sleeps she does not wake up. This must be nice but can be alarming to loved ones I found out last night.

"I can't do this sort of thing all the time. That was hectic! I almost lost you!" She had no conception of what had transpired, she was out on her feet, so she became annoyed at my editorial on the way back to my place. After a silly squabble she arrived at the simple fact that I care about her and to please not do that again if at all possible.

July 17 Sunday

I picked Tebre up, we met her friends at the train, then we drove over to Walter's party. My folks met Tebre's mother, all of whom came down before their respective social events. The weather was perfect, the moon was full, the food was great, the band inspired, old friends made new memories with laughter, I kissed a girl by the roaring fire, another moment at my favorite place in the world. Thanks Brother.

July 18 Monday

There are colors in the still life reprise palette that I haven't worked with in years, so I picked up a deep sky blue, a phthalo green and an electric violet. I blocked in colors between black lines of the composition, like the modernists and so many creatives in the 20th century have played with. Spatial complexity can be found in between the outlines, where colors vacillate, run together, play off of one another, vibrate visually like the striking of a musical chord, the color white in between often leading the charge.

July 19 Tuesday

I wrote and painted this morning before my brother Matt came over. We drove locally until rush hour died down before getting on I-95 to the Upper East Side of Manhattan, where my Mom grew up, my second home. I parked on 89th between Park and Madison, I picked up Tebre, who was a block away at her Aunt's apartment, and we walked over to Heavenly Rest on 90th and 5th. I noted Heavenly Rest Cafe next door with amusement as we strolled in and greeted our mother. My brother Christian and my father were milling around the last pew. My father greeted us and we walked over to the bench, where my mother's purse and the ashes of her parents sat, boxed.

"Little did I know all this time," my mother said, reaching into a cardboard box and producing a coffee can, "That my father was never placed in a proper urn."

She then opened the pull strings on a velvet maroon bag and brought out a nicely designed bronze-plated box with the dates of my grandmother's life etched in an attractive cursive. My family leans towards humor the way German Pointers get on a bird and just stay there, so we laughed about the coffee can my grandfather's ashes have been residing in for 8 years. 8 years and skipping right under the surface of time.

Brenda, the Rector of St. James, which is the church my mother's side of the family all went to, walked in and we embraced her. She went downstairs with my mother in preparation. I sat next to the ashes of my grandparents, talking to Tebre about her week and our plans. We were called down shortly, Dad carrying a grandparent in each arm, these grandparents that I had loved, these parents that had suffered the losses of two of their three daughters early and tragically. Walking through the wrought iron gates, Tebre mentioned that this was cool, that she felt medieval and perhaps she should become Episcopalian, to which I smiled.

Downstairs the Columbarium was open and we walked into

the wall of names I had never seen or been to. My mother's side of the family all reside there in a nicely engraved casing which contains urns that go way back. Our family gathered around as Brenda gave us all a prayer book and we followed with her introduction. I was then asked to read 'To Every Time There is a Season,' written by Ecclesiastes. I read it cold to the small room of we seven and tried to absorb the poetry of the words through my speaking voice. Then Brenda finished the short service before getting on an old mini-circular staircase so she could give a blessing as each of the urns were placed with the rest of our maternal family. This short service was emotional, poignant, closing in its own way, sweetly moving, but not too heavy as our grandparents died 3 and 8 years ago respectively. I loved them deeply as they were good grandparents to me. They lived, they rejoiced, they instilled in me love, history and family, they suffered, they passed on to another plane.

After thanking Brenda for her warm words we moved up and over to 92nd and Madison, where we enjoyed some hearty, witty laughter over an excellent lunch at a French bistro. The mood was light and airy and Tebre enjoyed some of the family history, humor, ideas that make us work as a nuclear unit. Lunch ended, we said goodbyes, I walked Tebre to the corner of 89th and Park, gave her a kiss, then got into the car and zipped home for a nothing afternoon with brother Matthew.

My grandparents have my heart, I am lucky to have had their wisdom and experience and love in life, and they live on with the people who knew them, loved them and tried to understand them. Such is the natural importance of family and honoring those who have passed away.

July 20 Wednesday

Sometimes the studio hums with the sound of its own creativity, work moving in and out like the churning of a well-oiled engine. Sometimes the studio feels bogged down, jammed up with small items that don't want to resolve themselves, ideas and creative juices frayed at the edges, skipping notches on the belt-drive, looking for rhythm. I felt rhythm today and this is a good vibration. I made progress on the small still life, I edited some pages on my expanding website, I corresponded with collectors, my patent documents came in on my Revolutionary Family Totems, I tinkered with a song, I worked on the Larry Lewis art catalogue, and I cleaned up my basement studio.

July 21 Thursday

I have to feel the sensation of creating new, original things. The energy builds up and then releases in new art. Always.

July 22 Friday

When I'm cranking on the easel I will do a morning session, an afternoon session and an evening session. Lately with public art, writing and music, my energy has been dispersed. It is challenging to balance all these disciplines while running the studio.

I have a good song that came to me last week. You have to sit around with your butterfly net waiting for melodies. They just float out of the air and you need to get them down or they will vanish into the cacophony of life. Once I have a melody the words are easy, even if the lyrics take time to flush out or are written first.

July 23 Saturday

The heat has altered the brains of everyone in the region. My friend called about an art project and I mentioned that Tebre was looking for a pool. He told me to go to his mother's pool as she is in Florida and not to mind the two guys staying in the house from Kathmandu who summer here for labor.

I picked Tebre up from the train with refreshments on ice and we went over to the pool. I brought a flashlight to find our way through the dark lawn, and after announcing myself to the house guests we hung out for a couple of hours. We talked in the summer burn about her gig next week on a movie set as a stand-in. I understand a lot of this as I made art for the music industry and was on music tours around the country awhile back. We shared funny stories and enjoyed being in and out of a pool after a 108 degree day in the New York Metro area. At one point we heard a commotion and I went up to the house to announce that we were heading out. My friend's mother had returned home to strangers in her pool, so I went in and she was relieved to see that I was a friend of the family. Pool etiquette, like all forms of etiquette, allow for the perpetuation of pleasant social activities through the years. I never actually thought about where to find a pool in my whole lifetime until Tebre tasked me with it this morning.

July 24 Sunday

I dropped Tebre off at her mother's home. She is going to work on a film in Cape Cod for a week or two. She never knows what she's going to get, if she will get stand-in work, stunt work, extra work. I always said after dating an aspiring actress who slept with a famous director while we were together, probably in the hopes of being included in a film of his that she was never included in, that I would never date an actress again. Maybe I should have expanded that to anyone in the film business, as much as I love film. We'll see. Tebre doesn't care about the fame thing, which is comforting, but she's flighty and a guy she dated for eight months last year is working on the set as well. Hmm. If the shoe were on the other foot she told me that she would be gone, so I'll just have to roll with it.

I spent the day working on Lina's Larry Lewis catalogue. He made these otherworldly collages, frightening commentaries about women, gender and culture. I scanned and shot a bunch of work, cleaned it up in Photoshop, and laid out a 64 page book, making big progress for my meeting on Tuesday.

July 25 Monday

It sucks having a piece of crap car that your girlfriend's mother broke down in last week, so I found a young enough silver Toyota 4Runner today, moving right along.

July 26 Tuesday

The Public Art Committee asked for a breakdown of the large mural budget. They already broke the budget down for me by cutting it in half. The reality is that I can't make a strong enough piece of fine art with half a working budget.

July 27 Wednesday

Today I etched a portrait of a German Shepherd named

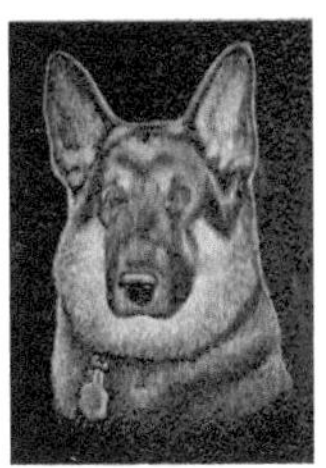

Bowe onto a family gravestone. The woman whose husband passed away came by while I was working on the etching. This is a large black granite stone and I sat on the floor of the monument shop with my etching instrument, which is a diamond-tipped buzzing stylus that scratches the polish away, white from black, chiaroscuro. I always see the people coming as their reflections frame themselves in the polished granite, my canvas, when they stand behind me and watch me work. She was happy and told me to keep going, which I did.

July 28 Thursday

I sat with a wise friend who told me I have to be stronger regarding the mural budget. He asked if I have an agent. My friend Kim has helped me several times, so I reached out to her. I would rather have someone else do the negotiating, particularly if nothing will come of it. I've spent twenty years working my own pricing out, but I have not been faced with larger public art budgets. Some people think I'm not smart for turning the mural down. Several friends who understand art and small business are telling me that I can't take a hit on this one, that sometimes it is empowering and the right thing to walk away.

July 29 Friday

I was an easel monkey all day, gunning through a number of canvases, fighting my distracting thoughts about Tebre.

I picked up the 4Runner in the early evening, a better car than all ten shit boxes I have ever driven were they to be combined into one super shit box. I don't care about cars as long as they work and are not a waste of money. I have a friend who put half a million miles on her 4Runner and mourns it like the loss of a beloved family member, so this one should do the trick for awhile.

July 30 Saturday

Tebre hasn't called in the past week, texting scantly that reception is bad on the set. Given that she called me eight times a day in the three weeks before she left, and given that an old boyfriend is on the set, this has been fair cause for concern.

I texted in the morning, "If you have time let's catch up this weekend."

July 31 Sunday

A day and a half later I received a text back from Tebre.

"No, not really. Was on a boat all day yesterday with friends. On boat today all day with friends," and got worse from there, ending in a text breakup.

I haven't opened myself up in a long time romantically, and Tebre is an old friend, so a breakup text after six weeks of fireworks hits hard. Common decency is lacking in the equation. That text was kind of open ended so I have a feeling text breakup chick doesn't know what she's done and will come back in a week from the movie set thinking everything's cool. I don't allow behavior like this into my life, so everything's not cool.

Making art is such a game of smoke and mirrors that I have to maintain a Zen-like balance; spiritual and physical health, excellent peripheral vision, honing the antennae for opportunities, liabilities, pitfalls, danger zones, black holes, vampires. Over twenty years I have built my network of solid family, friends, collectors, sublets, fans, supporters. Although my art career is tumultuous my life is rock solid spiritually, otherwise I would fail.

This experience has damaged my spirit, so I will try to mend and move on quickly as I don't have time to lie around and suffer. I'm trying to find my footing again quickly. My inner council went right to work on me today and I will need them this week to regain my strength.

August 1 Monday

I sat with close friends and family regarding the failed romance and they were supportive. Run for the hills was the clear message, which is very logical, although it will take time for the heart to catch up.

I've spent my adult life honing a deep radar to keep my energy patterns simple and clean in order to negotiate the art game. Weird energy and nasty behavior are not allowed anywhere near my world because these energies are like a broom handle in the spokes of a spinning bicycle wheel.

Although I had trouble being productive, I got 50 pages into the family book by evening.

August 2 Tuesday

This morning I made gravestone etchings of a book and several crosses. I feel the history of monument making, of honoring death, the pain of the living. The spirits shine down as if to thank me for helping their family members with my art. Sometimes I feel the spirits coming through, in a very abstract way as they don't want to freak me out, or sometimes they answer when I ask for inspiration or vision to finish an etching properly... not always, but sometimes.

In the afternoon, as I dug into the layout and design of the photo book, I found a rhythm and started enjoying myself. I like design work when a deadline is not blowing too hard on me.

Even when the pressure is on I have to drop into a relaxed pocket of creativity or I will be doing busy work around the project and not working on the project. I started with my great-great-grandparents, which are very old photographs; chipped, ripped, scratched, scarred, so I went down the rabbit hole and began cleaning each image up in Photoshop. I got to page 75 by midnight.

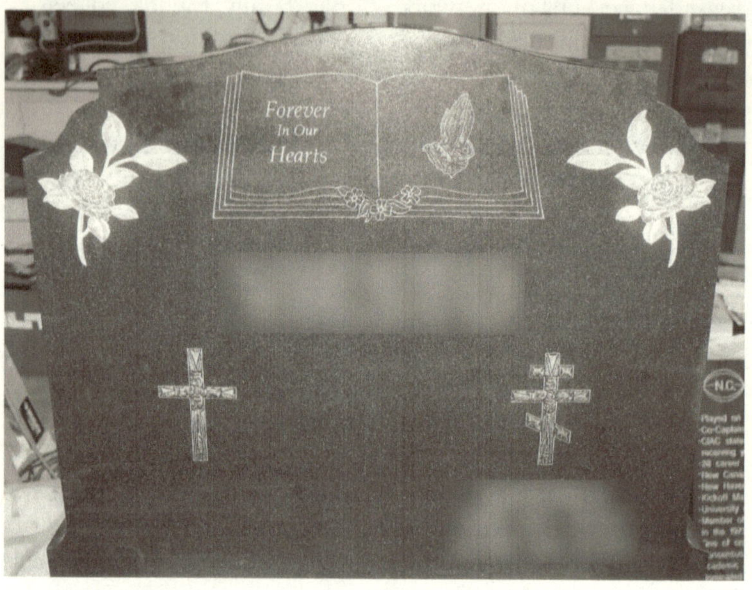

August 3 Wednesday

Jurying my first art show was fast and interesting. I followed the format that this Association likes and it went well. The co-chairs asked for a statement from me that I will write this week for press. They seemed pleased with my jurying duties.

August 4 Thursday

I sat with a friend and mentioned to him why I'm ornery. He pulled out an envelope and told me his story.

"What do I do with this thing I received yesterday? A love letter from a girl I proposed to 40 years ago. She declined and married a guy who looked like he might do better. She has no kids, she's 62, she's pissed, bitter, divorced, and she's now knocking on my door again after all these years."

My friend Jake is married for 35 years with 4 kids and 5 grandchildren. He said that the letter in his drawer doesn't change anything all four decades later. He said that I'm better off letting this one go, which I know intellectually, the heart slow to follow.

In the afternoon I bought and prepared a laptop to work on the family photo book while I'm away.

When fishing for a week, the most important thing is to bring good humor and nothing else. I filled a bag of fishing gear and leaned it against the front door.

I have to get out of here and into another space. On the other side of this fishing trip may be a brighter perspective, like being on the other side of a painting, another year, another love.

August 5 Friday

I'm all wordy on my new laptop, facing Long Island Sound, listening to my crew members laugh about their rods and new hats and new coffee maker on board. This, brother, is the perfect speed for my busted wing. I fished on a 35 foot Carolina Classic for ten years and I miss her, but Walter went in on Nathan's Downeast 41 foot Guimond, and this boat is another animal. There's a cabin table I can type on as we cruise east out of Long Island Sound at 18 knots, which is a lot different than standing next to Walter while surfing at 24 knots in The Canyon Lady on a flat day of travel.

A fisherman's idea of a good time is sitting in the wheel house or cockpit and remembering, bringing the best things into the present, bringing the best things into the future, where we might catch the next best memory on the new reel Walter just showed Nathan. Nathan is at the helm and I am on the port side bench, which might as well be a twenty foot long mahogany table looking down at all of New York City with the world in the palm of my hand. Here is a boat I can get creative on.

Red has made me the office manager with my computer aboard. When we get to Montauk we need Trip Sec, Tequila and two sandbag ashtrays. Walter just showed me where the life vests are, where the e-purb is, where the fire extinguishers are, where the key to the shotgun is. A poppy love song was just on and Nathan told Walter that we should change the music because it might not be good for me to hear at this juncture in my life, to which we all laughed. Fishermen know tough love in hard laughter.

Onion, garlic, celery, these things Walter is concerned about, but Red brought all of that. I am a character in the mix, in the cell with four other lunatics who have big hearts and do life pretty well. The sun peels layers of my soul away and I listen to my two captains mesh their spirits together as some ridiculous tune comes on and Walter does his leader dance. He cheers me up without talking about the things that don't matter any longer.

Walter sat down and we worked the bets out. We are going for the 250, 500, 1000 Tuna, the Tuna Jackpot on Monday and Tuesday for 250, the largest yellowfin tuna for 250, the Tri-Fishecta for 250, 500, swordfish for 500, Lay Day Fluke for 100. The captains are in on the 2500 tuna Calcutta as well, where I hit with 10% on that 249 mako six weeks ago. I asked if I could get in 20% of that 2500 and the captains said sure, so I'm in for 1840. The week will run me another 2 k so this is a pretty penny for some chill time with my boys, but with my father staking part of the ride I'll take the bet.

Walter is a paramedic and fisherman, Nathan is in the fine jewelery business three generations deep, Red runs a landscaping company and his family does real estate, I make art for every penny of my waking life, and my idea of a vacation is getting on a boat with friends and going high stakes fishing. They can afford more leisure time and travel, but every day in the studio is a spaceship ride to planet Pluto. Non-creatives will never understand this.

There is motion on the boat. The water curls by, my friends are busy doing random crap if not joking as the Fish Pig moves along at 17 knots. I go out to the cockpit, which has a massive 16 foot beam, and I am mesmerized like Ishmael by the trail of the ocean, the flight of the birds, the rolling of the clouds, the hum of the engine, the disappearing of my recent past, which feels like it's sliding out of me slowly, gently, like the releasing of a bad memory, an unfortunate episode. I feel peace and friendship, with people who treat me properly like everyone I vet before allowing into my life to make for a richer experience.

On a boat you focus on balance, on the horizon line, on your crew members, on the tasks at hand. When you are taking a four hour stroll up to the tournament everyone goes into their own head spaces that fishermen do. You know you are moving in the right direction, but you've got plenty of time to think about life if you want to. The picture gets broader when you are moving around in life.

The intensity of focus that comes along with running a fine

art studio is a completely different animal; in one space, in one's brain, exercising one's spirit, high stakes spiritual yoga that brings in the bacon if you crush it hard enough against the walls of your solitary studio. A lot of people need to go outside of themselves for life, money, love, activities. Put me naked in a rubber room with a pencil and I will fly away. No walls can contain me. I'm not even here. I'm an aberration like we all are, a momentary stop on this planet, in this skin, catching a vibe, doing a minute's work on the soul in a long, timeless path to unity. We are one but we don't know it in this life, or some people know it and others follow, swinging to the music of several pied pipers per generation per nation. Only room for a handful of names whose power stretches over the centuries. Who will be remembered in this new century? Last century was a blistering nightmare the world is still coming to grips with.

It's cool to see Walter and Nathan bullshitting with the water in front of us while I write. I can't paint a picture without full physical attention, and I usually write in solitary, but I can type while peering out at the water line, which reminds me why writing is one of the best things to explore when I'm not painting a picture.

August 6 Saturday

Yesterday we left the dock on the Connecticut side of Long Island Sound, the boat ran out at 18 knots and I slid into another world, which is what people who spend their leisure time doing hobbies or passions excel at. We stopped at Fisher's Island to get some equipment, picked up crew member Marcus, then we went to Montauk Marine Basin to fuel the boat. We filled the boat with a ton of ice and were off to Block Island. We pulled in and docked the Fish Pig around 5 pm, cleaned her up, had clams and steak on the ice box, which doubles as a table in the cockpit, and went out to listen to Warren play guitar at Mahogony Shoals, a short walk from the marina.

Today was a rainy piss storm of a day. I worked for 8 hours on the family book at the captain's table. I have 400 images that have been placed in the book layout, but my family renamed every image they had to rescan so I spent 8 hours finding images and relinking them to the book file. I got halfway through one section that will take 15 hours to find and relink the new scans. Nobody knows to care. They just want their books.

In the evening our friend Danny brought us back to his place that he shares with his fiancée Ashley. They are living over a store they set up and are running this summer. Danny is an integral part of our crew but he won't be fishing this week, which tears him up. They made a great meal for us and we sat at a circular table outside on the second floor balcony in downtown Block Island as the streets stirred with activity. I want a circular table when I have a house for entertaining, like my friends the Beans taught me.

August 7 Sunday

It rained all day until 4 pm, then the hazy sun emerged as all the tournament boats lurched in from the Eastern Seaboard and started to greet one another; crews laughing, recounting stories, sharing good energy, reigniting bets and feuds that will never go away. The mood on the Fish Pig was festive as friends jumped aboard to have a drink, everyone fishing for information, where the action is, where the boats are going. The shop talk is meshed with very good storytelling, the humor on our team is heating up as every experience makes for a new laugh, behavioral patterns spawning nicknames, the best of which will embed themselves into crew lore.

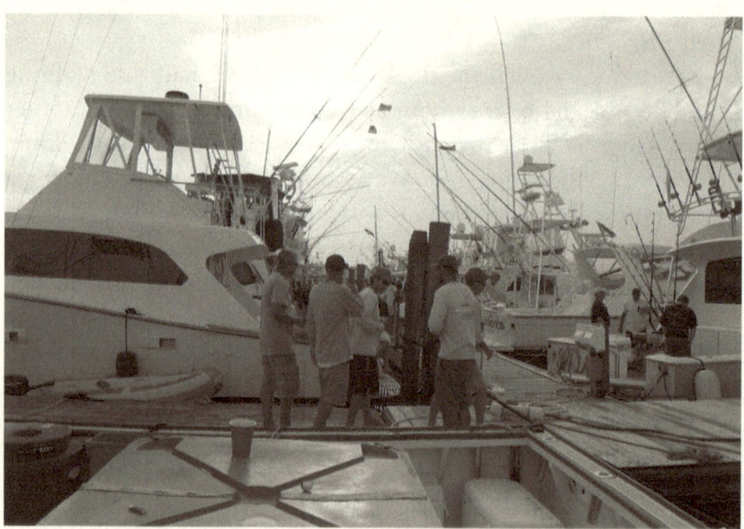

I was seated at the table on the family book project all day, just trying to find and relink images. I did not sign on for this job. My job was to design the look of the book once all the files were linked into the layout program. No such luck. I've got another hundred hours minimum with these major design setbacks. I have to get this book done and out and not look back.

At the captain's meeting we got some shrimp cocktail, a tournament bag with shirts, drink tickets and meal tickets, the rules of the tournament, and we said hello to fellow fishermen under the huge tent. Red has been whipping up the best food on deck so we didn't stick around for dogs and burgers provided by the tournament meeting. We went back to the boat and determined that we will take off tomorrow morning. We leave at 5 am and have 36 hours to get back to the dock with whatever we catch. As we talked strategy we caught a couple squid who were attracted to the transom lights with a little squid jig.

August 8 Monday

We were up at 4 am to prepare the boat for departure. We pushed off with 40 other boats and left the harbor at 5 am. Captain Nathan ran his boat and we had five or six hours to get out there, so the crew went back to the sheets for a spell, as a lot of the fishing time is every single hour that is not traveling time.

I returned to my bunk for a little more shuteye like everyone else. We got tossed around like potato sacks down there in these bunks on the bow that take every wave. When you are on a boat and you have a moment to sleep, you take it. You take anything you can get, and you smile about it, otherwise you are an ungrateful, shitty crew member. If you can't make a joke out of your last injury or the last fucked up thing that went wrong, you aren't worth much if you can't make them laugh. This happens to fit my disposition, which is why I get along with Walter so well. We've seen all sorts of shit, and whatever the situation, we come away with laughter, maybe a story, maybe a concert, a life lesson, a fish, some kind of journey to remember, 25 years of adventures.

Walter was not feeling too good, which is unusual given his iron stomach at sea. I remember when he graduated to Montauk shark fishing and I was with him. He insisted on Dramamine, which helps people with motion sickness. My father has always said that he's never had a problem on the water, and so it went years ago when brother Matt, Dad and I were crew for one of Walter's early shark tournaments. He had a 28 foot Mako at the time, a great boat that nevertheless can kick the crew's ass getting around Montauk Point and spending days out fishing for sharks. My father sat on the bench reading the paper in his cross-legged, sock-less tassel loafers as we shot out at 20 knots in 3 foot swells, the bow crashing down, one bumpy ride, my father completely at ease, no candy-ass Dramamine for him.

Walter looked back at my father and said then, "I could never do that shit, read the newspaper in this slop."

The Dramamine knocked Matt and me right out, so after a couple shark tournaments I stopped doing that stuff. I've never been seasick. I know it is unwise to never say never, but I think I'm like my Dad that way. There is something to the rhythm of the ocean that makes sense to me, although the ocean can get pretty tough, and I haven't seen much compared to any commercial fisherman. I do one or two tournaments a year, and if the weather is really bad Walter does not go out. Better safe than sorry. Some tournaments lose boats and people, which is a real shame.

Five hours in we slowed down and started placing rods in their holsters. We set the spreaders, which fan the lines out so they don't tangle, and got eight rods going, trolling at 7 knots. The weather was perfect, and we moved slowly through the mid-morning rollers. There were three other boats from our fleet in view. Sometimes you find a spot where nobody in your fleet is fishing, which is good and bad in the same way.

We trolled all day, picking up a little yellowfin that we released. No action otherwise. Humor and fishing meditation go hand in hand. Fishermen like to be here, to empty their minds out, the anticipation of a good fish, memories of successful trips in the past. Our crew clicks and as with any team this is most important, so there is good communication and clean energy running through the boat.

Things were slow so I climbed the ladder up to check in on my old friend looking for action at the top of the boat. I spent an hour in the tuna tower with Walter and we talked about the decision to come all the way out here, the 'life' that was here earlier in the day; tons of dolphins, a large turtle, some marlins jumping, three mantas flying out of the water. But by the time I got up in the tower, it had been hours since we had seen life or activity.

When you are on a boat in a competition, waiting for activity is its own language. You have to make your move and see what happens over the course of a twelve hour, twenty-four hour, thirty-six hour cycle. The fleet gets action over there and you can't help but wonder if you should have been over there the whole time. I suppose it's like making your career or life decisions. I understand this as an artist because there are often no creative boats in my vicinity when I am fishing for the next painting. I can yell out across the water and nothing comes back. This is the beauty, the curse, the Zen of making your moves and standing by your decisions every hour, every day, every week, every year of life, of an art career. I should have zigged, I could have zagged, but hindsight is its own terrier.

At dusk we had clams and tuna on the deck. Red prepared the food with a pot boiler and a grill we kept in the cockpit. There is nothing really like gathering around the bait box, like a tall bar table, trolling your way, communing with your boys, eating fresh seafood, laughing, having a drink to good music at August dusk 100 miles south of Montauk Point.

Red likes his handle of rum, and in making a swift move to avoid being burned by clam water, Walter accidentally tipped the bottle off the bait box. We all watched in slow motion as Walter and Red tried to swipe the handle out of the air, but it fell and broke over the metal hatch on the deck, which threw Red into a tailspin. I've never seen Red so anguished, 100 miles from civilization, suddenly 24 hours away from another taste of his trademark rum. I thought I saw a tear in his eye as he hung his head in despair and walked into the cabin to investigate the remaining wet bar, secretly hoping to find another magical handle of rum. No such luck. Walter apologized with compassion, almost with a severity as though he had run over Red's dog. We had to do our best to raise Red's spirits, which went very low.

The weather was perfect, aside from the tragic fact that now Red had no more rum on board. We were the only ones out here but the crew was getting feisty. A day of fishing and one tiny tuna that we had tossed back. Red got up in the tower and Walter slept while Nathan drove the boat, Marcus slept in a port side camping chair and I sat in a starboard chair, facing our wake, letting my mind go free. 9 pm, 10 pm.

10:30 pm. The line to my left pinged off the spreader, I stood up and said, "Hey!"

Marcus woke up, Nathan ran back, Red shouted "Fish," and Walter came right up. That line went slack but a second starboard reel tip went cranking down and away.

"Put the fucking deck lights on!" Nathan huffed as he took control of the boat from the cockpit wheel. I put a fighting belt on Walter while he picked up the rod. We started to clear all the lines as Walter set the hook in the fish by pulling hard while reeling.

The crew was chattering but Nathan likes his boat quiet and calm during a fight.

"Shut the fuck up and listen to me!" I never say anything because I'm taking orders and don't want to piss these ornery bastards off.

Walter brought the fish around to the starboard side and Marcus assisted with the fighting harness strap, which was tangled. Walter made some ground on the fish as Nathan steered the boat with the fish. Everything was right.

"This is fighting exactly like that 280 big eye tuna last year," Walter said as the fish started to take line again, the rod spinning, our crew starting to look at one another.

Marcus said, "We were looking for one bite. Here it is."

"You're doing great. This thing's a fucking stud," Nathan said to the deck as he followed the fight with the çockpit wheel.

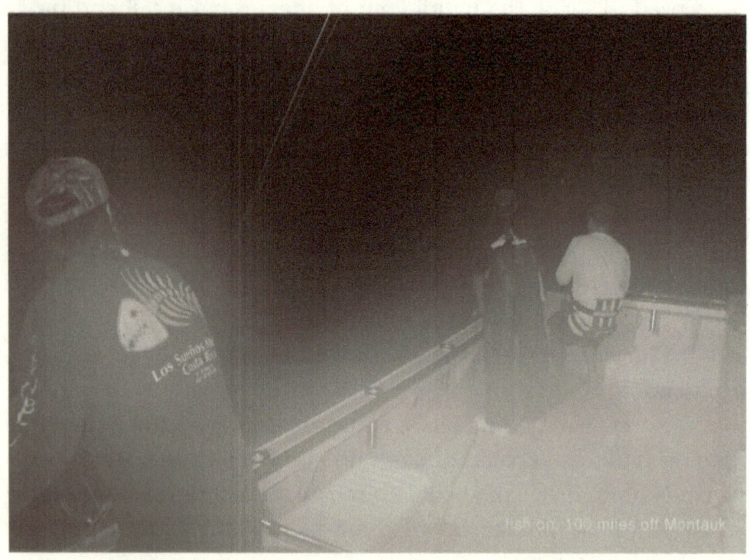

fish on, 100 miles off Montauk

The fish kept peeling line off the reel as the crew did everything right, namely stay the hell out of Walter's way. I stayed out of Nathan's line of vision, just behind him, doing the little things he was asking me to prepare for. I got gloves on and Marcus came over.

"This will be exactly like the stud mako in our last tourney. You are going to hand me the starboard gaff, then you are going to hand me the black gaff," Marcus pointed to the port gaff sticking out of a rod holder attached to a cooler next to the center bait box.

"I'm going to gaff the tail, gaff it in the head, then you and I are going to pull this stud into the boat."

The fish kept taking line and Walter mentioned it again.

Nathan said, "We have to turn the fish," and Walter started banging again. Everything was smooth, everyone was doing their job right. There were no mistakes.

The line went slack.

Oh boy. Walter reeled the line in while everyone's dreams of a huge tournament purse, this victory with the big one, drained away. Shouting, cursing, swearing, collective disappointment. No blame, just the nature of tournaments, the nature of fishing, the nature of the sea.

A deep, brooding depression overcame the crew as we worked to get the lines out again. The fish was on the line for 25 minutes and hadn't budged. The hook showed the teeth scars. The leader was bent to shit but would have held. The one that got away.

One of the hundred thousand that get away in every person's lifetime. I thought I was holding the one who got away but had returned then flew away again. The timing of cosmic chemistry with another human being. Why do there need to be so many stars aligning for true love to blossom? Don't ask this beaten up artist fisherman. I know how to paint pictures that will hang in museums some day, but eternal love? Evasive.

I sat out there with Marcus while Red and Walter got some sleep. At 12:39 am Nathan shut the engines down and turned in for a nap. Marcus and I brought the trolling lines in and started chunking. We laid out five lines off the starboard side with balloons attached to glow sticks and I started throwing chunks of butterfish. I did this until about 3 am and then Marcus went down, relieved by Walter. Every fresh mate enlivens the tired crew member who is keeping watch and soon you find yourself working together on new projects. Walter pulled out the chum chucker, which we attached to the side of the boat. You plug it in and it has this arm on a belt that pulls a little chum out of the container and dumps it overboard. I poured two buckets of fish heads and guts into the chum chucker and watched the thing do its job. It worked too well, taking too much chum at every pass, so Walter jerry-rigged the platform to slow it down, jerry-rigging being one of Walter's specialties. Presto... good as new. Then he started cutting up butterfish as we stood there at the bait box talking about the big one. Watching someone work is boring so I got a knife and started cutting butterfish up with him. We gunned through the flat of frozen butterfish quickly. I guess the big oil spill in the Gulf has made for smaller butterfish lately.

Nathan woke up and started the engines around 4 am. We pulled the chunking lines and set up the trolling lines again. Walter and I found ourselves sitting together after all the work was done, as old friendship goes in life, looking back at the glittering lines in the ocean, illuminated by glow sticks to attract the big fish. He told me I should take a rest and I listened to him.

August 9 Tuesday

They trolled, I slept from 5:30 until 9 am, then rolled out of the bow bunk and got into the depressing humor my crew mates were throwing around. We were running out of time if we wanted a chance at anything, so the skipper was going for yellowfin and mahi. At 11:30 am a marlin pinged through three baits, which we quickly reset. At 12:30 pm four reels went off at once and I pulled in a 46 lb albacore tuna. Red pulled in a 50 pounder and Walter pulled in a 40 pounder. We got the rest of the lines in and headed back, thinking we might make the weigh-in. Walter checked the rules and we had to be in by 4 pm, so our chances on albacore were dashed as well. At least we weren't blanked today and we had our shot at the big fish. A 206 Big Eye was on the board back at the marina and a 238 was weighed in. Walter thinks this one was like the 280 last year, so with his experience I'll just think to myself that we had a winner on the line. At least a nice money fish.

The ride home was peacefully solemn. We were all disappointed that we didn't bring the big dog in. This fish could have won us $150,000. That's a lot of clams to pass around, enough to make a starving artist rich for a spell.

In this way tournament fishing is like the art life. I have this mural on the line but there is not enough fine art in the fight, so either I get more money or have to clip the line. I never know where my next art fish is coming from, and I know what it feels like to lose a big one overnight, take the beating and move on. I remember losing 25 grand in two separate painting commitments one Tuesday morning, which sank my art boat studio that summer. I got her floating again. Love of the game, resilience, the ability to take a shot, stay alive and keep the light shining.

August 10 Wednesday

I went down early last night like a pussy and got up at 6:30 am. We left the dock for the fluking piece of the tournament and had a good day. We all caught a bunch of fluke and some small sea bass. There were tons of reels out so there was a lot of action for hours. Our fluke weighed 7 lbs. 13 ounces, which just missed second place for a couple grand. Shut out.

We went to the awards ceremony dinner and watched other jubilant fishing teams rejoice in their glory. One boat took $188,000, and there was another boat that took $78,000. Those two big bites in deep water could have been a game changer for me and the studio during a challenging year, but I try not to spend money I don't yet have. We ate our dinner and joked around about several running themes on the boat. Everyone has different names now. Walter is Neil, T. Rex, Peggy and Honey Badger. Nathan is Peggy, Skip, and Honey Badger. Red is Waye, Cook, Cat Dog, Honey Badger and a host of other names. I am Sandman and Honey Badger.

We went to Kittens, which is a massive, ridiculous meat market with music so loud that you just nod when people talk at you. I am not good at lip reading so I can't understand what anybody is saying in places like this. Nobody could get a drink so my crew drained out of the place in pieces. Marcus and I caught a ride with Mike and Tara. We stopped by Mahogany Shoals for a mudslide, a bar which is more my speed, before returning to the boat, my home for the week.

The dock was rowdy and festive, flush with cash and new stories about fishing conquests. Nathan asked if anyone wanted to play Beirut and I went along with him. The beer pong or Beirut table was 30 x 96 inches, a thin table to allow for passers-by placed midway down the central dock.

Between 1:30 am and 5:30 am Nathan and I ran our side of the table with a perfect record of 10 wins. In the middle five games we bet twenty a head but only collected 40 out of our 200. Guys fresh out of college who were masters of the game we crushed into the dirt. We didn't care about the money. It was some form of retribution for missing that big bite. That 200 k would have been great but the pride of the win is the thing that makes the people around here tick, not the cash. Four hours at the table draining 15 x 10 = 150 ping pong balls into red and blue score cups.

The second to last game meant the most, as Nathan had

an old score to settle with a young gun who had taken him for a lot of money one year at this game. We went into overtime with three cups per side. I nailed the right front cup, they reformed, and Nathan hit the front cup. The last cup stood there in the dark, around 30 people who were our audience. I let the ping pong ball go... eight feet and swoosh. Our friend Mike behind me screamed, "Holy shit! Larry Bird!" as I turned and walked away from the game into the darkness towards the end of the dock, feeling total victory. Nathan called me back for one more game and we spanked the last team. Game over, we walked back to the Fish Pig with Red into morning dawn blossoming.

August 11 Thursday

We cleaned the boat and I worked all day on the family book again. In the evening we went for dinner and then martini night at the Spring House, which was cool, but Nathan and I were tired. I don't understand why martini glasses are shaped the way they are, a glass you should never walk around with as everyone is just spilling their martinis on the shoes of people next to them the whole drunken time. My crew wanted me to get lucky with one of the pretty girls who were clearly available, but this was the last thing on my mind. Somehow I felt the thought unethical on the grounds that there had been no communication with text breakup chick for two weeks. I don't have eyes for someone else, but I'm tough when I get burned and this girl doesn't know that yet. She just saw an intense warmth that I rarely share and that she will never see again.

August 12 Friday

We were up early and pulled off the dock to Noank for gas, then Fisher's to drop Nathan off, whose son is being Christened on Sunday. Marcus jumped off yesterday because he had a job to do today on the mainland. We helped Nathan off with his stuff, handshakes and hugs all around brothers. The Fish Pig pulled away and Nathan watched his old boat, his new boat, with a new partner and a shifting crew, as life moves along, things change, people come and go. I've seen the changes with Walter for 25 years; different boats, different memories, different adventures. Some things stay the same like best friendships if you treat them right, and other things change.

On the ride back my heart and mind drifted in and out of

the past week, the past month. It can be helpful to replace sad things with good things, fun times, new experiences. Some people spend their lives running away, immersing themselves in new skins so they don't have to look too long at their aging faces in the mirror, at the old things that haunt them which made them run in the first place. I spend my life staring into the mirror, trying to find every fold, every crease, every ripple in the wake of my spirit. I try to get the kinks out, try to work out the tough stuff, try to lay my world out art-wise in order to survive, in order to grow spiritually, evolve humanely, age gracefully, live fully.

August 13 Saturday

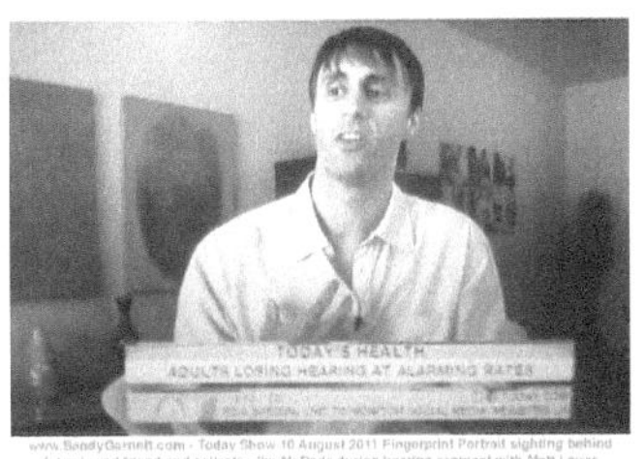

www.SandyGarnett.com - Today Show 10 August 2011 Fingerprint Portrait sighting behind interviewed friend and collector Jim McDade during hearing segment with Matt Lauer

My friend Liege sent a photo of my Fingerprint Portrait paintings on television behind my friend Jim, who was being interviewed at his NYC apartment for a network piece about the wellness business. It is fun to receive photos when friends and collectors bump into an original Garnett painting.

A number of articles on the 'Alternative Visions' show that I juried came out last week, and my prepared press statement was quoted a number of times. I found the cleanest, best article and uploaded that to the press section on my website.

I have been distracted by the large mural commission and the text breakup, neither of which seem to have worked out. My individual collectors have always kept me alive so I have to return to my roots, as my friend Don astutely noted several weeks ago.

August 14 Sunday

I was 205 lbs. before getting on the boat and I'm 212 a week later, so I have to shed a few pounds. My grandfather Gump always maintained his college weight. That guy did hand stands off the diving board into his 70's. When I was little he taught me to love Chunky soup out of the can or sardines out of a tin with a sleeve of Ritz crackers. Navy gourmet, World War II style. He taught me how to stretch, how to box a little, how to watch out in New York traffic, how to use a little fork to pluck sardines out of the tin and paste them onto Ritz crackers, sitting side by side at 420 East 79th watching football on the television.

I spent 15 hours on the family book, not leaving the studio once on this rainy day.

August 15 Monday

When I hang around the easel the answers come in to sustain my studio. I added three new collector placement pages to my website and put up some spec work for potential collectors in Maine, Houston, and New York City. I received an email from a new collector who has heard about my Fingerprint Project and wants to do something for a family member's birthday.

My studio has achieved just enough of a tipping point to tough it out in good times and bad. The key thing is to never stop, to always plug away, to grind it out, like my parents taught me. This is my reputation, that I am one of the hardest working artists around. People ask if I ever sleep. The answer is no.

August 16 Tuesday

I got from page 200 to 250 after another 16 hours working on the family book. The deadline pressure is intense and I feel it in the small of my back. I am making incremental progress and hope to clear the decks soon. Bed, rinse, repeat.

August 17 Wednesday

I went to my parents' house with my brother Matthew for an early dinner. My cousins David and his son Henry are in from London. They visited my studio in the afternoon and David, who has been a CEO for half of the career he is about to retire from, talked about how it feels like there is a tsunami in my studio waiting to happen, that I am sitting on a gold mine. This would be wonderful. I have heard votes of confidence like this for years from people I respect, so it's always a nice jolt to hear a new perspective confirming that I should find more success in my future.

August 18 Thursday

I spent 18 hours plowing through the family photo book. I finished my nuclear family section and got into my aunt's section. I have about sixty pages to go, so tomorrow my goal will be to open up the remaining 170 photographs, remove dust and scratches manually, resize, color correct and change them all from RGB files to CMYK files for printing.

Aside from the technical problems and a tight deadline, this book has been an engaging family exploration. It has been a lot of fun for me to revisit relatives as they were growing up and into life, taking good care to digitally clean each photo and create layouts that are respectful to each family member. Every family member gets his or her day in the sun, the design is fluid, and the best part is that nobody knows about the book.

August 19 Friday

I got on the road late afternoon and arrived in Newport at 7:30 pm, so I missed my friend John's wedding party booze cruise. I checked in, then I called to see where my friends were, two couples from college who are my favorites. I picked up some wine and beer down the street for the group before Ben and Julia arrived. Julia turned in so Ben and I walked into town to meet up with the wedding party after their cruise.

We went to a meat market on the water with house music blaring and women walking around wearing fishing lure dresses and sparkly high heels. I found the parade of talent flaunting their wares amusing, although the place wasn't exactly our cup of tea.

We couldn't find the wedding party so we sat for a last drink up the street. My thoughts hovered around the girl who I was planning to be here with me this weekend. The bars closed and we walked ten minutes back to base camp, enjoying the deep friendship that comes with spending half your life in someone else's brain. I have never had an argument with this old pal of mine. We are in lock step. I have a lot of people in my life who are like this when I get to spend time with them. There is no competition, no pettiness, no bullshit, only true appreciation for time spent together. These are the friendships I seek out in life that have made me a better man, a better artist.

Artists can be competitive like athletes are competitive, and a lot of competition is about one's search for self. When I commune with others I don't seek to measure myself up against that individual, and I certainly don't want to debate about politics or anything else, which is a waste of time. I want to laugh and sing and enjoy good times with people I care about. My art life is brutal so friends are a welcome break from the intensity of looking at myself in the mirror relentlessly as a matter of profession. When I get to sit with family and friends the best remind me that we should take a moment to laugh smartly at the absurdities of life.

August 20 Saturday

I have this posh room and my better-to-do friends have smaller rooms this weekend. I almost offered a trade just to be a good guy. My larger hangout room became the center for engagement. Ben and Chris hung out in the morning as their wives, super close friends of mine also from college, milled in and out. We went to Second Beach and tossed a frisbee around for awhile. It's not easy to find time to toss the frisbee around with your old friends who usually have kids to run after.

After a drink at the bar, Chris drove us to Jamestown. It was an easy shot over the bridge, off the first exit and straight down. You can always spot other wedding cars on quiet roads, so we tailed one to the house where John's wedding was taking place.

The wedding was an intimate affair on the hilltop of a beautiful home overlooking the ocean, sun streaking through the wind, boats sailing dramatically in the background as John and Allie took their vows.

There was a nice girl who John had told me might get me out of my breakup blues. She went right over to my friend Chris and asked if he was the artist.

"No, that guy over there is." Then she was smack by my side and we had fun talking throughout the evening. She has a sweet spirit, but I let that one lie like I did with the tall pretty girl in Block Island. My guy friends insist that the proper remedy after a breakup is to date other women. I'm in no rush. There are always pretty girls to have a nice time with. Someone to fall for ? That's a different story.

The reception ended and people were going to a place off Broadway in Newport. I drove Chris's big family truckster back over the bridge and up to the inn. We were planning to meet the wedding party out but found ourselves having drinks and laughing on the comfortable back porch, all to ourselves. It's hard to find time to sit with old friends outside the hustle and bustle of everyday family life, so we stretched out and night-capped the evening there.

August 21 Sunday

The commute back from Newport today was peaceful and reflective. I listened to the songs that I've been working on, composing a new song in my head as I drove through the morning sun, watching the foliage of Rhode Island fade into Connecticut greenery.

Back at the studio, I lined up some movies and took my primary computer down to the first floor kitchen island. I watched or listened to three movies between 2 pm and midnight as I sat at the table and prepared 170 of the last photographs to go into the family book.

August 22 Monday

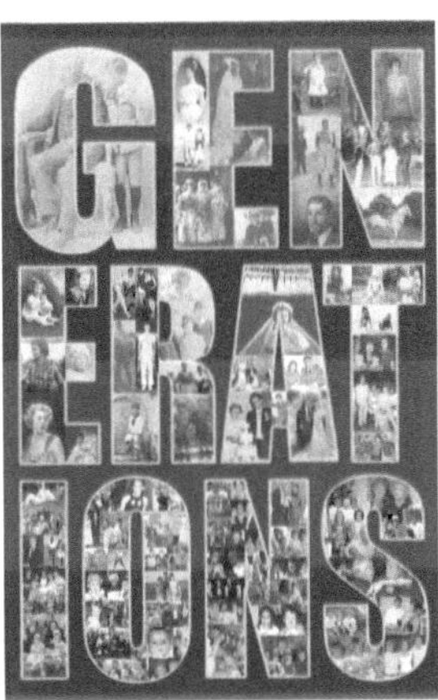

The title of this family book is GENERATIONS, so I spent 12 hours dragging old family photos in and creating a chronological photo-montage within the letters, one letter at a time, one segment of the family at a time. It took me several hours to arrive at a tan 12 point border around the type and even longer to determine that thick maroon and navy horizontal bands made for the best background, balancing traditional palettes with the mildly contemporary collage lettering.

August 23 Tuesday

Lina came over with edits on the Larry Lewis book. She thought it would take all day but we burned through the edits in a little over an hour because we complete each others' sentences, which is why we like to curate shows together. I'm also very fast at book design currently, the blades very sharp.

I spent the rest of the day on *Generations* and by 9 pm I was at the finish line. I called my father and he told me he will come over tomorrow after 6 am spinning to see what I've got.

I can't believe this monster is almost finished.

August 24 Wednesday

I was up at 6 am to tweak *Generations* before my father came over. I went through the 355 page book with him once, we caught some corrections, then I left him to take his own notes so I could go to a meeting for another gravestone etching.

I walked into Don's office and met his client, a nice woman who lost her husband recently. She had medieval books and wanted to do a kneeling knight with a medieval flag flying over his bowed head. I told her about all the medieval subject matter I enjoyed as a little boy living in London, drawing knights in shining armor, military figures, and painting tin soldiers. This got her excited. She said that they had put on a medieval-themed wedding, so she wanted to do something appropriate for his stone. This nice woman was happy that we connected, so I took some references home to do a spec piece for her approval.

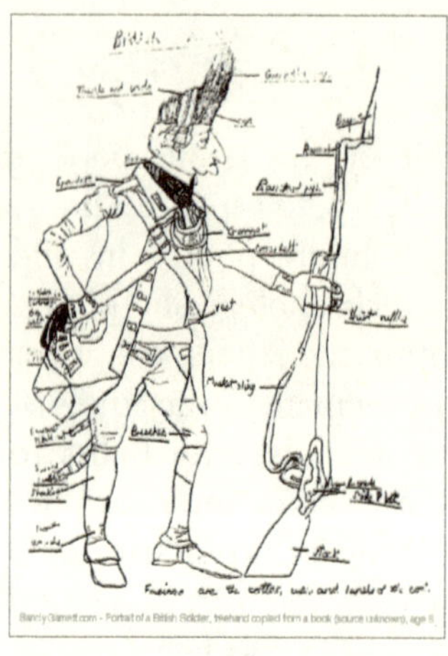
SandyGarnett.com - Portrait of a British Soldier, freehand copied from a book (source unknown), age 8

I returned to my studio and my father had found three or four corrections. We made adjustments and I created another PDF for him to review again while he got lunch down the street.

We had lunch and my father took one last look at the document. I don't like ordering twenty books without getting a proof, as there are always more small edits. You get burned with small mistakes that you don't catch until you are sitting with a hard copy in your hand cursing yourself.

I suggested that we print four perfect bound softcovers, which will definitely be here in time, and order 15 hardcovers, which should be here on time, so we agreed on this approach. In the afternoon I generated covers and guts for softcover and hardcover formats and sent them off for printing.

We finished at 5 pm and high-fived each other. A day well spent with my dear old Dad, a project long in the making, a combined 700 family hours to produce this project. My mother said I should start a side business as I have a knack for book making. I'd rather be painting or sculpting, but now I've checked a 360 page pictorial family history hardcover book off the list.

There is always relief and euphoria when a project finishes itself. The larger the project the greater the relief. I feel like the clouds have parted, time and space are sprawled out before me.

August 25 Thursday

My brother Matt's Godparents Bev and Dick visited my studio today, then they went over to spend the night with my parents so Matt and I joined them for dinner. The old stories were filled with laughter and reminded me that younger people should listen to the stories and wisdom of older people.

I returned to my studio and text breakup chick had sent me an email from her mother's phone.

"I hope you had a good summer. I need to get my things from your place. You can call me at this number as my phone is broken."

First correspondence since the text breakup almost a month ago. She hopes I had a good summer? A month ago she was placing clothing in the drawers of my bureau and talking about names for babies when we got married (her words, not mine).

I absorbed the blow and went to bed.

August 26 Friday

This morning I received a phone message, a text and a social networking message from text breakup chick about the same subject, getting her crap.

My cousin Steve called and asked if I wanted to come up to his Vermont farm. Yes, I needed to get away.

I responded only to one social networking message.

"I left your things at Bella's when I went with Walter to Block Island as I figured you would return and want to play your sport. Summer great off to VT with cousins."

The drive to Vermont is always refreshing, although text breakup chick fired back a bunch of texts, social networking messages and emails asking for our friend's phone.

One of these messages read, "Thanks. Have a good summer in VT. Need mutual friend's phone. Thanks. Best, TBC."

I wondered what planet she was on. Planet Not Well. I'm done with correspondence on this one. I think she figured her stuff was all nice and tidy, sitting in the drawers at my studio where she left everything... like she could return and everything would be fine again. The minute I had received that nasty text breakup I had moved her things out of my place.

I got to the farm at 4 pm and Steve had just finished mowing a field on his new tractor. He showed me the barn that he has been cleaning up. He has made an amazing workshop out of part of the barn space since the last time I was up.

Steve's wife Claire just had baby Lane two weeks ago, so this is big news. Usually I am cheerful and a good listener so I tried to keep it balanced, but I was hurting and Steve knew it. My family and friends are not used to seeing me like this.

We picked up drinks and steaks, shot clay pigeons for awhile, then I played guitar while Steve lit the grill up and cooked.

We sat for dinner in the dimly lit chicken coop that his family had made into a beautiful three season place with blood, sweat and tears. We adjourned to the sitting area for a night cap then hit the rack. I was happy to be in Vermont with my cousin. He called at the perfect time.

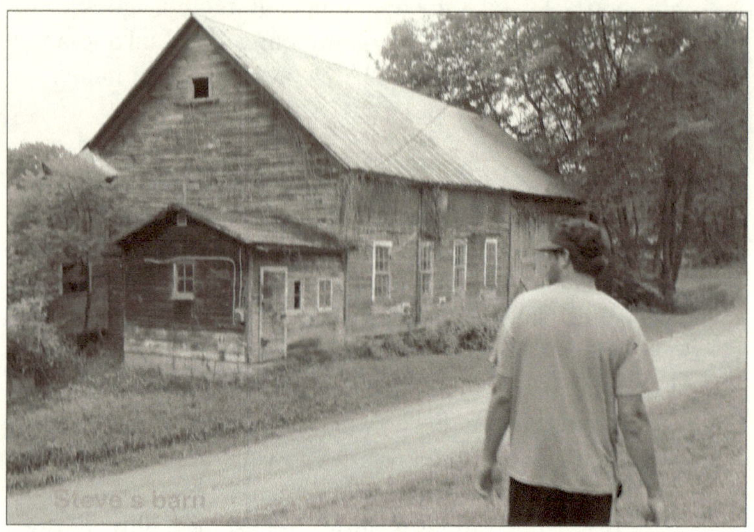

Steve's barn

August 27 Saturday

I stirred at 6 am but went back to Vermont sleep until 7:30 am. Steve walked in with a coffee and cheeseburger for me from the gas mart. Then he got the chainsaw humming and we cut down eight trees that were leaning against out-structures on the property.

Steve and I work well together, so we got into a silent rhythm of trading off the chainsaw, carrying larger logs under the chicken coop, which houses the firewood. There is a fluidity that develops between good workers, family members, athletes, when they are using their bodies to achieve a unified task that I find compelling and on the animal side of human nature.

These weren't huge trees so they came down without too much trouble. There is an intense amount of energy in a tree coming down, which is a charge. Cutting up a tree smartly is interesting and important. You have to look at all the angles, what is attached to what. You can't cut the wrong thing first or a limb could take your leg out like a catapult. Plus you are swinging around a chainsaw that will sever your arm in one swipe. The buzz of power tools. I wore my jack hammer headphones to dull the crank of the tree trauma as the sun poked holes in the gray clouds and made them white.

While we were closing in on the end of a tree, Steve's brother Reyn pulled in. Cousin Reyn is up here at his fiancé's family house forty-five minutes away, preparing for their wedding next weekend. The three of us went to work on more trees. We cleaned up a stone foundation that had partially crumbled, using Steve's shiny new red tractor to reposition 500 pound slabs of granite. The weather was good but the news was looking bad as Hurricane Irene made her way up the Eastern seaboard. Steve's wife Claire and brand new daughter Lane were in Greenwich, so we made the call to drive home after a lunch break. We packed, cleaned up the house, closed up the barn and headed out by 1:45 pm.

I got home and checked the weather. It would start getting bad at midnight. Steve called to tell me that his sister Jen was over so I should meet the baby before the storm came in. I went over to their place and hung out for a couple of hours, getting some cousinly insight from Jen and Claire. I don't have sisters so I rely on the feminine perspectives of my cousins and old, close friends who feel like sisters. 'Run for the hills' is the consistent message.

August 28 Sunday

Last night I slept downstairs on the couch that I designed and built as my loft skylights can be loud in the rain. The power went off at midnight as the weather drifted in. I woke up at 7 am, drank some cold coffee and started writing on my laptop.

370,000 New Yorkers were evacuated, they shut Tri-State mass transit down, closed highways, stores, businesses, and schools on Monday. This was a shitshow.

Sun broke in the afternoon while the East Coast picked up the pieces. The wind died down and the hurricane had passed. It's weird when you are looking at the trees outside your studio shake violently like toothpicks for twelve hours and then suddenly silence. I checked my car, our building, and everything seemed in order aside from a lot of small foliage in the parking lot and a pool of water behind one of the buildings. I bumped into the president of the condo and she mentioned that the large park across the bridge is completely underwater. She said that one woman was walking her dog on the raised path and it looked like she was walking on water in the middle of Long Island Sound.

My parents were okay and my brother's house did not have damage, but a number of friends were not so lucky. I saw pictures of one friend rowing his boat down a Rowayton street past the local deli, and I saw another picture of a friend's daughter in a row boat at her mailbox in Noroton Bay. This is going to take a long time for a lot of people to get through.

August 29 Monday

The entire Eastern seaboard deep into the Northeast is reeling from Hurricane Irene. My studio is okay but a lot of homes are underwater, boats and cars destroyed, expensive property damaged, tens of thousands of trees have fallen all over the place, power lines cut, cable lines cut, people living out of suitcases in shelters, people lost in the storm.

I am compassionate for others but I looked at my negative accounts today and started breathing fast and shallow. I need to find a painting sale but two of four active collectors have been in the eye of this hurricane. One is an old dialogue I need to rekindle. The building of dialogues is crucial the way I make my business happen, over complex emails that span months and years. I act as artist, designer, representative and shipping company. This summer I let some things go because I was chasing phantoms like that mural and love with a girl that didn't pan out. There is a vacuum that has threatened the health of my studio, which pisses me off. People are generally not allowed to come in and mess with my world, but I let two energies in that I should have been more cautious about. Live and learn I suppose. I need to start making things. The answers will come as they always do.

My brother Matt came over to watch the Giants lose to the Jets in preseason fashion. He left with the second stringers and I almost closed shop but my eyes fell upon a landscape that I placed on my easel to taunt me. It worked. I saw the unfinished painting and wanted to clarify the deep space in it, fall into it, move around in it. I have this, the Twister pictures, several new sculptures, some old Reconstructions to start chewing on again. Why have I been blown off the easel, this place of renewal, a place of survival? I'm not sure. When I'm locked onto the easel like an insect all the answers come. I have been stretching mediums, writing and music in this rough market, so that is a small factor. The easel hasn't quite been covering lately, so maybe I have to spend a week on there and let it bleed.

August 30 Tuesday

Complete freedom is the beauty of an independent fine art career. I wake up every day to create, to explore the human landscape and its relationship to new art objects, the best of which are timeless symbols of human existence. Our lives are an instant and then we move to the next plane, so I try to make every day count. Art is a gift that can be left behind for others to enjoy and be inspired by. Art begets art.

I waited outside and the overnight mail service came by at 8 pm. I signed for the box and brought it up to my studio, bladed the box open and found my four *Generations* books. What a buzz.

I got a good song out of the text breakup. I wrapped the lyrics tonight and continued to work on the single microphone recording as opposed to multiple tracks. Part of me feels like I am working on cursory performance exercises in this way. Lyrics work themselves out when you are singing them. A lot of lyrics look good on paper but phonetically don't roll off the tongue in melodies smoothly. This one has three stanzas and a refrain at the end, which is a little unusual but feels right.

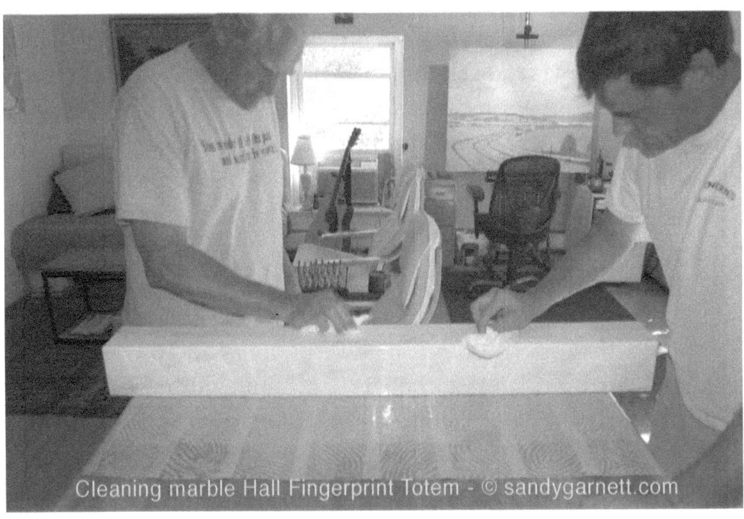
Cleaning marble Hall Fingerprint Totem - © sandygarnett.com

August 31 Wednesday

My father came over this morning. At one point he told me

to get him a tissue. I watched him look at the book across the table, so I was looking at the book upside down with him. He went through every page, then he high-fived me and remarked that our family will be blown away. I told him if the hardcover books leave the printing facility today we could get them tomorrow.

I asked my father to help me get the Fingerprint Totem stencil on the marble totem I just had polished. There are four sides to this sculpture, so the stencil needs to fall perfectly on each corner or the sculpture does not work. I was 3/8 of an inch off, so the stencil was no good and I had to start again. I let my father go, I altered the stencil design and sent it off a third time. I will sandblast next week.

Lina came over, we did another run of edits for the Larry Lewis book, and I sent the book off for another proof.

I set up a page for my friend Pierce in Houston, throwing up five or six landscapes and nautical pictures for above his mantle. Collectors appreciate the project pages I make for them on my website, which allows me to put ideas up there for easy reference. I try to take photographs of projects in progress as this is good for collectors to see and helps future collectors look through past sculptures, paintings and projects.

I chipped away at the new song and tweaked the lyrics. I'm surprised it plays between 3 minutes and 3:30, depending upon the speed at which I play it, as it feels shorter. I recorded a number of takes and I'm getting closer to one clean take with my vocal and acoustic guitar. Maybe I should record two tracks. Eventually I will instrumentalize the song so it's more like 'Busted Wing.' I have to play all the instruments on this first CD project as an exercise in excruciating self-flagellation in order to learn the hard way. I'm getting better at fleshing songs out in my home recording studio.

September 1 Thursday

The hardcover *Generations* books came in at 10:30 am. I brought the box upstairs, bladed it open and here was my major August work blast. Fifteen beautiful hardcover books. I went through the book again before calling my father, who was whispering because he was on the golf course, agitated that I would bother him out there, as if I knew he was playing golf. He called back later and came over to take the hardcovers back home. He couldn't believe the timing on this thing. It was a barn burner but we got it done on time as planned, as I do.

Before Dad headed out he listened to my new song 'Cruise' on the headphones and said it was amazing. You can only trust the praise of your parents so much, but they are no pushovers. They are masters at telling me if something I did sucked in a million ways as all good parents should be. At this point they don't bother candy-coating anything because they know I appreciate their honesty and I am not offended like so many children probably are. This took a thick enough skin to grow as a son and as an artist, but having good editors who unconditionally love you is rare.

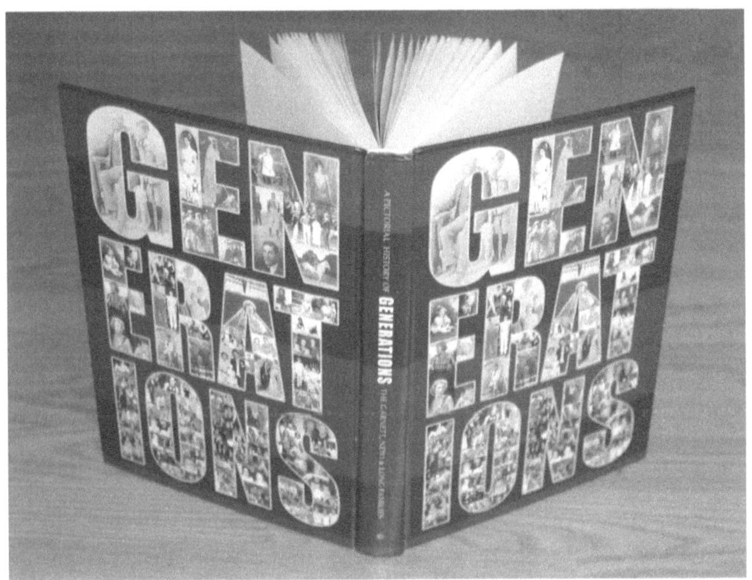

September 2 Friday

The ride up to Vermont with my brothers was hysterical, every one-liner punctuating the last observational one-liner. Humor is a complex bouquet and veers in all directions. My mother is responsible for instilling in us wide ranging humors of all shapes and sizes, which is one of her greatest gifts.

The drive to Wilmington from the exit off Route 91 was circuitous due to Hurricane Irene's blown out roads, but we made it to the Summit Inn by cocktail hour, got settled, then zipped over to the family reception. It was sad to drive through downtown Wilmington, where structures had been torn away by the raging water that had ravaged this community of good people. Workers walked around with paper masks to protect their lungs from the toxicity of old materials and particles which were floating in the air as they cleared away the devastation. I saw one guy smoking a cigarette through his disposable white mask, the dark tan rings keeping time. Homes and businesses were boarded up, police and yellow-bibbed construction workers in hard hats directed traffic, residents walked around with anguish in their eyes, and tourists like us were driving from one festive destination to the next.

The party was an informal place where wedding-goers could decompress from the week, the hurricane, the drive up, shake some hands, start to relax and laugh some of their worries away. Towards the end my father announced that there was something for the Garnetts, so I pulled the books and posters out of my Dad's car and took them upstairs where my family was gathering. My father and aunt Sally made an announcement and the books were presented, fifteen of them, passed around to family members, who all expressed varying degrees of excitement and amazement at the scale of the project they held in their hands. It was rewarding to watch everyone browse through the books, which went on for an hour of family reminiscence.

We headed back to The Hermitage Inn, where the wedding party was staying and where the house at the bottom of the hill on the property had been rented out. Fifty of us partied on the porch, dancing and celebrating, as wedding parties do. Matt wanted to head out at 1:30 am and Christian wanted to hang out, so I split the difference and left with Matt at 3 am. It was good to be away with my brothers, my cousins, my entire family, to feel the heartbeat of generations, to feel the strength of continuity, to feel the pride of family, leaving behind old things and looking into the future for better times.

September 3 Saturday

People look back when they are older and think about the times they never had, or so I've heard. Time is at the center of everything and time is nothing which collapses into itself. Events are held and exist in timespace whereas the best art is timeless.

Artists who live and think only in this time might make fashionable, ornamental art objects, but these things will not likely be measured outside of the time frames during which they are created. Timely art objects often become dated things, appreciated for their moment, their era. It is most challenging to create an object that lives outside of time, as it is to invent something that is ageless, as it is to write something that will be appreciated through the ages. It is a strange life to live with one foot in time and another foot outside of time, knowing that time is a fallacy in our spirits but also an accepted measure of our natural world.

In the afternoon I followed a runaway school bus filled with wedding people to a vineyard for the rehearsal dinner. The bus driver was trying to break a land speed record, navigating around orange cones (which indicated broken pieces of road from the hurricane) at an alarming pace that left me in the dust behind an old pickup truck. Brother Christian found the name of the vineyard in his notes so we navigated ourselves to the place.

The rehearsal dinner at the vineyard was large and entertaining. The caterer had canceled a week before as one of the company employees had drowned in the hurricane, so like every wedding detail the families had to rally to save the weekend. Another caterer agreed to step in at the last minute so 170 people were seated after making their plates at the burger buffet line. Perfect. I played frisbee and football with the kids before dinner, which the kids appreciated but my clothing didn't, as the temperature hit 90 degrees. I spent the rest of the evening sweating, but who was I trying to impress?

During dinner the toasts started coming and they kept on rolling until it was time to drive my brothers back to the Hermitage, where we returned to the house that was rented for the weekend at the bottom of the property to party for a few more hours.

September 4 Sunday

I took Christian to brunch at an eatery that had not been severely damaged by the hurricane. Various elements of the wedding party were there, scattered about in casual Sunday diner comfort. Christian reminded me that it was his birthday on the way back to the hotel and I gave him the card I had made him with a gift certificate to a sports equipment place. He said that cash would have been better in a way that only the youngest sibling can do... bluntly and with a smile.

We drove to the church and it was a scorcher outside. The programs were glued to popsicle sticks so they doubled as fans, which was smart, interesting and funny. Bernice's cousin played a nice acoustic guitar during the service, which lent an intimate warmth to the wedding ceremony. My cousin was married, the church was jubilant with applause, the special moment was behind us, and it was time to pull out the party hats once again.

There was an outdoor tent at the Hermitage with a dance floor and seating inside for dinner. The first dance was the most original and amusing that I have seen. There was a Georgetown street sign up and the wedding party was announced two by two. Each couple walked in, tapped the Georgetown sign and did a little dance act, all very animated. Reyn and Bernice came in and did a great dance to Meatloaf's 'Paradise by the Dashboard Light,' bringing the house down. People danced for awhile and then moved inside for dinner.

The rain came and went during dinner, where more speeches awaited. Wedding speeches are a real art form and there were several excellent speakers. My eyes wandered around the large room, taking it in, seeing various elements of my family moving through this moment, trying to appreciate the ephemeral nature of events and memories.

After dinner I was on the dance floor and uninhibited, getting into the flow of humans in concert celebration, the pretty women in motion, attracted to various rhythms and pulses that rolled throughout the music. One cute girl expressed direct interest in me with words, speaking into my ear that she wished she could be with me right now. This felt nice. The band was excellent and played a wide range of music fluently and with enthusiasm.

The wedding adjourned back down to the party house, where some of the guys jumped into the pond and tried to coax the girls in with them. When it started pouring the cute girl came up and asked if I'd like to go back to the hotel. A quick run through the rain with a sweet girl for a nightcap? That was an easy call.

September 5 Monday

I got up early enough along with the cute girl and her roommate, in the bed next to us, who was pissed off that her new cell phone had been thrown into the pond by the naked dudes along with her friend last night. Two other girls came in and flopped down on the other bed. I threw in my two cents with the stream of conversation when appropriate, lying there in my boxers for awhile as these four cute girls recapped the evening. The two visitors left, I said goodbye with a respectful kiss, which was all that had occurred the previous evening, and off I went.

Matt and I packed up like the efficient experts that we have become over years of traveling together, completing one another's tasks to save time. My father picked Christian up and brought him back to the suite we were sharing, he got his things together and we hit the road. The ride home was filled with more laughter, the humor cranking at every turn, back to the studio, back to pressing projects and new art creations, back to the stack of bills I have to deal with, back to the strangeness of the text breakup still fresh in my mind yet starting to feel behind me ever so slightly.

September 6 Tuesday

Cousin Steve's wife Claire brought her parents Bill and Hildie over in the morning. They just renovated this 1840 house in historic Charleston so they are thinking about art. Bill and I talked about doing two paintings that would face one another, allude to the city of Charleston and work together in some way. I pulled up some examples of diptychs that hang apart from one another by design, although they can always hang together as well.

I could talk to Bill for days about all sorts of cool things. This is one of the best things about being an artist. I get to research, explore, flip over stones, find particles of truth, beauty, fresh ideas and fuse them into new art objects.

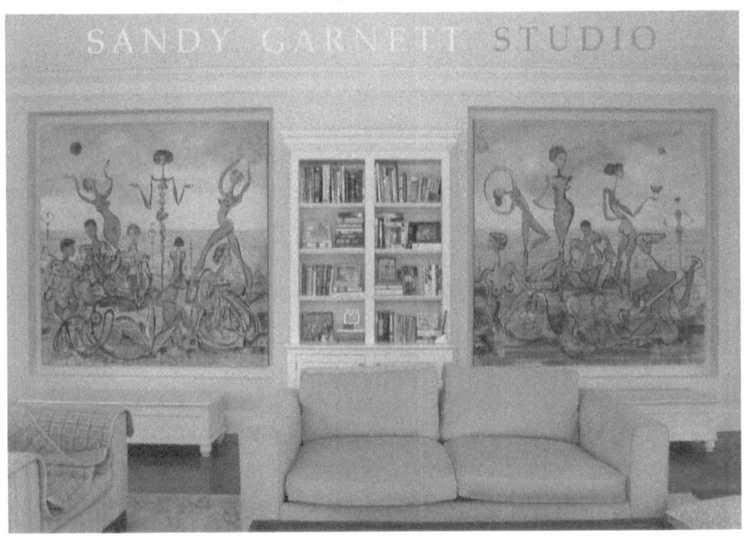

Fueled by the good energy of a studio visit, I designed walls to Bill's specifications, placed some virtual paintings on the walls I had created, and made a collector placement page on my website for them.

Lina checked in, we made final edits to the Larry Lewis book,

I prepared pdf files, uploaded them to the fulfillment service, and placed an order.

In the evening I recorded some vocal tracks to the new song that I need to expunge from my soul. I got an acoustic track on either side and recorded the basic vocals to the beat of a drum track that is suitable. I want this song out of me.

September 7 Wednesday

In the morning I chipped away at my website, organized the office, did correspondence with some of my collectors, and I straightened out some lines to the new song. Once I have the percussion down it is much easier to build out the parts. I started layering vocals with melody. The structure of the song is three stanzas and then a fading refrain, with a cadence that might be construed as quasi-country, but with a straight backbeat rock vibe.

In the afternoon I modified the gravestone etching spec piece, placing a cross on the knight's chest. They asked me to illustrate the ground on which the knight is kneeling, but that would not read well. Spec work on gravestones is always in reverse, which is confusing. Gravestone etching is one of positives and negatives, like monument work in general, like my Fingerprint Totems to a certain extent. It's important to gently direct people who can't visualize what something is going to look like when you know it won't look right in the end.

I picked up the third stencil for the Hall Fingerprint Totem, weeded the negative pieces out of it, and got it ready for the stone while alternating between work stations; writing, chipping away at the timing on the refrain of the new song, painting while a movie played in the background, back to the stencil. Pause movie, go upstairs, music, writing, hit a painting, repeat process.

September 8 Thursday

I finished a rough cut of the song this morning, put it to a slide show, then posted it to my website. I made a CD of the songs in progress, which sounds pretty professional. It's new for me to listen to and work on my music in the car running errands.

Back in the studio I applied the rubber stencil successfully to the marble, which is a little nerve-wracking with only two hands. The corners have to line up perfectly in order for these sculptures to work, as symmetry is paramount. I spent an hour carefully laying the stencil on before pounding it down with a hammer against a hockey puck that was moving along the stencil in a methodical pattern. A hockey puck is rubber so it will not damage the stone. The sand is very strong when sandblasting and can peel the stencil off in places if the stencil is not pounded down properly. The corners always make me nervous with these things. I spent the next three hours cleaning up the corners, blading out bits and pieces where necessary. Then I got a drill and tried to clean out the 8 inch deep center hole that is 5/8 inches wide. I could not get my steel mounting pin flush because there was a small piece of marble that had not been cut out, so I went to the hardware store and got a longer drill bit. Eventually I managed to get 7 1/4 inches deep with the steel pin after two more hours of fussing with it. You drill too hard, your marble splits and you are screwed. You go too soft you can't solve the problem. I am hoping the steel pin on the base is strong enough to support this eighty pound pillar of marble.

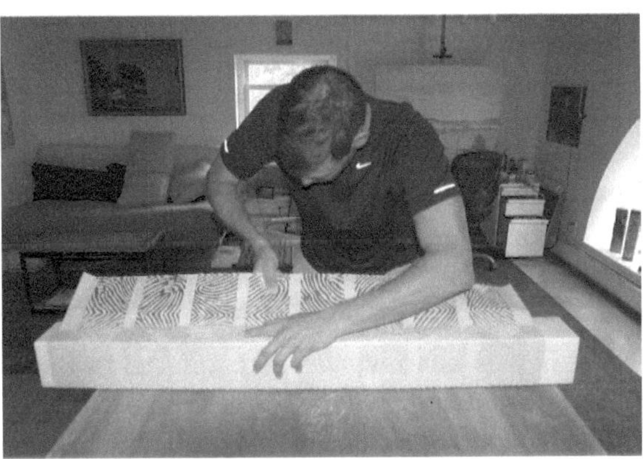

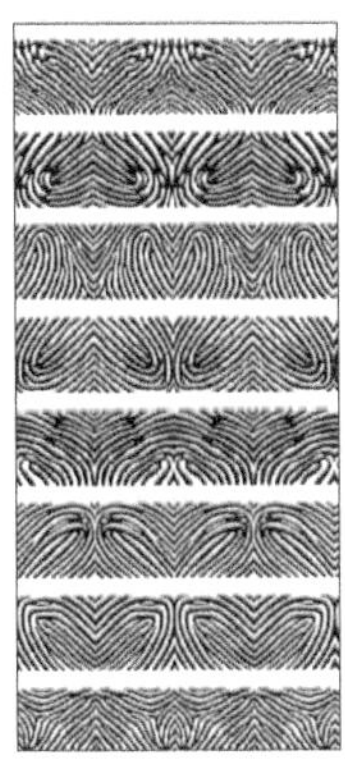

September 9 Friday

I called my friend Ned at the monument shop and he told me to come over at 12:30 pm to blast the stone. I spent several more hours making sure the stencil was clean and symmetrical, taking a blade to parts of the design that needed some attention. I taped the ends with duct tape and put the marble in my car.

On the way to the monument shop I stopped to talk to Skip about the angle iron pedestal that I had brought along. I told him I thought that welding a 7 inch long 5/8 inch pin to the top would do the trick.

"Alright, do you need this today?"

"Whatever you can do."

"Otherwise it's Monday."

"I was hoping to deliver this weekend if you can."

"Okay."

"What's the number?"

"Hundred bucks."

"Thanks Skip. I really appreciate it," and I was on my way. Small business owners have their own clients, their own schedules, their own ways, so you have to give them respect and appreciate the things they do to help you stay afloat.

I remember right out of college I left an angry note after missing my then new accountant a second day in a row, who was at lunch. I remember how that didn't work out too well for me. You don't want to piss off a nice, decent small business owner because guess what? They don't need to work for assholes. The key thing is to learn the most from the smallest mistakes. That note to my then (and still now) accountant? Fifteen years ago. I give my subs time and respect, I don't complain about prices too much, I try to bring fun stuff to them, and the years build long working relationships.

I drove up to the monument shop and pulled the marble out of my car. Ned finished with a customer, then set up a table in the driveway next to his truck. He put sand in the hopper, fired up the engine on his truck and we sandblasted the stone. The sand carves into the exposed part of the marble and the rubber stencil protects the rest of the marble, like silk-screening a tee shirt or inking a plate on a printing press.

The stakes were high as anything can go wrong at any point. I should have delivered this sculpture weeks ago were it not for my jammed schedule. Redoing the stone would crush any profit, I needed to get this spiritual energy out of my studio, and I needed to pay bills with the balance. All of these things swirled around my head as sand cut the stone and shot off into the wavering winds.

The totem blasted deep and evenly, I put the sculpture back into the car and talked to Ned about the money. I had three stencils to make, there was the time, materials, and blasting expenses to consider. He gave me a number, I thanked him for his time and told him I'd send a check next week.

Back at Skip's, he showed me how the pin was almost perpendicular, but the crossbars from another welder were not true, which explains the minor hedge. Skip's a good guy. He doesn't take any crap, he's always busy as hell, but you know he cares about what he does like a lot of small business owners I work with.

I brought the totem back to the kitchen island and spent a couple hours peeling the stencil off, cleaning the marble up. Then I placed the Fingerprint Totem on the pedestal and was able to see the sculpture in my mind that had emerged into reality. This is such a buzz, when you have an original idea and over the course of months or even years that idea develops and one day snaps into being.

September 10 Saturday

I shot my new sculpture and posted images for my friend Ed and his siblings on their web page, I made an email invitation of the Larry Lewis show for Lina, I wrote several handwritten thank you letters for the Vermont wedding, I cleaned the loft up, I chipped away at a song, I designed shelving for my bathroom, which I will also paint a mural in eventually, then I stretched an old nude that is of interest to my friend, who wants a painting for her new apartment on the Lower East Side.

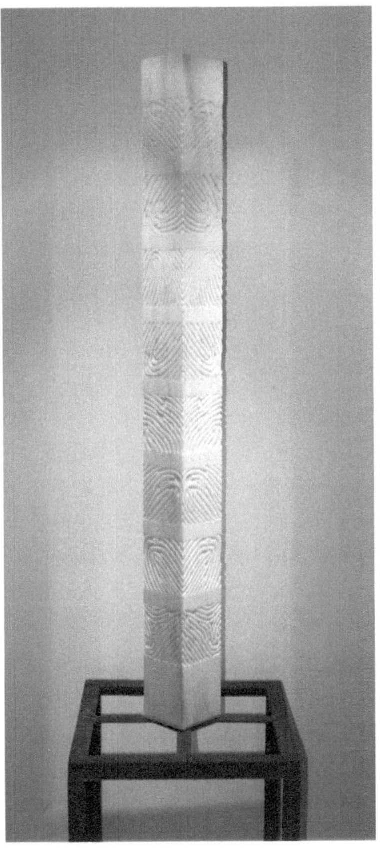

In the afternoon I watched Djockovic defeat Federer in an amazing five set U.S. Open semi-final during which Djockovic came back from a 40-15 deficit with Federer serving 5 games to 3, which included two match points. I watched the last two sets over with my Dad, who is one of the best people in life to watch sports with, when he's not watching three games at once on the television. My father is the reason sports bars were invented, so patrons can watch ten games at the same time.

September 11 Sunday

I am thinking about the families who lost loved ones on 9/11 ten years ago. I am wary of all the flag waving as this seems propagated by the media, which I have no faith in. The implication, the messaging goes that if you are somber and say the right things on this day you are being an honorable American. 100 things about that day of infamy will never add up and were never properly brought to the public's attention. The 9/11 Commission Report was filled with Swiss cheese inaccuracies that defy logic, science and mathematics. Our nation changed that day and has suffered for it. Armed paratroopers in black, bulletproof jumpsuits with intimidating weaponry are common sights in-country nowadays, while the phones and internet activity of Americans are routinely tapped and tracked, body cavities searched, children x-rayed at airports, private lives turned upside down under the auspices of defending against 'Terror.'

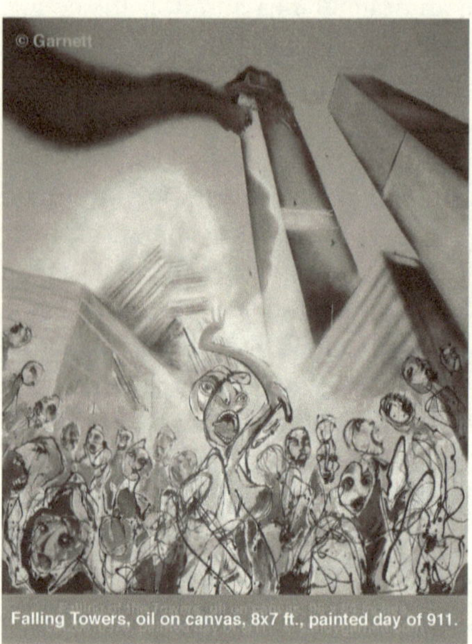

Falling Towers, oil on canvas, 8x7 ft., painted day of 911.

By design, 9/11 chipped away at my cautious optimism as it did for every countryman, a day of dread and grief that altered the course of history. Preventive, responsive, militaristic, civil maneuvers after the fact have not made ours a better nation, as much as I love my country and as proud as I am to be an American whose lines stretch back beyond the Civil and Revolutionary Wars.

In every day there is a heartbeat. In love of life and creativity I quickly return to the powerful sensation of peace that washes over when I stay in light and am grateful for my lot as a professional artist. When I return to this central pulse which propels me I am on a timeless rail where life and death are unified in layers of consciousness that blur the senses into clarity.

September 12 Monday

Yesterday I went over to best friend Bill and Sheila's new house in Pleasantville. Bill gave me the tour and I played with his 2-year-old daughter Catherine, who is completely conversational now. She showed me her brother Thomas, who was waking from a nap and all smiles, lying on a floor blanket with puffy mobiles spinning over his head, his little sausage fingers reaching for the stars above.

The Giants and Redskins kicked the season off, so we talked about old friend business as the game drew to a 28-14 Redskins win. We happen to be Giants fans so this was depressing, the deflation of a crumby loss a particular type of misery that clings to the spirit for awhile. The bigger the game the more unforgettable the disappointment, as life goes.

After twenty years in the D.C. area, it's good to have my oldest best friend since the age of 12 close-by again.

This morning I arrived in Harrison, New York at 8 am, shook hands with my new collectors and brought in the angle iron pedestal. I went back to the truck and retrieved the marble totem, which I had wrapped and taped. I set the totem on the steel pin in the place they have designated and called them in for the unveiling. They were taken aback by the Hall Fingerprint Family Totem and we discussed it for several minutes. Judy wanted to know where the fingerprints were, so I explained that each band was a portion of a fingerprint that I had mirrored so it would symmetrically wrap around the four-sided totem. People are used to seeing the ends of the fingerprints, or the whole fingerprint, as opposed to a section or series of sections of fingerprints.

My new collectors have wooden bases for their sculptures, so I offered to make a stained wooden base for them instead of the angle iron base. We decided on a base that will be 22 x 15 x 15 inches, they told me they were very pleased with the sculpture, and back to work I went. Mission accomplished.

Completing and delivering a painting or sculpture is a buzz that I have gotten hooked on, a buzz that is better than most sensations; better than a wine or beer buzz, better than a dip in the ocean, better than catching a fish, better than sex even on occasion, as some people don't excel in that department. When commissions are in the studio they are constant reminders of relationships with collectors, pending projects, things to be chipped away at. Completion, delivery, the cleansing of the palette, the clearing of the studio always lightens the load and changes my creative patterning from week to week, which is a good thing. It means there is flow to my creative process, a cycle that is moving in and out of my studio, a little commerce to pay the bills, and new ideas that now can take center stage. There is also the enjoyment of the old 'atta boy' pat on the back when I pull off a piece of art that really pleases a collector, which is for life. People remember purchasing art, they remember the process, the deliveries. I drove back to the studio satisfied and looking on the horizon.

September 13 Tuesday

I received an enthusiastic email from my old friend CD, who asked about downloading my new song and others, which are currently attached to videos. I told him I am getting closer and he will be the first to know.

Throughout my career I have always had one or two commissions in the studio and a growing stream of inventory sales. When the market crashed, while continuing to paint and sculpt, I went right into building a new website from the ground up, writing, editing, archiving, book making, music. All of these mediums are valuable to my studio but don't cost me much to make. As my wise friend Bill E. said, when I am not selling things, time is cheap to do my own projects.

It will take time, but people are starting to note that I write books, make music, their kids are telling them their favorite books are my Rainbow Riders. Several years ago my audience had no idea there were other facets of my creativity other than visual art, so this starts to broaden the base and strengthen the platform, if ever so slowly.

September 14 Wednesday

I chipped away at the 1000 Paintings book today and the project is massive. I have an uphill battle to climb there, but once that book is in hand I feel like this might be some sort of key, some sort of code. People come into my world for a quick glance and are gone, unless they are astute and patient, as I have a lot of history to share if they have the time. A big catalogue will do what a studio visit cannot do, as 700 of my paintings are placed(sold) and gone from my world. The chronology of creation is a point of interest for collectors and also a footnote in the art world I would argue as well, the way I sift through genres from one painting to the next. I can't reference another artist who has meticulously catalogued his first 1000 paintings, remains unknown, yet has made a living strictly by his art for two decades. The book will be the record I suppose. I just have to keep my head up while marching to my own drum beat.

September 15 Thursday

This morning I continued working with the layout of the 1000 Paintings book. Work flow is crucial, so I got into a sustainable, repeatable pattern. Today I got through 1997, an 85 painting year. I'm onto page 110 and up to career painting number 330, so the book will be around 450 pages long.

It's odd to start to see the chronology of my creativity, where my mind goes as the catalogue numbers evolve. There is a clear exploratory bent that is inevitable, stubborn, fearless and intense in this passage of pictures. I pick up a genre, learn to swing it around, and lay it back down or combine that in with the next genre or style I am working with. You can see this most with my Reconstructions, where I am literally meshing and blending genres into one another, which was the point of the Reconstruction series, my Reconstructionist philosophy; genres are like letters in the alphabet, and when combined make words that tell new stories, the best of which reflect aesthetic truth and the era during which these art stories or objects are produced.

The art world, which I have stood outside of in order to learn self-sufficiency, in order to find my own heartbeat, in order not to rely on the heavy opinions of others, may frown upon this picture and that picture in my first 1000 paintings, but taken as a whole I have forged my own place without the assistance of any galleries or institutions. I think this will make me a curiosity at first, an interesting story, before it helps me get to a larger platform in my career.

At lunch I went to the monument shop and finished the knight with the epitaph. Etching small serifs is a huge pain because serifs, the points and lines on the ends of letters, determine where your eyes go when looking at a line of text. You have to 'draw' the impression of perfect typography that is straight, which is challenging to etch very small.

The knight came out well, I finished the etching and thought about the 1000 etchings I have done, most of which I have not photographed, these etchings that sit on gravestones all over Western Connecticut and Westchester, New York. This is the only area of my portfolio that I did not archive properly, namely because shooting granite is like shooting the image painted on a mirror, and because when I started I did not want to focus on the gravestone work. Now I see gravestone etching for the original karmic accoutrement to my fine art that it is, and my collectors find it a compelling sidebar.

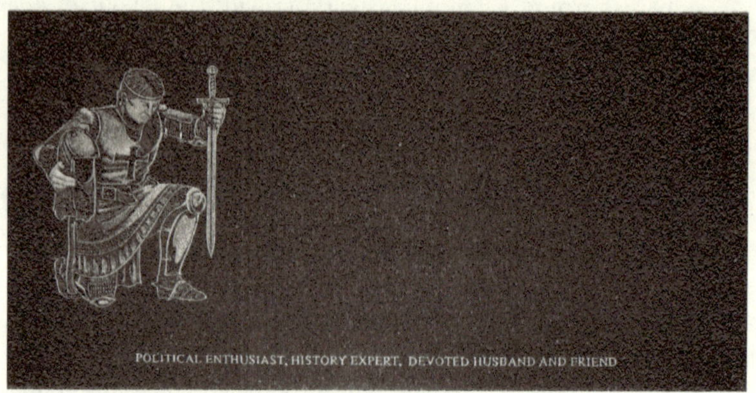

Etching of Knight and Epitaph, 20110917, www.sandygarnett.com

On the way back to my studio I stopped by to say hi to my mother, who wanted to show me some heirlooms. I opened an old box she gave me and in it was a bracelet with a note that was written by my great-grandmother in 1950.

The note said, "This is a bracelet made from my grandmother's hair. It is over 100 years old."

The bracelet was in fact a gorgeously woven hair bracelet with a monogrammed gold clasp. I told my mother that this was the most interesting and beautiful thing I had seen today, and this is one of most fascinating family items I have ever seen. It belongs in a museum. The intricacy of the weaving is incredible.

Today I looked at a bracelet woven out of my great-great-great-grandmother's hair from before the Civil War.

September 16 Friday

Sometimes it's quiet here on weekend nights and I think about the swirl of humanity around me, the celebration that people can feel when they commune, family and friends uniting and sharing life together. Mine is more solitary but I don't mind. Sometimes I miss the chatter but it is only a phone call or a step away. I juxtapose this existence with others who are busy with people around them always. My thoughts and creativity surround me and egg me on when I am in the pocket, which is comforting like a warm blanket. I feed the fire and it feeds me back, the circle of life in the short time I get to spread my wings in this artist skin until the next go-around. I'm trying to learn and become a better human being all the time, which is part of the art process, at least for me. Somewhere in this is the root of something deeper; a deeper sense of love, appreciation for life, understanding that we are all unified on this planet we call earth, that conflict is an illusion of the isolating, defensive man, that living in the solution is the way to build bridges in the studio, between fellow human beings, between states and nations, between the lives before us, the lives ahead of us down the path. It's the mystery and the journey that keep me on my toes and awake fully into the next day.

September 17 Saturday

"Have you forgotten about me?"

I awoke to this morning email from my collector Nevan, who last year commissioned me to paint a portrait of his friend, an appreciated model in her country. I was emailed 15 pictures, an eloquent description of Kara, and Nevan told me to paint an original 'Garnett,' not a traditional portrait. I'm not sure why but this confused me for a year. I was not given a deposit and there is no deadline on the painting, although it seems this morning Nevan is mildly disappointed that I have not arrived at some creative epiphany yet.

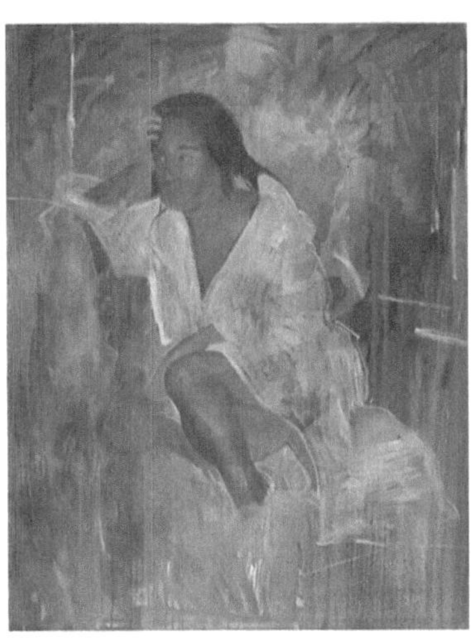

We have these sporadic, intellectual communications about art, life, philosophy, which makes him one of my favorite collectors. Engaged collectors want to open their minds and see with you, fly with you, subsidize your vision when they can, when they are inspired, if they find themselves on the same page with you. Nevan has become one of these friends so I don't want to disappoint him, but he set up a tricky riddle to solve.

In order to properly slip into a particular work of art, I have to feel a certain way. I have to let go of all preconceptions and allow myself to float, to flow through a painting or sculpture. Time means nothing, so if I am playing too aggressively I will lose. With a commission like this Nevan painting, knowing what he likes in my painting catalogue, knowing where his writer brain goes, I have to meet him halfway, take the leap. On the other side of that canvas can be a new understanding of myself, of Nevan, of painting, of what else can be an original Garnett.

September 18 Sunday

I spent 24 hours all weekend working on the First 1000 paintings book. I got through 400 images in the layout, which now stands at 180 pages.

September 19 Monday

My friend Steve dropped off the maple pedestal I designed for the Fingerprint Totem. I completed the installation with my collectors this morning and they are very pleased.

September 20 Tuesday

I charged the balance for the Fingerprint Totem I delivered yesterday, which gives me a little wind in the sails. I hold my breath, grow weaker, hold, hold, then pop! Bills are paid somehow. Lately I have been wondering if I ask for this edge in life, if this is what I'm here for, if this is what I've grown comfortable with so as never to become complacent. On the edges there can be very clear visions, which are paradoxically obscured by the blinding pressures associated with living in search of edges.

September 21 Wednesday

My art sales subsidize creative research. Today I spent 15 hours working on music; uploading songs, tweaking files, working on a CD cover image, measuring the conceptual differences between an EP and an LP, considering songs that would round out the 7 I posted for download today. At some point I need raunchier electric stuff, so I found some heavy bass filters and worked on electric leads for several hours into the evening.

September 22 Thursday

I have been thinking about forgiveness lately. As I drift away

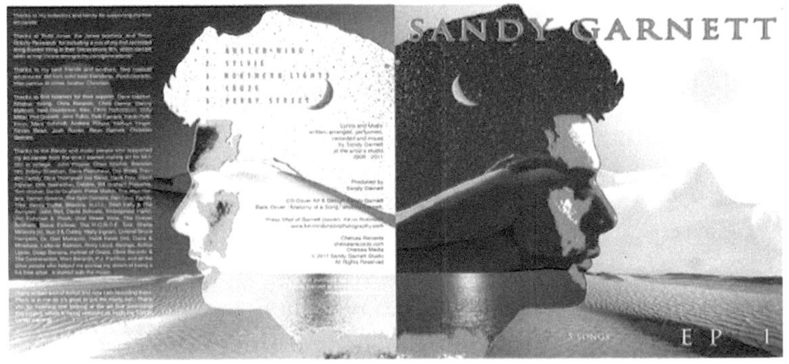

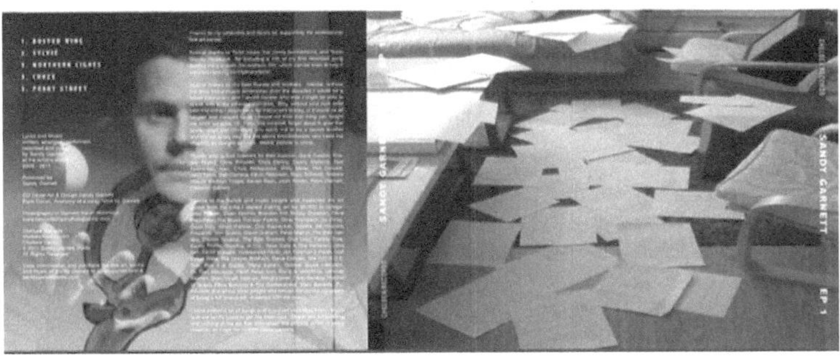

from the recent love tangle I am starting to feel relieved. The indicators were not healthy but I overlooked them. I enjoyed being swept away for a moment.

I don't really have skeletons in the closet, I have few regrets, I walk with a clean spirit, I do my best to forgive and forget, to avoid hangups, to avoid projecting frustration on others.

This planet is all about the flow of energy. If I'm angry I will make angry art, which is self-perpetuating. I am not an angry person. I live my dream, so I need to perpetuate that dream with the mutual exchange of good energies with friends and collectors. This creates a magnetic attraction that can be sustainable through good times and bad over the years. You add up the months into years, then decades, and you've made a career, a life, your own philosophy about the way things tick. You've learned how life can work for you, how you can work for life.

September 23 Friday

Today I met a family about a gravestone etching. I am doing a portrait of the father on the left of a 3 foot wide by one foot tall black granite stone, the Virgin Mary on the right side of the family name, and an epitaph at the bottom. The family was very nice, a mother and her grown son. I returned to my studio, designed the etching and sent it to Don for approval.

My friend Bill E. checked in and needed a compressed file of his book cover for 'Wine Killer' that I designed, so I made the alteration and fired a new file off to Bill E. for his e-book sales.

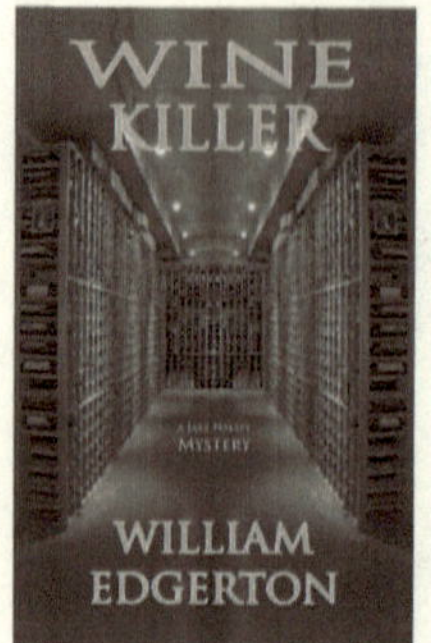

My friend Rob called in about a public art project. He needs spec work and I will furnish it. It is refreshing to work with people who get the big picture. We talked about themes for this project, then the conversation drifted in several interesting directions before Rob mentioned that he had listened to my first 7 song EP. He found my voice original and my lyrics 'killer,' a compliment that made my day. Rob comes from a musical family and sang on albums that were famously produced, so he does not compliment lightly. He asked me where I got my singing style. I've never been asked this. I don't know the answer. There's a little country twang in there, a little rock and roll, a little irreverence, a little sweetness, a little roll of the tongue, rolling on words, changing the way words round out of the mouth to rhythm and melody.

September 24 Saturday

Last night at my friends' dinner party I met a very pretty woman and there was zero pressure, particularly as she had to race home to her three children at 9 pm. It was good to get out of the studio, have a drink, laugh and catch up with my longtime friends. I hung out with my friends' kids, who filled me in on how they are doing in life, with school and sports and the other things they are interested in. Kids are the wellspring and it's fun to be friends with them as they grow up. Ted asked if I would see one of his games this season and I said of course.

I went over to the high school field today to watch Ted play football. They beat the best team in the league 14 - 7. I sat with Ted's Mom, who was on the phone trying to negotiate the sale of a house our friends are flipping. Ted's siblings were bored, so we bounced my racquetball around. The kids had one of these skateboards with a single axle that you have to twist to move and not fall over on, which I almost got the hang of.

Keil asked me to come over for lunch after the game. Cope

asked if she and her friend Lex could go back to their house in my car. I buckled them in and we talked about the bake sale they wanted to have. We got to the house and I lettered a bake sale sign for them before a casual lunch, picking at food and talking around the kitchen island. Keil told me she had an old tee shirt I had designed that Walter and I had sold at concerts in high school. She brought it down and I took a picture of it to put on my website in the 'formative' works section.

The 'Alice in Wonderland' themed tee shirt I designed at the age of 16 and sold in parking lots at Grateful Dead concerts took me back to my rock art roots. I was hell bent on making art for bands back then. I chased that passion, I got in with some bands that were on the rise, I made art for 50 bands and production companies in college, then migrated from commercial art to the easel as soon as I could get there. I haven't seen this old tee shirt design in decades. It's interesting how an image, a song, a fragrance can take you right back in life.

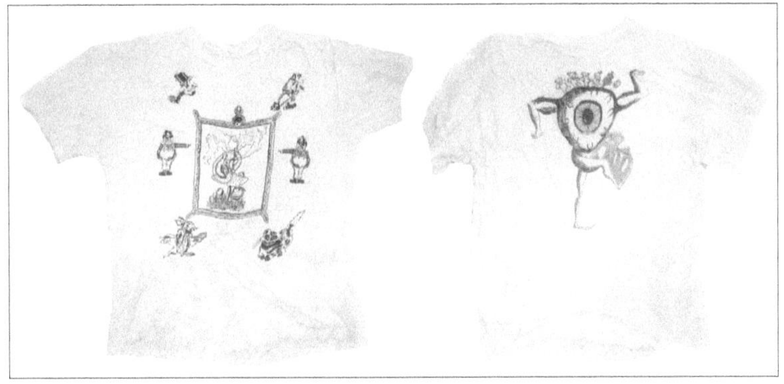

September 25 Sunday

This morning I worked on the 1000 Paintings book, a painting, and a song, mixing up sight and sound.

Creative sessions are where new works develop, in this soup, in the brew, in the batch, so you have to stay there, put your wizard hat on and stir the pot patiently. I find myself here all the time, sometimes in quick snippets, sometimes in long meditations, part of the magic that makes an art profession so rewarding. It's all about the journey, the quest. I don't need accolades at the end of each challenge, I don't care if people can see the elusive spark that is hard to define.

It is rarefied ground to feel this way. I couldn't explain it to text breakup chick, who is competitive, needs to jockey for silly things, needs to prove herself every day like an unrewarded athlete. I have no bones left in that closet, no mountains left to climb to know who I am and where I stand. Sure, there are a million projects left to do, and I will always try to grow wiser, but I have done the good work, I have walked in the desert, I have suffered, I have blossomed, I can see 360, I can make what I want, my cup runneth over, I am a grateful human being, it all lies within.

September 26 Monday

At Silvermine Guild Arts Center yesterday I saw the Larry Lewis collage show I had done the catalogue for and said hello to Lina and Sharyn, who were beaming about the completion of a year's total immersion into this exhibit.

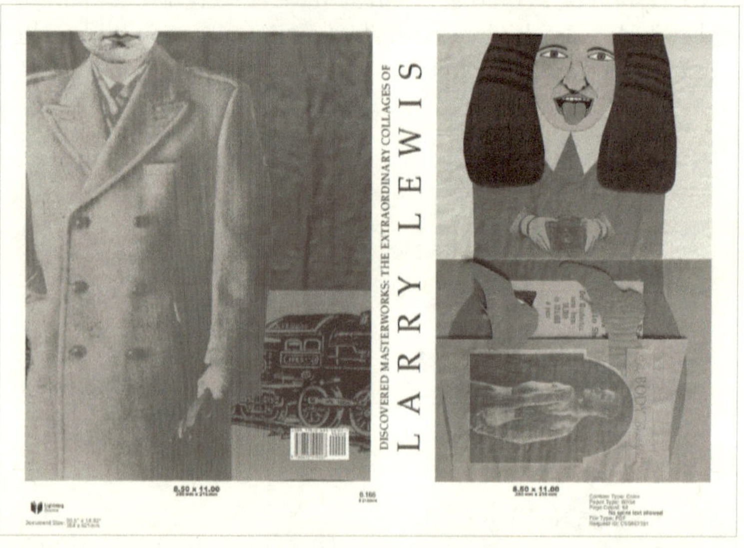

At the show a fellow artist wondered how I make every penny by my art for decades, if I have to fall back on one series of paintings or another. I can only talk about certain genres with certain artists, as every artist seems to have some philosophy or genre or series he lives in, thinks in, speaks in, sees in, is protective of. I always find my answers at the easel, a broad enough and true enough thought that creatives across spectrums can appreciate.

I don't know what my answer is this week. I have to keep cool, stay collected, and go into the right meditation. I don't know why but I feel protected by the good work I'm doing now, like the spirits will make sure I'm okay. This is where a professional needs to be most quiet, when the heat is on HIGH.

September 27 Tuesday

I spent yesterday and today from 6 am to 9 pm working on books; writing, designing covers, editing, tweaking layouts, merging files, cleaning up images. I was productive but I felt like I blew off 'real work' at the easel.

This is the way my studio goes. I am feeling heat, but my spirit resists and tells me I'm on the right path, I should continue moving in this direction, everything will work itself out.

It's hard to walk a line alone that rails against all the traditions of Western civilization. Most of the people in my life get up, go to work at an office and make a decent living.

The exchange of creative energy for financial energy is a strange one. I can't bend, buckle, alter my course or I'll get screwed by karma in the end. I can't go to the money energy. I have to make something with creative purity that will be received for such and rewarded with spiritual energy that has a component of financial energy. Business people who think this is bullshit will never understand that money is a tiny portion of my creative wilderness, where most of the time I can live off the land without too much trouble. That is unless you take the economy and chop it in half, which changes the face of the nation and the face of the world very quickly.

I find myself dancing in the studio at night to the sound of my own spirit, chasing ghosts, trying to sit still, trying to meditate, trying to hold on. I have no idea where the next ten large is coming from, but what I do know is that I'm in some sort of protective pocket I can't describe better, some kind of space where my energy is aligned and I'll be alright if I continue to go to the source, the pulse. On a cyclical basis I am rewarded or relieved of financial burden, which is just an illusion, when I tap into the right spiritual truth for me at that precise moment in time.

All of this sounds like hocus pocus but it is twenty years of living life as a professional artist. I'm not green at this game, and yet the experience is fresh and edgy every step of the way. There is an unknown quantity to what I make, what I am about, what I am tapping into, how it affects humanity, how art heals, how my art can move people, how my art can inspire me to make the next object on the lunar calendar. I have nothing this week and yet I am full in spirit, I am grateful for my lot in life.

Gratitude goes a long way towards peaceful existence. With the proper spirit, the proper energy, the right art, the patrons will come, I will be fed by nourishing other souls with my honesty. I pay for this life in every walking step, the razor blade I balance on, filled with paradoxes and energies that are way more powerful than my small footprint in this realm. My format of work, of art as life, is endless, sometimes terrifying, and most people could never live this way. Most people need to plan a year ahead, three years ahead, five or ten years ahead. I could not be an artist in this time if I could not wake up like this morning and wonder how it will all work out. Tomorrow I will wake up with the same question, and then the next day, and then the next day, for another fifty years or whenever I move on to the next spiritual plane.

September 28 Wednesday

Today I etched the Virgin Mary's portrait, a man with a wise, happy smile, and the epitaph, 'Will Always Be Remembered.' Gravestone etching, like painting, puts me in the zone and calms my spirit like all healing meditation.

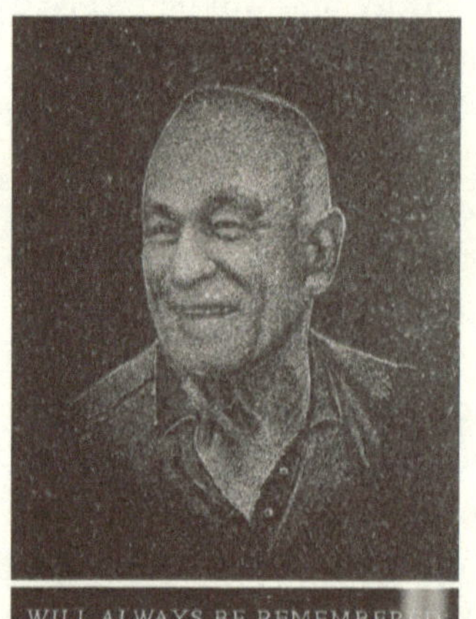

September 29 Thursday

A professional artist's life requires many hours of setup time in order to paint, sculpt, write, compose a song, propose a public art project, in order to make anything. Half of life is keeping a house, a studio, a car, a family, a social calendar, paying the bills, all that stuff. This is all important stuff, but it is not creative time.

Creative time belongs behind a glass case because it really is the magic time. The beauty of creativity is that nothing can touch it. I can't be taxed on it, no bad energy can come in and take it away, it cannot be tapped or sucked out of me unless I allow it. It is something that only the creative possesses. I don't say this out of ego so much as I say this to myself when I start to feel the wolves gather at my door, their toenails clicking as they pace, wondering if this is their time to get a piece of my ass or if I will produce the fire to drive them away. I know intellectually and spiritually that the wolves are a part of me that I am here to work out. After all these years it remains a perfect labyrinth.

September 30 Friday

After painting and sending out an email newsletter, I picked up my father and we drove to Chuck's hunting club for a Texas Hold'em Tournament. There was an open buffet, an open bar, and a five table set-up, with a dealer at each table. I was giddy when the buzzer went off, and I couldn't pick up any cards. I kept folding as the dealers changed every 15 minutes with the increasing blinds. The format was professional and interesting. We all had 2500. ($100), you could buy back in several times in the first hour only, and only if you lost on an all-in call.

The two guys to my left, Ray and Mai, built early chip leads, so they were betting more aggressively and knocking people around. My cousin George was to the left of them, and he picked up a nice nut flush to pull down a good pot pretty quickly. I went in with a 4-5 suited but stalled on the flop. I almost picked up a pot with nothing on a 300. bluff, but at the last minute the fourth guy hung in there and got me. The cards weren't there for me so I was on the sidelines. I went all-in and picked up a grand with a pair of threes as I had no other move, then a couple minutes later picked up another 1700 on trip threes. I made a mistake laying down 10-6 suited, as the dealer flopped a 10-6 with no high cards, a hand I would have pulled in 3 or 4k on because a couple of bulls would have pushed back. Right before the hour I was dealt A-9 hearts, and after A-9 flopped I doubled the 400 bet at one remaining guy. He came back and I went all-in. I turned my cards over and had an A-8, my error, very rare and very stupid. My opponent had an A-J high. I bet the right way with the cards I THOUGHT I had. I was pissed and got up from the table, declining to buy back in. I should have but didn't have $100 in my pocket, although cousin George or my father would have happily spotted.

Everyone broke for food and refills, then the game resumed, with blinds starting at 300-600 and moving up every 15 minutes. The carnage was quick and the Boss consolidated tables. Five tables became two and two other cash games started up in the back. I was having fun watching my cousin George take chip lead on the second table and my father hang in there on the first table. Dad was doing very well but he was a little happy, so I told him to focus as he was very close to making the last table. He nodded and reset while I egged him on like a prizefighter. The hands got wilder on both tables, players falling overboard every second hand.

The ninth guy went all-in, was burned and the Boss yelled, "Hold your cards! Table two gentlemen, please bring your chips to table one." My father had made the final table, facing cousin George, who had amassed a fortune.

Half the guys at the first table barely had gotten there, so they started dropping out as the blinds got up to 500-1000, then 600-1200, then 700-1400.

The fifth guy crapped out and the dealer screamed, "Winner! Fifth place!"

I shook hands with Joe as he walked out on the porch and Chuck gave him an envelope with $800 winnings. The fourth guy dropped, making the final table cousin George, my buzzed up, ass-kicking poker player father, and John. My Dad nicked John up a couple times and insisted that John high five him, which three John off guard. My father is filled with camaraderie and good sportsmanship, although if he had just lost 20 grand he would not want to high five the guy who took him for it. John got knocked out and my father took the hand down with trip 10's. This left cousin George and Dad.

Dad kept saying,"This is so cool! Right over there, he's my nephew George and also my Godson!" to which George would tell my father to simmer down.

George was concerned that the guys at the club would be pissed about the fact that two of Chuck's family members had made it to the final table, which nobody cared about but I thought was funny. The blinds were crazy and after a couple lay-downs my father had to take a stand but didn't pull the hand down. Cousin George won first place and my father won second. They were exuberant, happy as two pigs in the mud.

We had a nightcap, thanked Chuck, said goodbye to George and some of our new friends, and were off into the Friday night September rain. My father couldn't believe his luck. Before the game he had suggested that we split whatever was won between us, so he kept saying, "You're getting half of this, baby!"

When we got into the car my father insisted on pulling the cash out of the envelope and waving it around like a fan, making me hold the bills as well so I could rejoice in the victory. My father is like no other person when he is excited by life, and all he wants to do is share it with the people he loves. This quality is one of his finest, and his boys, his family, his friends bask in it as if they are sitting in the midday sun on a beach, enjoying the shine for however long it lasts. I wish I could bottle it up and always have it with me when the going gets tough.

The drive home was uneventful as we recapped the evening. Dad insisted I come in for a nightcap so we could split the cash. I didn't want to wake up Mom down in Dad's basement office after the money was counted while we laughed about the evening.

"Who's going to wake up your mother? Nobody. She's fast asleep! Relax!" I turned around and there was Mom, opening the door, my father unawares.

"What's going on down here?"

My father said,"It was awesome! George came in first and I came in second!"

I backed up Dad, saying that he had played a helluva poker night, telling Mom I was sorry we had woken her, then I excused myself and headed home to bed after giving Dad a high five.

In these moments my father reminds me, "Fuck it! You only live once!" when he is not being very conservative. A good balance goes a long way in life, the work hard, play hard thing.

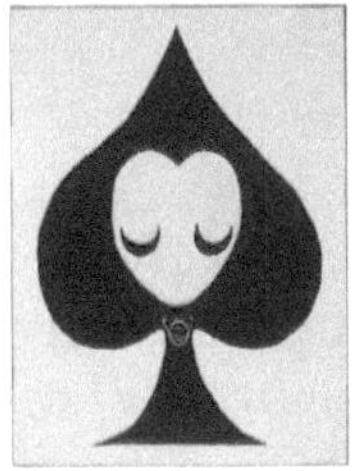
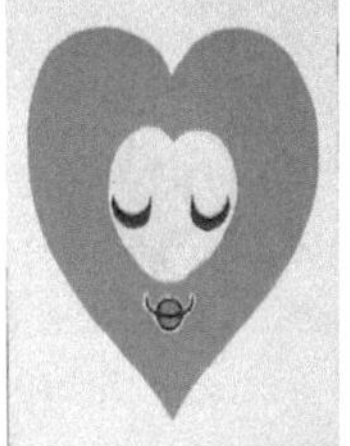
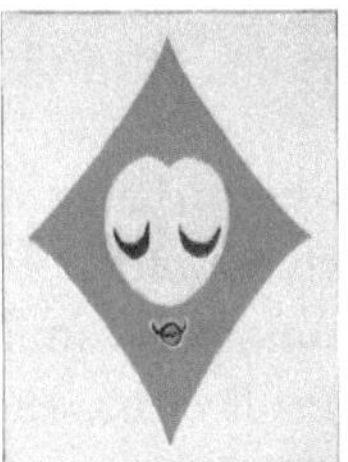
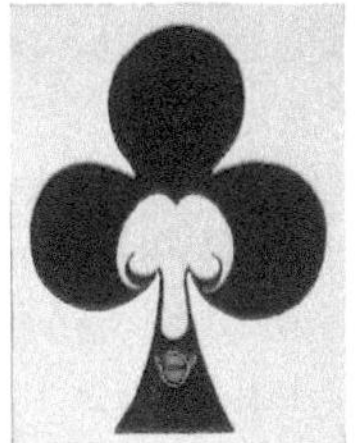

Suited Garnett Girls, acrylic on canvas, 2010, © Sandy Garnett

October 1 Saturday

I was in the lab experimenting all day, moving between work stations, letting ideas drop into all areas of the subconscious, trying to distill some good visuals and sounds.

Thirty people checked in regarding my email update yesterday, rooting for me, talking about how I am inspiring to them. I can never bitch and moan about why I don't get support because I have tons of supporters. I just have to hang tight. I work with a smile pasted on my face in a freedom that belongs only to me, so I know that I am a lucky man.

Dinner with great friends was a nice way to remember that

there are these things called weekends, where people meet up, socialize, try to relax and have a nice time.

October 2 Sunday

Vision is a tricky thing and every medium or field is a completely different discipline. I have a fluidity in painting that I don't have anywhere else. The feeling and the act are merged when I am in a state of painting flow because my technical capacities in that mode of expression are a natural extension of my body and spirit after 20,000 easel hours.

October 3 Monday

I am developing a song that is going somewhere. I can hear the notes as they crystallize; the left side, the right side, the guitars, the drums, central vocals, backing instruments, backing vocals I haven't met yet but will some day be recorded on this song.

I am starting to feel the beginning of space with a guitar, that there is a voice in there, like I might one day feel free in that medium. I am constructing the lead on another song carefully because I'm not good enough to be free with instrument, but I know where all the notes go. It seems a lot of people are great technicians, but when making their own stuff they don't know where all the notes go - regardless of medium.

October 4 Tuesday

Fall has arrived and my studio feels cleansed in a way. I don't have any complex commitments, I return to my one-on-one relationships with collectors, and I get to solidify some of my own projects. I have a fresh palette so all I need is a little good energy and a few painting sales to see me through the end of the year. I just have to roll out the red carpet of my spirit, open my arms, smile, and sing to those paintings which belong to people who don't know it yet.

October 5 Wednesday

A rhythm is returning to my studio after months of feeling pressed in strange ways, off kilter, out of sorts. Maintaining balance of one's studio is paramount. The sailing goes smoothly and then the storm, so you have to be prepared for anything to come at you, the way life works. I feel some sort of equilibrium flowing back into the studio as I am feeding my studio in the right way. I am staying grounded, healthy, exercising, my heart is mended, which clears my head for better field vision and frees my spirit up to work on art. I am back at the easel, my books are coming along, my communications with collectors have picked up and I'm feeling their energy, so I have to stay on this train to the next stop.

October 6 Thursday

Before racquetball I was saddened to read that Steve Jobs, Co-Founder and CEO of Apple Inc., passed away at the young age of 56. He thought differently and he helped me to think differently. I typed my first book on his first consumer grade Apple II in college. I built my fine art studio over the course of twenty years and twenty Apple computers, one of which I'm typing on right now, five of which sit in my studio ready for use at any time.

The home desktop computer became ubiquitous and now is almost outdated, as Mr. Jobs made sure that we would be able to travel with his laptops, ipads, and iphones, Apple computers in our pockets. He changed the way I thought about making books, websites, recording music, editing video, using the internet, buying music and videos, playing back media. Essentially his vision was crucial in allowing me to rely on his company's tools to build my small business from nothing into a 1030 painting studio, with a back office assistant whose name is Apple. The programs are important sure, but the way that Apple approaches work flow and interface, user experience, speed of use and learning, has made it what it has become. Steve's baby is alive and booming. It only took the whole world way too long to realize the genius of Apple. Here is a company whose name is tied so intimately to the vision of the CEO that he is really one of the most important corporate historical figures. He made his products for creatives and for the people, even if he was a tricky people person. I never needed to be friends with the man. I am friends with the powerful tools he made that help me run my art enterprise. Steve Jobs Rest In Peace.

October 7 Friday

I was up at 6 am and worked on the 1000 Paintings book for 16 hours straight. This project demands a master file archive that I am currently building, as my first 1000 paintings have their own respective catalogue numbers (1-1000). I make a folder for every painting, and each folder will contain all file iterations of that painting for future applications, which I am starting to realize will be a valuable resource that I hadn't originally anticipated.

I got word that a family friend died today. The life and death around us are constant reminders that we are ephemeral creatures. What is not ephemeral? The best art, the best of one's spirit. Truth is not ephemeral, truth is there for the ages. Beauty in one moment is not ephemeral. A beautiful woman caught on canvas is eternal. The actual model will grow old and die, but her visage, captured by the artist, will live for hundreds or thousands of years to inspire others regarding eternal, fleeting beauty.

October 8 Saturday

I spent another 16 hours on the 1000 Paintings book and got to painting number 700 in the book layout. I have 300 to go.

October 9 Sunday

Matt and Jess and Jackson set up a spooky graveyard in their front yard, so Jackson was pretending to be the Mummy, Frankenstein, a vampire. We drove up to a farm and met their friends Michelle and Garrett, who is also 5. Matt and I took the boys through a cornfield maze. I was the ghoulish uncle who chased the kids around and Matt was the voice of reason, trying to read the illegible maze map he was handed at the start, telling the kids to slow down, worrying and so on. My job was much more fun. The sun was beating down and the boys had a ball.

We went back to Michelle and Chris's house, where Garrett and Jackson played while the big people watched the Giants lose to the Seahawks. Five turnovers. Chris did a boil with corn, potatoes, onions, and sausage, which he dumped on a picnic table of newspapers. Now this is a good way to spend a Sunday afternoon. Chris is starting a spice company so we talked about a logo. He showed me the mock-up for one of his spice bottles and I liked it. I rarely do commercial stuff, but I have references if he needs graphics people. Artists can be useful and entertaining wherever they go, which is a good thing for artists to remember. I've been happily singing for my supper many years gone by now.

October 10 Monday

I went down the street to O'Neill's for my Condo Board meeting to discuss the owners who have not paid their assessments to renovate the lobbies and hallways of our condo. I happen to be on that list of six people, so I came right out with it.

"Sorry, I know this is a little awkward, me being on the Board and everything," to which my three fellow Board members smiled nervously, "But I need to sell a painting. I had a live one last month that didn't come through, so I'm waiting for the next sale."

My friends laughed with me and said not to worry, that I always pay, which I do.

"I paid a grand last month, so I owe $1600 or something."

"$1711.65," Ed responded. Right, that number.

The Board discussed what should be done about these deviants who had not paid their assessments and I led the charge, citing by-laws, talking about liens, what we could do about one of the owners who says he will never pay. Ultimately this was an absurd meeting for me to attend, but I try to do my duty. I voted to impose a fine on myself and the five other owners who still have not paid up, which was a unanimous Board decision. It was the right thing to do.

October 11 Tuesday

Honest Vinnie got $1200 for my green shit box, so that brings my Condo tab almost up to speed. If only I had several gallerists who could place my paintings like Vinnie sold my old car.

Today I laid out the last two hundred paintings of the 1000 Paintings book, all 420 pages. The feeling of partial completion is complete elation.

October 12 Wednesday

I sat with my friend Ann today, who is very spiritual and inspiring to talk to because she understands what it's like to spend so much time in another place, like I do as an artist. I go into the art head and I return to 'this reality' after long stretches of meditation as a daily ritual. This practice allows an artist to tap into things that lots of people don't spend time thinking about or meditating on. Ann has dreams and visions that often come true, and sometimes this happens to me, although with less frequency than Ann. She talked about how she feels a room without looking at people, which I do as well. Energy vibrations from people bounce all over the place. There is a way of thinking that we selected our respective lots in life to work certain things out. I agree with Ann that learning how to be compassionate, how to love, how to give back to our respective communities is what it's all about, as we are here for a short blip and we can't take anything with us in the end.

October 13 Thursday

My musician friend, who does not mince his words, checked in regarding my first 7 song EP. He wrote, "You are fearless. In the best of ways. The rest of us should be less afraid by the sound of our own voices." This message will inspire the next music.

I fight fear like we all do, but part of my response to fear is to lay it out there and see what happens. The funny thing is that I feel no vulnerability in my art making as I don't care what people think anymore. The fears I have are about keeping my studio alive, which most would consider a much smaller fear. If this is so then I have conquered the big dog and just have to solve the illusion of money energy, because this is the only thing that I really get hung up about. My ego smashed long ago on the rocks of art, I make things with the editorial eye of a hangman, tossing out anything that makes no sense in building upon the foundation. Tossing the wrong idea is often more enlightening than finding the right answer, strangely enough, because by tossing dead weight accurately, with the right spirit, one is being true to oneself, exercising the good judgment of what not to make, what not to do. The truth always makes way for better concepts and energy patterns to emerge and enmesh themselves into a vibrant studio ecosystem.

Friday 14 October

There are few better sensations than waking to a waiting canvas, like your dog at the beach who wants to play fetch all day.

When the easel warms up anything there is possible. This is the language and the head space I enjoy as an easel jockey. When the easel is hot, when it's my best friend, which is most of my career, it's like riffing with a band. How about this one, what about this? Turn this on its side, take this canvas over here, give this one a good beating, take no prisoners. Different ways of seeing, different 'genres,' if you have to use this archaic terminology, are different energies, and I work with many of them. How does a composer pull off a symphony without horns or strings? A genre or style of painting is like a string instrument, if it's big enough it might be an orchestral section, a letter in the alphabet, maybe a set of consonants. When the easel starts turning I am not content to sit there on one genre, so I have my Reconstructions, my Garnett Girls, my Garnett Figures, my Green series, my Fingerprint Project, some traditional work, all riffing off of one another. When the easel gets moving I'll go from one head space to the next, from one canvas to the next, from one floor to the next, from one day to the next, from one week to the next.

October 15 Saturday

I insisted from the outset to teach myself a number of styles and genres in painting. I mean this not as a passive observer, I mean that I dove into these genres and lived by them, sold by them, paid my rents and mortgages with them, learned them to survive and make new work. If you are making a living at painting the way I have, you don't just get okay at something. You have to master these ways of seeing.

I have always maintained that representational painting is far and away the most challenging thing that I have had to teach myself. There are a hundred types of representational picture making that I have studied and explored. My traditional commissions have subsidized this research, inside the nooks and crannies of numerous sub-genres of representationalism.

In representational painting you need to hone your subject down from large abstraction into smaller abstract peaks and valleys. You map out enough small abstract details and an image takes shape. Abstraction lies in all the great paintings. You just have to zoom in. If you look at the corner of a Rembrandt painting you can often find an Ab-Ex painting in there.

The art world often thumbs its nose at 'contemporary' traditional work but I would rebut by asking this question. Should I have worked as a bartender in order to keep my vision adequately pure for the likes of taste arbiters, or did I cut the right path surviving by my art alone, methodically mining the genres for all these years? Does it make sense that the high art world only qualifies representational art if the representational art is practicing shopworn irony during this blip on the historical radar? Irony falls flat outside of time in much the same way that critics often fail to comprehend timeless art while it is being produced.

People only know you for one or two things. If you are more than one or two things people get fuzzy. As an artist you have to find your audience. In my case I have collectors in a pretty broad range who support various aesthetic cornerstones of my career. Unusual as designed. I have completely different aesthetic conversations with all of my collectors, which keeps the game entertaining while allowing me to continue my research.

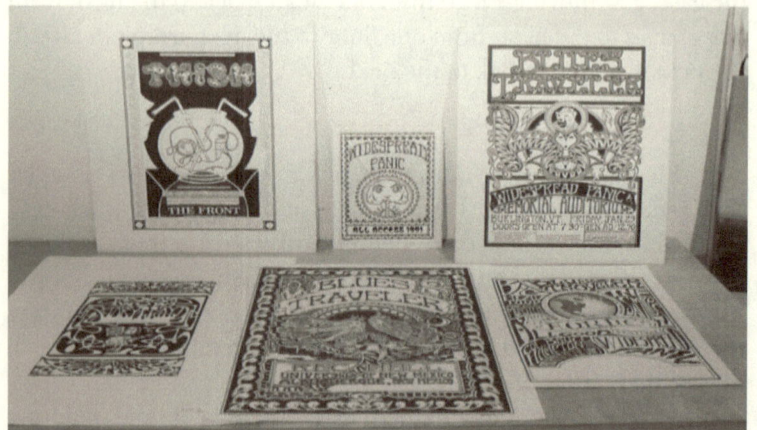

© SandyGarnett.com, Old School BT and HORDE Art, original ink drawings. There are hundreds of originals inventoried from the college years.

October 16 Sunday

Today I shot hundreds of original pieces of ink-on-paper rock art from college that jumpstarted my creative career. I've learned that as time goes by people forget everything, but a well documented artist archive is a useful and often inspiring library for collectors, fellow creatives and people who appreciate the arts.

October 17 Monday

My mother called at 11 am, frantic. They had just gotten back from a pleasant trip to see friends in Richmond.

"Sandy, I took a shirt off the couch in the den and there was a mouse on the pillow. Oh my God! There he is! Running on my couch! Please help me!" She was hysterical.

I talked my mother off the ledge, we agreed that she would go exercise, that I would meet her over there with some mouse traps and help her in an hour. I had just ordered lunch to be delivered but I didn't want to tell her that this was my delay, lest my shrimp fried rice sound trivial. On the way over I picked up mouse traps at the hardware store.

I arrived at the house before my mother and upon entering the family room I saw a flash behind where my father's chair would have been. My mother had rearranged the furniture in her rodent insanity. Poor Mom, I thought. The last thing she needs. The mouse was small and seemed to not know where to go, so it kept darting between the curtain and the adjacent magazine rack, where old reading material goes to never get read again. I kicked the mouse out of the open screen door into the shrubbery. Then I put traps in the basement. This little mouse could have siblings.

My mother returned and I gave her the thumbs up. She wanted me to toss the couch out, as though I could just lift it with a pinkie finger, or zap it and make it disappear.

"Your father doesn't care! We've been talking about getting rid of that couch for years."

"Mom, everything is fine, you have time to dispose of the couch. No need to toss it out the window this moment." That one caught her funny bone and she told me to stop it, trying to wipe the smirk off my face with her responsive humor, or maybe asking for more where that came from. I sat with her for lunch and got her onto subjects other than mice, like how great her trip to see old friends must have been. She cooled off, I felt like I had done my duty as a son, I got a sandwich out of the deal, kissed her goodbye and off I went to etch Mother Mary on a gravestone.

October 18 Tuesday

When I stand here in the strong winds, naked to the world, perched at the pinnacle of an art studio I have built with blood and sweat for twenty years, a point of light that is the center of every soul, an overwhelming peace and joy, showers me in a new skin every day. This is my sustenance. This and Ramen noodles.

When I began to paint I would spend 90% of my time with brush to canvas, eyes on the surface, trying to answer all of the questions right up close. This is how you can paint yourself into a corner or drive a painting off a cliff. Micro is as important as the macro, so over the years I learned to paint, then roll my chair 12 feet away until it hit the counter, look, contemplate, then go back in. I call this the runway. The more fluid I became at painting the more I spent looking and not actually painting. The actions an experienced painter makes, depending upon the genre, are often decisive, after the artist has contemplated the move he is about to make. Now I look 90% of the time and paint 10% of the time.

Happy Birthday Dad I love you.

October 19 Wednesday

I picked up a Fingerprint Portrait commission yesterday. This will be a 40 x 30 inch painting to accompany three existing Fingerprint Portraits as the family has grown. I have not heard from my friend in four years, then suddenly a commission.

As an independent artist, outside the walls of the high art architecture, I often identify with independent minds who really cut their own brand new trails in life, which is half the battle and not even the hardest part. The fight to stay independent in order to see original things that people in systems do not see or will not see or cannot see, this is the real test.

October 20 Thursday

I was at the computer working on the 1000 Paintings book from 5 am until 2pm again, chasing down 25 or 30 rogue paintings whose original references needed to be found and rescanned.

In the afternoon I finished a gravestone etching of Mary with the epitaph, "Mother Mary Pray For Us."

Gravestone etchings are the only things I have not archived properly, and now these are in many cemeteries, so shooting all of them is likely never going to happen. I have been good at shooting etchings in the past several years, but I would like to see that Cat in the Hat etching I made ten years ago, I would like to see the huge Harley Davidson Eagle I etched in the same time frame, I would like to see my massive etching of Pope John Paul that is in Bridgeport somewhere in front of a church, I would like to see all 1000 etchings laid out smartly in a book some day.

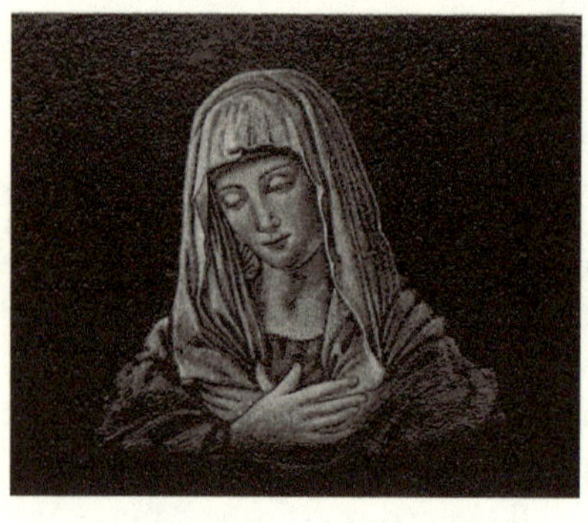

October 21 Friday

I woke into the fabric of art, which had tossed and turned me all night in deep sleep. Waking into a fresh studio with art on the easels asking for love, this is what the dream of life can be for a painter. I paid attention to the dog portrait, which was barking at me this week. I got most of her down quickly and the details have been skipping past me because I have not meditated on the visual mechanics of a proper finish, which is all very mathematical. You darken the left ear and the right cheekbone pops out too much, you highlight a whisker and the background recedes too deeply or loses its space, you put a rouge on the tongue and the highlight on the right eye loses that special sheen. All of these parts must be built together into a highly complex visual network that replicates or riffs on representationalism. Many people can do the pyrotechnics, but few can lace the spirit of the subject into all of the inner workings of a strong portrait. This language is something an abstract painter who can't paint portraits knows nothing about, amusingly, so when I hear a non-artist like Clement Greenberg or Arthur Danto preach about why some artist is amazing it's like sticking a finger down my throat and waiting for the gag reflex. I have little faith in art criticism made by non-artists who can sway art markets, and I have little faith in visual artists who place conceptual Trojan horses before the non-verbal visual language they are busy talking about while not mastering by making.

October 22 Saturday

I picked up some small brushes at my art store and met the new girl at the counter while talking to Jon, who I've known for some time. Picking up brushes is part of the dance. I've burned through hundreds of brushes over the years. I like to paint oils and acrylics with the same synthetic acrylic brushes for the slide and nuance these brushes give me on a canvas.

When painting begets more painting, the dust stays off the easels, the tools stay sharpened, the palette stays cleaned after every sitting, always ready for the next painting session. When painting is the daily mantra this energy builds and crescendos in cyclical patterns that are filled with light.

Right out of the gate my goal was to make a living as an artist, and I knew that if I did other things I would become something different. This stubborn adherence to making only art for my sustenance was the best decision I ever made. It forced me to survive or die on the vine, which leads to a 99.9% full time career drop-off rate, leaving one in a thousand.

The sun was shining so I took a balsa wood airplane over to nephew Jackson and he was delighted by the surprise I hid behind my back. He is getting more patient with things like breakable airplanes, so I involved him in the process of constructing and flying it. He did the countdowns. Then we took turns playing monster and roughhousing until dusk.

Before bed I received an email from text breakup chick.

"Maybe we should talk at some point," then another that read, "Leaving for Cali soon. Would like to talk before I go."

Interesting that three months later she feels compelled to communicate. I don't reengage with that type of energy... happy to be away from it. She burned a sturdy bridge.

October 23 Sunday

At Ben's house I walked into turmoil as the new pet hamster had escaped from her cage. I went down to the basement and got on the carpet with the girls, who became amused with the notion of recapturing Daisy. Daisy was stuck behind the radiator cover, so she scuttled back and forth as I tried to migrate her in the direction of the opening. I had a flashlight and Nel was standing on my back, as if I were a surf board. Cece screamed, "There she is!" several times and I got up to move over to where Cece was. She let on that she had been joking about spotting Daisy so we laughed about that. After two near captures I finally flushed her out of the radiator and cornered her with her own cage, which she finally climbed into.

In the evening I received an email from Julia, Ben's wife, Cece and Nel's mother. I've known Ben and Julia since college.

"Sandy - I want you to know how much Nel adores you and your Rainbow Riders book. She got in the car Friday to go to school with a notebook, pen and your book. She was trying to recreate your characters with her little magic marker, just as you had done for her on the yellow paper. Then she took the book in to show her teacher. Thank you not only for catching the hamster but for being such a positive influence on our little friend. You are the best and so is your book! xxx."

This and a little nephew time made my weekend.

October 24 Monday

Late to bed, I woke up early and tired at 6 am. I have art to make today and I am exhausted, not feeling the surge. This is a minor complaint but relevant for the art journal. If I don't take care of myself, if I don't plan ahead, if I don't remain healthy every day my art suffers.

I was thrown off, basking slightly in the 90 day check back from text breakup chick, regardless of her motivations. She let me go in a dismissive, disrespectful way and never gets to have my attention again. This played like a circus ring in my head all weekend, so I just had to let the energy run its course.

I spent the day painting one of my nudes, starting a

Reconstruction painting, chipping away at music, writing, relishing some peace and a couple of new gigs that keep the sails up and the wind pushing the vessel along. I'm hooked on this Garnett figure I keep coming back to, and tonight sketched her sister in a similar scale and palette. They would live nicely together but will probably end up halfway around the world from one other.

October 25 Tuesday

When I wake up into a new day on the easel with a paintbrush in my hand, my outlook is brighter, things sort themselves out better, it feels like an affirmation that I am doing what I was set out here to do, and I check back all day to the works on the easel, as patterns strengthen and become routines.

I finished a gravestone etching of a Greek cross in between easel sittings today. Etching sometimes feels like being a session musician as I am given the subject matter, the style, and my job is to knock an etching out professionally in one take.

October 26 Wednesday

I woke up at 6 am onto the easel and started sliding paint, which my body and brain want to do, moving between several canvases that are half committed, abandoned, lying around waiting for attention. My energy was loose as were the paintings, but they started opening up over several hours. This is the best way to paint for me, when I have a number of canvases in my sights and migrate from one to the next over the course of the day, the week, the month, as my mood changes, as my palette falls in line with this one or that one, as a quick insight drifts me in another direction. Sure, I can sit on a painting for 15 hour clips as I've done hundreds of times, on cue if necessary, but having works in progress keeps things interesting, dynamic, free. I mediate as several canvases in completely different genres start riffing with one another. They have a cool conversation, one influences the next, but the paintings often look nothing alike so the relationships are hard to trace. The traces, the bread crumbs are there for those who can see deeply enough, but not many people can see or make fluently in so many ways, so this is an obscure game, although highly engaging and entertaining as the seasons go by.

October 27 Thursday

I focused on the 1000 Paintings book today, going page by

page, making sure the images worked, moving images around if new ones came into sight, incorporating press and show images into the existing document, and labeling or captioning images, which requires me to cross reference each image with my database. Some of the images looked dark, so I had to go into Photoshop and color correct them again. I concerned myself with the overall flow of the book, as 440 pages is a lot of flow. Most people will pick the book up and do a cursory single flip through, but collectors and art people might chew on this document over the years. I have to make a book that can stand the test of time.

October 28 Friday

I communicated with three collectors today about five paintings that will cover me through the end of the year. It is refreshing to have collector energy accumulating in my studio, which will spin off into other fine art projects that have been waiting for ancillary patronage.

My favorite thing about the new autumn is that early in the morning on sunny days a yellow beam of sunlight floods my first floor in warmth that cannot be felt outside in the chilling air. I have built this cocoon and I am preparing for another winter.

October 29 Saturday

I have a 40 x 30 Fingerprint Portrait to paint for my friends Jen and Jim. They have three Fingerprint Portraits hanging in their New York apartment, so now it's time to paint the fourth family member Max. The thing is that these paintings share a palette, so I have to go in, pick the paintings up and modify them, introducing the fourth color into the other paintings so they pop together on a wall. Some art snobs might find this a capitulation of sorts, but I made the rule when I started to work with families who wanted to do Fingerprint Family Portraits. It's interesting work.

The weather was iffy so I drove into the city early today, which was alright until the Hutch exit on I-95, when snowflakes the size of potato chips started shelling my windshield and cars started slowing down. I still got in without too much trouble. Over the Triboro my E-Z Pass didn't work, so the exasperated toll booth cop came over, smacked my E-Z Pass on the meter and the light went green. I said thank you but he couldn't muster a response. I don't blame him. Once I heard that toll booth operators have the highest suicide rates of any profession. That's got to be a tough job.

The FDR was fine, sailing down the East Side Drive, with eight thousand memories of this drive and New York City spinning my wheels the whole way down. It was getting hectic out there. Before the underpass at New York Presbyterian I barely made out a tug boat on the East River, steam coming off the surface of the lapping water as the cold snow was starting to pelt it, sky and sea doing their dance. You take that slow right curve and up you go, over city roads for a minute until you sail back down. The 14th Street exit has been closed for too long, which is a pain in the ass, so I hopped over and off at 23rd, zipping straight down to 14th off the exit, going partially back under the FDR I'd just gotten off of. Right on 14th, pass Broadway and University, left on 5th, turn west on 13th, and there was an illegal spot right in front of Jen's building.

I put the hazards on and called. Three minutes later Jen and Jim and their kids came down. I painted Mia seven years ago and Max I have never met. Max gave me his Fingerprint Kit and I high-fived him. Jen and Jim gave me their three Fingerprint Portrait paintings and I made it for the car, stuffing them safely in the back seat and out of the rain as fast as possible. I said goodbye and was off in a flash. Right on 6th, up to 23rd, right all the way to the FDR North.

The visuals driving uptown were trippy, as huge snowflakes or groupings of snowflakes pinged my windshield while the flow of traffic slowed, even on the FDR, which is filled with some of the most insane drivers the world has ever seen. By this time the East River had become invisible, the fog had rolled in so deep, my view filled with tiny asteroids I was driving through. I felt like Han Solo navigating his junky but trusty Millennium Falcon through the asteroid fields. I skipped off onto the Triboro, which they just renamed the RFK Bridge, and I wondered how much the family paid for that one. Traffic was getting clogged and the shitty drivers were starting to wave their hands in the air saying, "Hey, look how bad I am!"

I shot through the toll, over the bridge, up onto the Bruckner, and the traffic fizzled to a crawl. I anticipated it was that dip down and right which was causing the bottleneck, that and accidents starting to litter the highway, the first snow freaking the masses out, drivers losing their cool or just hitting an ice patch. The ice was piling up and people were starting to rely on the heat of warm rubber that made ruts in the road which bad drivers never stray from. The 50 minute drive in took 90 minutes out. I was tired of driving and happy to spend the rest of the day into the evening on the easel.

October 30 Sunday

I hung around the campfire and worked on my 1000 Paintings book last night and most of the day. I am editing, designing and inserting information for each painting from page to page. I am remembering old paintings and wondering if I have references to yet others that were destroyed. I had a habit early on of destroying paintings, sometimes before I had photographed them, which is a mistake. Shoot the work before destroying it or painting over it because you will miss it at some point in the future otherwise.

October 31 Monday

I talked to my friend Pierce in Houston and we solidified the triptych I will be painting for him. I have done spec work over the past few months on this project, we agreed on painting dimensions, we covered the business, the project is clear, so we are a go.

I was planning on Halloween with Brother Matt so I could hold the fort while they took the kids out, but due to the storm and regional power outages Halloween has been 'postponed.'

I got my first call from text breakup chick in 3 months. I deleted the voicemail without listening to it. I'm getting better at not allowing that energy to rent space in my head.

November 1 Tuesday

I worked from 6 am to 9 pm on the 1000 Paintings book and arrived at the end of 438 pages. I spent hours preparing files of the cover and the book guts, then I sent the files off for a printed hardcover proof. I have trouble believing that 20 years of painting will soon be something I can hold in my hands. I've earned it.

November 2 Wednesday

My accountant recently said that I should have no problem with finances as I live modestly and because I am 'so talented.' I am short this month but I just finished my *First 1000 Paintings* book, living in the paradox. Frustration, like the illusion of money, these things are insignificant. Watering the spirit, giving back to humanity and growing more compassionate while making new art, these eternal truths outweigh all the small stuff.

There is a vacuum now that *First 1000 Paintings* is done and out. When I am in a post-gig funk, often the next flash of inspiration is self-generated by going to the easel, which has always held the answer, the medicine, in good times and in bad.

November 3 Thursday

I lost the first two games to Matt and won the third this morning. I like getting to the gym when it's pitch black out.

My friend Lisa is out of town and has kindly offered her studio to me for the weekend where Open Studios will be held with 50 other artists at the Loft Artists in Stamford, CT. Over the past 15 years I have made many friends and collectors through this annual Open Studios weekend, so it will be fun.

November 4 Friday

I loaded my van with paintings and took them over to the LAA building. Some genius had left the second floor slop sink faucet on, which had overflowed and created a flood, so maintenance guys were wet-vacuuming as I passed them on the stairwell up to the third floor, where I found the freight elevator.

Freight elevators are interesting creatures. You never know when they are going to work and when they are going to screw you. At my old building probably 40% of the artists got stuck in one of the freight elevators during their time there. The landlord doesn't care as artists are like cockroaches. The elevator today had no lights, so I had to go by touch, which can tear your hand off in those decrepit things. I managed the piece of shit elevator, got the art into my friend Lisa's space and put up a show.

I returned to my studio at 9:45 am because the mail service indicated a delivery before 10:30 am, which I did not want to miss. Sure enough, my book arrived. I cut the box open and had a look. It will take time to absorb this accomplishment.

The Open Studio started at 6 pm so my door was open at 5:30 pm. It is always nice to see friendly faces and some of my collectors. The evening skipped along from 6 to 9 pm and I enjoyed the visitors. We are open 12 to 5 pm tomorrow and Sunday so there will be more activity on the weekend. Some people asked where my sculptures and portraits were, if I still did this work. It's hard to show everything in one shot so an artist has to make selections and not worry too much about it. I have collectors for wildly different series of works, which is unusual, so I have trouble representing it all. There will always be another show, and there will always be a segment of the audience that wishes I was showing something different. This is a little like the person who sees a red dot, indicating 'sold,' and tells the artist, "Oh, I really wanted that one!" This happens to all artists every single time.

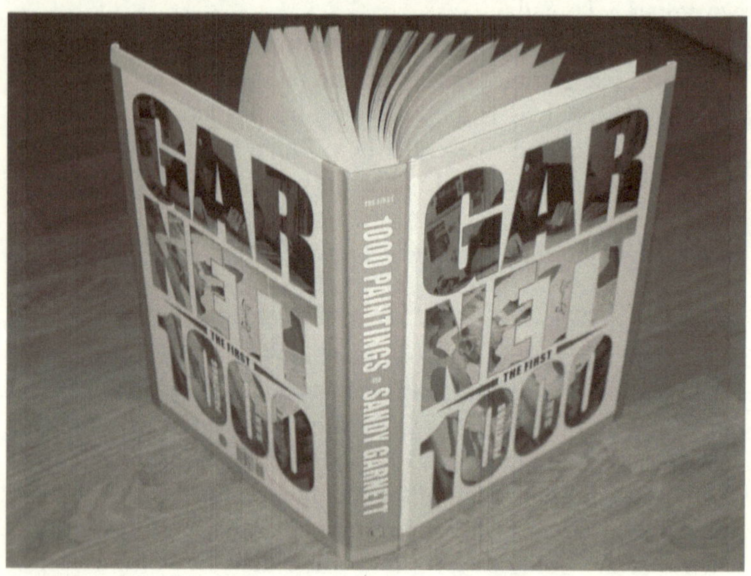

November 5 Saturday

Today nothing sold but I found some new potential collectors, I shared my *First 1000 Paintings* book with fans and current collectors, I had some nice conversations with artists, friends and visitors new and old. The governor stopped by so I said hello to Dan, in between his linebacker-sized bodyguards. He and his wife have been very supportive of our art organization for many years, which is helpful, as art organizations are often besieged by the breakneck pace of commercial progress around them when their buildings or their areas or their ideas get hot. Artists just want to keep their organizations ticking, and when business people feel that heartbeat they often want a piece of it, in every way, shape and form. The paradox is that there is no way to own a piece of another spirit, although throughout history people have coveted the thought, striven for wealth, power, domination, all dead ends to the life of one's soul. A couple of bucks for an artist or an arts organization? This is always helpful to the overall health of society but often gets lost in the shuffle of hands changing money.

I heard today that the big mural I respectfully declined went to the runner-up, who will do a vinyl-printed 'mural,' or more accurately a vinyl billboard. Part of me stings for letting the business go, but it didn't feel like a fine art statement, so as much as it was a tough lay-down, I know I made the right call.

Halloween was rescheduled to this evening because of the snowstorm that knocked power out all over the East Coast this week. Jackson was waiting at the front door eagerly like a Norman Rockwell painting in anticipation of simply giving candy to trick-or-treaters. He was beside himself when the first visitors came to the door and I was inspired by his unabashed generosity, the purity of his heart and mind, the beauty of his childhood.

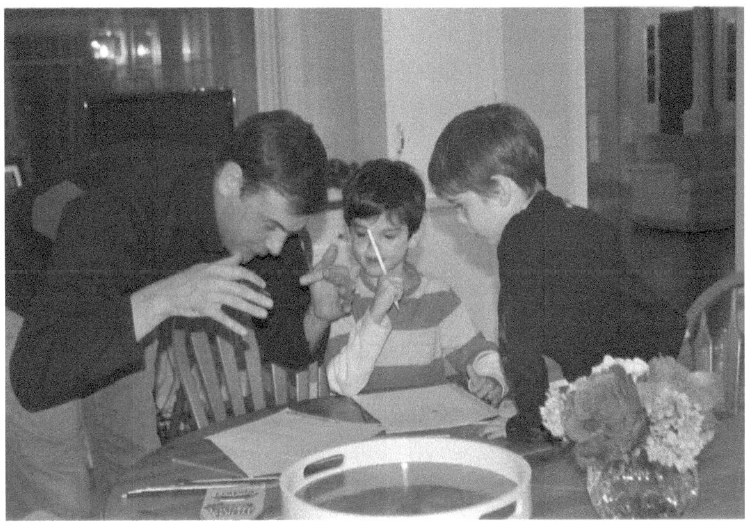

After Halloween with Jackson I went over for dinner at Bruce and Pam's with a dozen of my closest, oldest friends, couples with families taking a fast break from parenthood to catch up, laugh, eat, drink, be merry. Pam reintroduced me to her kids, who at first were not interested in another boring adult. After they learned that I had done the big Hindley Elementary School mural my stock went up, and once they heard that I did the Rainbow Riders books for kids I was alright in their eyes. They got the books and I started drawing Rainbow Riders for them. They were totally into it and so was I.

As an artist I find it very rewarding to reach people young and old, as the magic of creativity is ageless. The spark of inspiration from one human being to another lights a long fire which can blaze many trails and elevate the spiritual journey.

November 6 Sunday

In the morning I decided to change up my presentation for the Open Studio so I peeled my Musicians painting off its stretcher, rolled it up, took it over to the Loft Artists building and tacked it on the north wall of the studio, replacing three paintings that had made the wall feel too quiet. The Musicians painting is a large, bright canvas and livened things up.

I sold a small painting of a woman seated on a beach looking at the water, which delighted people. This was the last minute painting I brought over, which is how it often works. I found several new collectors, kindred spirits, and I fell into some interesting, technical, artistic subjects with new visitors, which is always fun. One guy has a friend who wants a portrait of his 12 million dollar car. I said that I'd paint a portrait of his friend's car for the paltry sum of one million dollars and I'd give this guy a 10% commission.

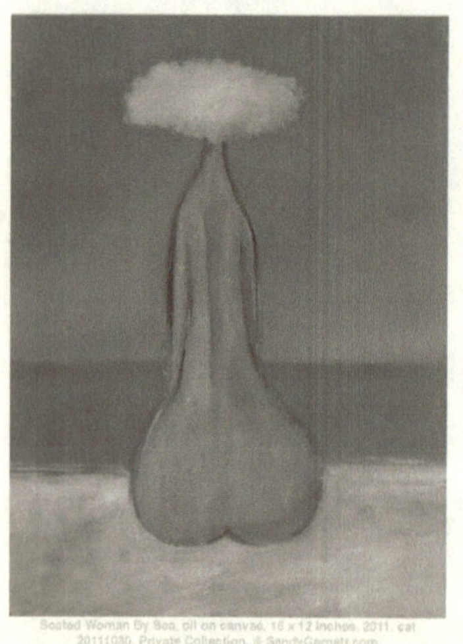

Seated Woman By Sea, oil on canvas, 16 x 12 inches, 2011, cat 20111030, Private Collection, © SandyGarnett.com

My football team was playing at 4 pm so I wanted to leave early but Lynda convinced me to stay as she was having people over after the show. At one point there were five of the past LAA presidents in the same room and I mentioned that we were in the midst of LAA royalty, an observation that amused the room. Hats off to people who pledge their time and energy to non-profit organizations. We laughed and told funny stories while the wine and cheese made the rounds. I have been a member of this art organization for 15 years, so it is nice to have long friendships with artists who have common memories of the old building, of old art shows and projects, of old friendships, creativity, incidents and accidents that bind and weave humans together.

November 7 Monday

I removed all of my art from Lisa's space at the LAA building, loaded it into my trusty van and brought it back to my studios in South Norwalk. Artists spend their lives making voluminous objects and then fretting about where these things should go, moving these things around endlessly, from studio to studio, gallery to gallery, show space to show space. Art that sells? I still find myself handling it - borrowing an old painting to shoot it again, bringing it back to the studio to put a frame on it, re-stretch it, make a repair, whatever.

My father helped me get the big Musicians painting tacked up in my loft this morning. I was feeling lazy after working all weekend so we walked over and watched a big popcorn movie about robotic boxers, shameless action entertainment for the boys in both of us as we banged down two big buckets of popcorn and exclaimed, "Awesome!" to one another anytime one robot beat the shit out of another robot.

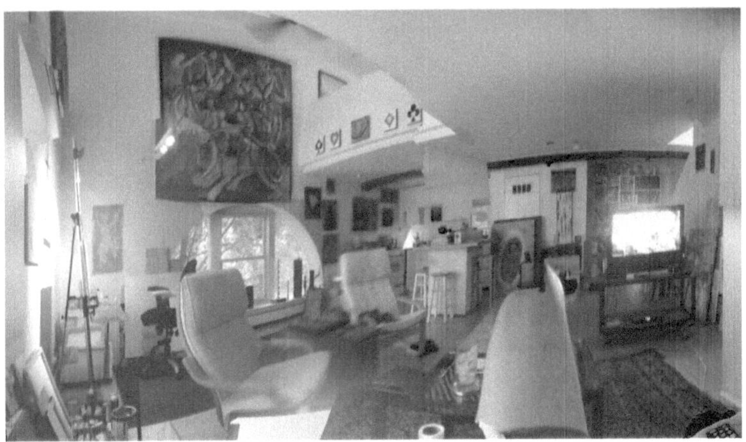

I went over for dinner and watched Gregory Peck's "The Keys to the Kingdom" with my parents, one of my father's top ten flicks of all time. He said the movie gets better every time he sees it, every five years or so.

I have learned to love cinema through my parents, and over the years the family movie dialogue has been something that all of us have enjoyed sharing. It is special to watch one of my father's favorite films with him, to receive the message he is passing along to me. I try to be aware of the lessons my parents have to give every day. I've gotten better about this over the years, the decades, and I am very grateful they are close to me, happy and healthy.

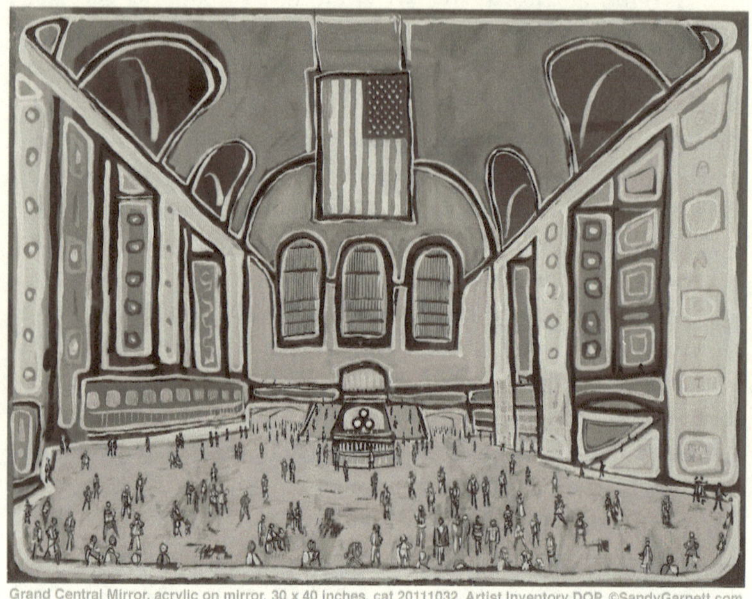

Grand Central Mirror, acrylic on mirror, 30 x 40 inches, cat 20111032, Artist Inventory DOP, ©SandyGarnett.com

November 8 Tuesday

I got Matt in two fluid games of racquetball before going to work on a new 30 x 40 inch Reconstruction acrylic painting of Grand Central for a show deadline I committed to this week. The surface is a mirror, which was challenging but proved to be an interesting exercise. I had to clean the mirror thoroughly and layer acrylics, building up the painting, letting other regions of the picture bleed through. There are parts of mirror rattled throughout the composition, which does spatial things to the eyes and to the mind. For this reason it is tricky to paint a mirror, as I was looking at myself the whole time, trying to see through myself, trying to paint myself and my easel lights out of view, distractions I never have when I am painting on a canvas.

My new collector Robin called and asked about three paintings on my website today. She wants a second painting, one in particular, but she can't do it now. Collectors bring with them new energies, new enthusiasms, new opportunities that charge my studio. I have another friend who is serious about the painting in progress I have been doing for my friend in Jamaica. Maybe I start on that one again and find a home for this continuing sketch.

I have some energy flowing into my studio at just the right time. With another Open House next weekend and some proper follow-up maybe I will be able to see through the end of January. The winter months need to be survived, so if I get another sale or two I can hunker down with a calm mind and clean spirit into a productive winter of creativity.

November 9 Wednesday

Today I split games with Matt, then returned to the Grand Central painting, which came together in fits and spurts, measured blasts of creativity. This one will be a crowd pleaser. More importantly, as usual, the painting pleases me.

I finished the painting and signed it in the afternoon, then I went to the art supply store and found a discount frame. I epoxied the white frame on the back of the frame-less mirror, then I set two granite Fingerprint Totems on the back to weigh the frame down against the mirror while the epoxy sets overnight. Tomorrow I will wire the work and deliver it to the group show where it will hang for a month. The effect of a reflection coming through various parts of a painting makes for an interesting original work of art, which is the point of the mirror show. I am intrigued to see what other artists will do with a mirror. I have painted on mirrors before and I'd like to do more of that, but mirrors are temperamental bitches, heavy and fragile and always telling you to screw off if you don't treat them right.

Creativity can be cheap, meaning that I can be low on reserves but make my best stuff if my spirit is in the right place. This is a saving grace for the fine artist, who is accustomed to making something out of nothing. My overhead on a painting is very small in terms of materials, but I have to run a small business, pay taxes, insurance, the monthlies, the mortgages, maintenance, keep the car running, fuel the body with food and exercise, all of these things before art materials.

There are so many talented spirits in the world, yet only few can wake up every day of their adult lives and make art for a job. In the United States, where the business of money making is held to the highest regard, art support is scattered and often reliant upon the individual collector, foundations, philanthropists of various sorts. Then there is the raw art market; the auction houses, the art fairs, the commercial galleries. There are many avenues to find support, but artists have to be at the top of their game and claw tooth and nail for every dollar to keep their dreams alive. Maybe this is just the nature of any business in our country, or anywhere in life.

November 10 Thursday

I split games with my brother this morning. It is good to wake into the morning with a racquetball careening at my head, which keeps me honest and sharp.

I wired the Grand Central mirror, prepared it for delivery, shot and archived the picture. People have no idea how much time is spent doing all of these important steps to preparing a painting for release. When a painting leaves the studio many artists don't think about the fact that they might never see it again. I learned that even if a painting will come right back, I have to pretend I'll never be able to shoot or archive that painting after it leaves the studio. Once I have catalogued a painting, shot it, color corrected it, put it in my archive? It is mine forever. There is nothing worse than trying to remember what a painting looked like that I forgot to shoot early on in my career.

I received another message last night from text breakup chick. Four texts and a voicemail in the past two weeks. Three months after a text breakup dark energy is seeping back into my studio. I worked through this awhile back, so I would prefer to be left alone by this person.

November 11 Friday

This morning my father spent the entire day helping me set up my Open House for the weekend. We moved forty paintings from my basement studio up to my loft studio. I grouped paintings by genre in various sections of the loft; traditional works around the kitchen, Reconstructions up the 16 foot wall of my easel area, Veil paintings around the seating area, a Twister relief in progress by the book case, my soft landscapes upstairs in the gallery area. We cleaned and talked about life, family, the weekend show, my father injecting his good energy into my studio as a Dad and as a best friend.

November 12 Saturday

My parents brought lunch, which was nice of them. Someone came over before noon and she likes two small paintings for her husband. We will see how that goes. People started filtering in and I sold a 20x16 inch painting 'Mother and Child' quickly to my new collector Robin, who came to pick up her 'Seated Woman

By Sea' painting that she bought last weekend. In the afternoon another couple came by and I recognized them for the painting that they had almost bought four years ago, which was the last Open Studio they had been to.

"Still Life with Guitar?"

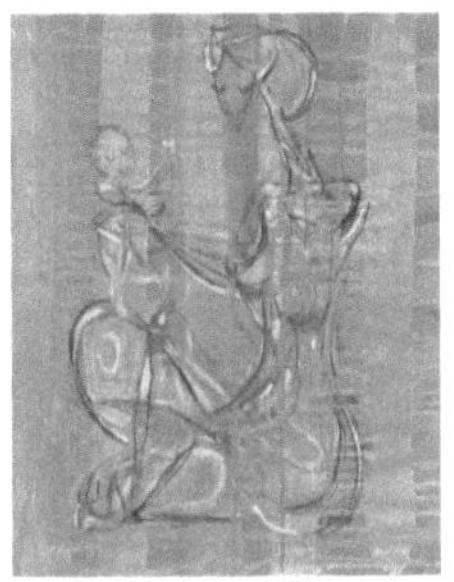

Jeffrey said, "Remarkable." I had sold the original 'Still Life with Guitar' they wanted, but I had prints, so Jeffrey selected a frame for his print and asked about the 'Mother and Child' painting Robin had purchased earlier today. People can always sense the energy around a sold painting for some reason.

November 13 Sunday

I had a good day yesterday so today was relaxing. My parents came over early with lunch, great parents that they are, and helped me throughout the day. A couple came in, friends of the family, and took a 36 x 24 inch painting entitled, 'Woman in Landscape,' a Reconstruction picture with a muted palette that I signed last year. They were uncertain about how the painting would work in a particular space and mentioned a realty website where their room was photographed. I found the image online and did a parlor trick, placing the painting on their wall in Photoshop while people watched. My technical side helped to solidify the sale.

Towards the end of the day I sold another painting, a 14 x 11 inch Garnett Girl canvas to cap the weekend. This little picture was hiding behind ten paintings and my mother told me to put her out, saying that she would like to borrow the painting if it didn't sell. It sold. Who knew. I didn't.

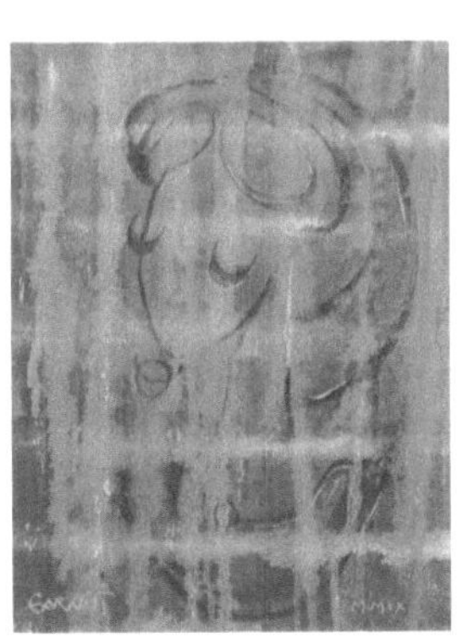

When I put on a show or an Open Studio I have gotten pretty good about having no expectations, which is really like a muscle that needs to be developed over the years. This weekend I had no expectations, I sold work and saw some great people in my life. I am inspired and peaceful this Sunday evening while the energy from good people drifts around and will resonate nicely as the Holidays approach.

November 14 Monday

I worked for my audience all weekend so today I was lazy. Almost all Americans don't understand what's it's like to take it easy on Monday, but after two full work weekends in a row busting my ass I needed a break.

Selling paintings you never expected to sell fills one set of sails and takes the wind out of a second set of sails. It's relieving, thrilling, and exasperating all at the same time. Why was it so easy to sell these paintings? Why were these paintings sold and not others? Why do I have to struggle for months only to have an easy weekend of selling paintings? Why do I have to make the work, inventory it and sell it as well? Why don't I have a gallerist selling for me, taking my work to auction and art fairs so I can focus on making new things? This is a constant stream, all day long through life, the questions of being an artist. I have to mute this stream of thinking, the questions, and live in the solution, practice gratitude for my lot in life, find the next original thing to spring from my heart onto the canvas.

November 15 Tuesday

I started a gravestone etching of St. Jude at the top of a black granite gravestone, centered above the family name. There is an I-Beam rail that the stones come in on, but they can't get these massive stones tall enough for me to sit in a chair, so I have to be a contortion artist as every new etching is in a different location on a new stone in an awkward position.

In the afternoon my friend Jeff called in about showing some New York City prints. I stopped what I was doing, went downstairs, found some prints and visualized a wall of my work in Jeff's gallery that I know. This one can go on the left, this one of the right, and you can have an original painting in the center. These are colorful spatial studies, I sell the the originals, and I will always paint this series, love letters to Manhattan.

Jeff's energy got me thinking about making a new large city painting for the space above my easel, that 16 foot wall. The energy bubbled and percolated and almost negotiated its way out of me, by which I mean I almost dropped everything, got a big canvas and went to work on a massive New York City painting. It didn't happen, but here is an example of a friend inspiring creativity. It doesn't take much to get the ball rolling.

November 16 Wednesday

I open my studio to visitors, I sell some work, there is a natural flow of income to cover the business, as it should always be. When something comes in another thing goes out, so I try to be careful what I wish for. One day my life may be very busy, with little time for myself. I have this time, where I struggle in peace and solitude, here in this studio, in the last studio, scraping away the layers of my spiritual amnesia, remembering what I am here for, in this skin, trying to learn compassion, now that creative fluidity is a laser beam twenty years in the making. Flashy pyrotechnics are good party tricks, but when accompanied by an unwavering spirituality the works shimmer in deeper ways that attract other human beings to act, react, interact with me. If not for my collectors, my audience, I would not have this career. Gratitude.

November 17 Thursday

I finished the St. Jude gravestone and spent the afternoon painting. The opening for the mirror show in Greenwich was early evening. I saw some fellow artists there and we talked shop about art making, mirrors, life. My Grand Central painting was well positioned in the speaking hall. The gallery directors were standing right in front of it, saying that it is a crowd pleaser, hopefully it will sell, and then they pointed to the reflection of the mirror on the floor. I met a pretty photographer and wanted to spend more time laughing with her, but off I had to run.

I picked my fraternity brother Chris up from the train as scheduled and we went to a bar where old friends of ours were gathering to see a band play, some old friends and family involved in the band. It was nice to see Liege, Sarah, and other friends from college. We all laughed, drank, and danced, as communing with friends always feels like when it is good.

I brought Chris back to the studio and we solved the world's problems for several hours, talking about art, friends, work, life. I showed him how I play my song 'Busted Wing,' a song he likes. This song has a weird rhythm I do with the upswing of my hand, which confuses some of my friends who can't understand how to strum that way. I will be painting a portrait of Chris's son soon, so we talked about that for awhile as well before calling it a night.

Old friends are like old trees. Things change, but true friendships can grow deeper with age, often directly relational to the excellence of people we choose to have in our lives and the hard work we do in life on ourselves.

November 18 Friday

Cousin Antonia is flying in and speaking to a gallerist on my behalf while she is here. She works on the authentication of art, finding stolen art, forgeries, all things interesting about the corruption that can revolve around this vast field. We corresponded and I gave her some details about my career that she thought might be useful to communicate during her meeting.

I have a lot of work and could use an established gallerist to help place my fine art, in the same way I could use help with marketing and distribution of the books I have been making. Finding the right people is a challenge, but maybe this is stating the obvious of any career. I am not around art professionals or publishing professionals on a daily basis. I built my studio to be a peaceful respite that would shield my spirit from all the dangerous ways that artists fall down and fail out there. I am doing this for the rest of my life, so buying and renovating my first two spaces is the story of my thirties; owning a sturdy vessel that can survive the storms year in, year out, modest but strong as an ox. This methodology does not often lend itself to the fashionable winds which sweep through the art markets, and I don't like chasing the phantoms of false hopes, so I have made my own luck, I make my own wind, one painting brick at a time.

One of these years, one of these decades I'll find the right partner, and this gallerist who I find? She will make a mint off the blood I have spilled in this studio.

November 19 Saturday

After my monthly greasy spoon burger at Pat's Hubba Hubba, a legendary locale reserved for old school in-the-knowers, I passed a tattered estate sale sign, which I followed deep into the wooded streets, glimmering pavement, sparkling leaves, the sunlight pouring through the dying canopies of autumn on this bright, warm Saturday.

The house was tucked away and thriving with activity. It was a hybrid colonial that seems to have been expanded upon several times. The house was something to behold. There were nooks and crannies to the house everywhere; old accoutrements like bar cutaways, strange pantry spaces, storage spaces, outdated sun rooms that had become irrelevant to today's architecture and culture, odd paneling and fabrics, amateur art, table decorations that had been collected and had never moved. There is a poignance to rummaging through the lives of others after they have passed away, but there is also great interest, a story around every corner, so I walked with respect through the house, observing how clearly this family had spent so many years of their lives. I find estate sale goers interesting to watch as they sift through a house, carrying arm fulls of random items, these things they can't live without. I attribute this fascination with my mother and her New York City roots, this Central Park bench observationalism. Just sit on a bench and a thousand stories walk right by.

The man, the father, the husband, had been to war and had spent his life as a doctor. They were fond of electrical gadgets which filled the home; the latest space heaters which were designed to look like fireplaces, complete with flickering red flames, the storage rooms packed with every new-fangled kitchen tool that had come off the press in the past four decades. They had enjoyed rangy subjects on their bookshelves, which tempted me, but I moved on. This man was a hunter and avid fisherman. In his basement he poured buckshot with an assortment of machines. He had closets filled with clothing and hunting equipment. Upstairs in his game room of sorts hung the heads and horns of 20 creatures from this continent and others. He had hundreds of buck knives in glass cases that delighted visitors, bronzes of bison, carvings made from ivory tusks, paintings of big game hunters, ash trays made from buffalo hooves. He was a collector of experiences, an adventurer, like other friends of mine whose favorite things to do are hunt and fish. I like to check in on the hunting and fishing worlds several times a year for the camaraderie, but most times I generally prefer to be making stuff. Rather than kill, catch, collect things, I make things that spring from my head and heart which immediately enter my own art collection. I collect art, I collect collectors, and every painting tells a story of another safari in the studio.

November 20 Sunday

I picked up my cousin Antonia, in from London, and had brunch at my parents' house, where she will be staying. Antonia's great-great-grandmother and my great-great-grandmother were sisters, and the family has kept in closer touch more than many other strains on either side of the pond. It is nice to have family in other countries, which is not uncommon of course, but it opens ones' eyes to the world at large in the best of ways.

I brought Antonia to my studio, where we rummaged through my work, talked about how my art might fit into the larger context of the contemporary art market, as she has friends in the art world due to the fact that she has worked with stolen art and forgeries for some time now as her job profession. She enjoys my Reconstruction city pictures and interiors, mentioning that when she saw them she knew they were mine immediately. She also found some of the figure work intriguing.

After running through all of the family news and updates we were off to a football party, as I thought Antonia would enjoy the sight of Americans jumping around in football jerseys. I pulled into my friend Liege's drive and had obviously missed the memo as his house stood dark and silent in the crisp November evening. I called and Liege apologized for changing plans at the last minute, I laughed about it with Antonia as we drove over to my brother's house for drinks and dinner by the fire.

November 21 Monday

I went into the Fingerprint Portrait series I collected from Jen in New York City. I had three paintings from 2004 with palettes of red, orange and light blue. The new Fingerprint Portrait of Max has a yellow background, so I wanted to incorporate yellow into the existing paintings in order to unify the four works. This has become my rule but it works well, it is logical, and I've only done it with several paintings in my history. I changed the red sidewall on the blue background painting to yellow and I changed the blue fingerprint on the red background painting to yellow, which took hours and several washes. Then I changed the colors of the signatures, tweaked colors, cleaned edges up, mixed colors so they blended. I shot the modified paintings, color corrected the images and placed them in the archive. It was fussy business so it was a good day's work.

I ordered a frame from my frame wholesaler for the print that I sold at my Open House. I don't sell many hand signed, numbered prints, but it is a way for people to collect my work if they are not ready to spend money on an original painting.

When visiting yesterday, Antonia, who is constantly at Art

Fairs, pointed at one of my 24 x 30 Reconstructions and asked how much. I said between $1500 and $2000, then I asked her how much she thought it might sell for in the right market. She responded $5000, which confirms my continuing suspicions that I remain well under-priced. Friends who know art drop in here and there and remind me that my work is not priced high enough, but I sell and mostly don't split sales with a gallerist, so it has worked to this point in my career. When I do go with a gallerist my prices will be able to double with a little more exposure so the gallerist can get her 50% share for an inventory painting sale.

November 22 Tuesday

I spent the morning finishing Max's Fingerprint Portrait. After wiring, shooting, color correcting and archiving Max's painting I placed the four paintings in my truck and got on the road.

Traffic slowed to a crawl in three places driving into Manhattan, which cost me an extra half hour to get to 13th and 6th. I should have gone in on the West Side because the East Side was jammed. I parked out front of Jen's building with my hazards on and ran my work inside. The doorman was okay and told me to put my art on the rack. I introduced myself, told him I was just parking the car and would be back. I found a spot with a meter that was broken, which usually means you get a ticket anyway, and ran back into the building. I rolled the cart to the elevator and went up to the 9th floor. Judy the nanny was poking her head out expectantly. I introduced myself to Judy, parked the cart at the front door, walked the four paintings in and started hanging the three paintings back where they had been. The paintings were hard to hang because I could not stand on the glass table which came out two feet from the wall, but I got it done. The fourth painting went up on the facing wall as there was not enough room to run four paintings in a row.

I had not seen this space so I pulled out the camera and got some good shots for my press and website. These paintings look great in a nice two bedroom loft in New York City. I thanked Judy for her time, rolled the cart down the elevator to Jerry on the ground floor, shook his hand, ran back to my car and was off, into the Lincoln Tunnel traffic.

When you pop up onto the West Side Highway above the streets in the 50's that ride can be swift and sweet. I love driving out of the city on the West Side. It flows more and is a cleaner ride. On the FDR it's more like tight quarters and you are jockeying, doing battle with cars around you, with all sorts of quick on ramps and off ramps in tunnels underneath buildings that were built to the edge of the East River. The FDR is windier with pot holes and the drivers are more pissed off, more aggressive. I have two hands on the wheel when I drive the FDR, and that's rare.

I got out of town and back to my studio to clean the office up and think about the rest of the week, the next paintings, the next projects. I emailed my new collector Robin about delivering the 'Mother and Child' painting she reserved, and she came back saying that she really wanted the 'Central Park' picture, which is 3 times the price. I have another collector for the 'Mother and Child,' so I suggested she reserve the 'Central Park' and I can approach my other collectors about the 'Mother and Child.' She liked this idea, so I may have sold another painting today.

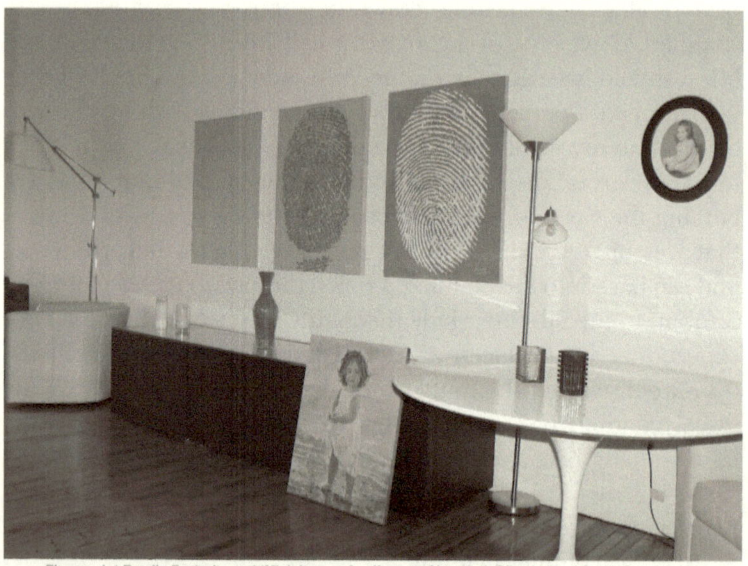

Fingerprint Family Portraits and 'Mia', home of collectors, New York City, 2011. ©SandyGarnett.com

November 23 Wednesday

I am feeling the flow of studio right now, which is the best place for me to be. There are paintings moving in and out, there is maintained interest by friends and collectors returning from years of projects on hold, elements of my office are coming into order. It could be a year's end that is peaceful and not pressing.

I picked up twelve thick stretcher bars for my friend Pierce's triptych commission and returned to pound them into three stretchers. Two of the biggest mistakes that people make when stretching canvas is they allow stretchers to lose their right angles and they often allow their canvases to warp. It is important to be plodding and methodical when stretching canvas.

I painted after lunch into the evening. All of the preliminary work is done, the composition is established, so my collector has a general sense of what he has signed on for. He wants my water, my sky, my landscape, my sense of movement, all these things I get to play with in his paintings. The project will be good fun, but I want counterbalance with another pet project that I have been holding back on, which always injects exciting energy into the studio.

November 24 Thursday

Last night I sent an email to my new collector Jeffrey, making him aware that the collector who had reserved 'Mother and Child' had chosen to buy the 'Central Park' painting, leaving 'Mother and Child' if he wanted it. I gave him the same price and flexible terms on installments. This morning I awoke to a painting sale. Effectively I sold the 'Central Park' painting this week and resold 'Mother and Child.'

I went into the triptych for four hours of peace and quiet, getting paint on the canvas, making a horizon line, painting whites and grays and blues into the sky. I started to move the clouds around, find some motion, pop some highlights, build some depth as the sun peeled through my southern arched window and made yellow spears of light that grew longer on the maroon carpet in front of my easel. The canvas that I stretched yesterday is okay, with a little bit of a dry tooth or texture, so I had to butter the surface up with plenty of paint. I don't like toothy canvases when I am painting representationally as the tooth slows the drag on my brushes, which can frustrate my process when I light the easel up with fast motion. Toothy, dry canvases are excellent for my veil paintings, when I drip sheets of colors and single drips plinko through the grid of teeth into very intricate patterns that a hand could never create.

Oh yes, Happy Thanksgiving. I went over to my parents' home and we had a nice Thanksgiving lunch, then on to my aunt Stepanie's for an evening Thanksgiving with my cousins. I am going to Vermont tomorrow, so we discussed projects and the foot of snow Chester got while cousin Steve was working up there this week to get the hearth in. It will be good to get away with my brothers and cousins this weekend.

November 25 Friday

Holidays are reflective when I'm not on a hamster wheel, running for my life, about to be thrown off. I have had a rash of luck lately, just enough to relax the prickly spines on my back in order to hit the road for a weekend in Vermont.

November 26 Saturday

We were up early into the chill of Vermont morning. Reyn made egg sandwiches while Matt packed up because he has to get home to the family this afternoon. We wandered to the big old barn and looked at a section of floor Steve wants to replace. After cleaning this area up for an hour it was resolved to remove the three floors that have been stacked on top of one another over the decades. Steve got the saw out and cut away the 9 x 16 foot floor, which groaned and collapsed into the open dirt ground ten feet below.

I climbed down and took a ladder to the other side. There were two beams facing each other that we could build off of, but one had a round face with only 4 inches of purchase, so I resolved that we should screw on a flat 2 x 12. We cut down an old 2 x 12 and got that in place, then ran 2 x 4's the length of both facing beams. This allowed us to cut 101 inch 2 x 7's and lay them on top of the 2 x 4's before hammering three or four nails per end into the foundation beams. We cut some twenty inch spacers so we didn't have to use a tape measure with each new cross beam.

This process took us from 9 am until 5 pm or so. I was on a ladder all day and the ground beneath the ladder was completely uneven and muddy, so it was a real core workout. I couldn't rely on any beam to hang on really, as I was busy building the skeleton of a floor with Steve, Reyn and Reyn's friend Mike, who pulled in at 1pm. My brother Christian pulled in at 4 pm and they went to shoot clays while Steve and I worked to finish the floor framing. The end got a little tricky but I got her done, tacking into one of the large beams under the barn to solidify the floor framing. I was swinging a hammer all day from odd directions, so the last nails went in slow, my arm not working right, missing the nail heads at the very end down below, a dead arm swinging in darkness, apologizing to cousin Steve, who tried to be patient as he watched me miss the last two nail heads while making fun of myself and telling him, "Almost there."

Once the bones were in strong, Steve and I rapidly laid down the sub-floor, finding barn board in varying widths. We found long sections and when that was done we screwed them all in. Reyn, Mike and Christian returned so the last section of floor was a team effort. I used the circular saw to cut odd angles and drop in the remaining sections of 48 inches that finished the floor while Mike screwed them down, Reyn and Christian fed us barn board and Steve laid down the wood as he liked.

The sub-floor complete, we went right in again on the top floor, this time laying boards across the short side to where the trim cap will go to conceal the old floor meeting the new floor. We kept the same system going, so I was on the circular saw cutting strange patterns on the fly that fit in closely to the end pieces of the old barn floor boards. We were done by 8 pm and celebrated by putting the tractor onto our new floor along with the wood chipper and two lawn mowers.

There is nothing like manual labor with people you get along with. We're a bunch of goons, so working together like a sports team is in our DNA. We got the job done and it felt great, one of my favorite projects, one of my favorite days of 2011.

The evening was spent eating and laughing around the wood stove, listening to music, playing with Handsome, Steve's golden retriever, reveling in a day well spent, talking about family and friends. I have never spent a full day working with Reyn, which was fun, and Christian has never been to the farm, so this was cool. I've done a number of projects with Steve and we work like animals together, feeding off of each other, the chemistry of good workers. I enjoy construction stuff, carpentry stuff, which is a combination of thinking, problem solving, math, manual labor, an assortment of tools, a finished product at the end of the day. Today was just what I needed, up at the farm with my cousins.

November 27 Sunday

We were up and off early after cleaning the place up and shutting everything down. I was sore from being on a ladder in challenging positions for 10 hours, a good sore, although this made me feel like a wimp, like I should do some core workouts when not playing racquetball.

The fog from the snow burned off by Brattleboro so the rest

of the drive home was clear and fluid. On the highway I chanced upon Steve's truck and followed it most of the way home. We hadn't started out together but this happens when driving home from Vermont with brothers and cousins. There was a steady stream of traffic coming home from Vermont, Maine, New Hampshire. You could tell by the cars, trucks, school stickers, ski racks, the nature of the drivers, the style of the driving. I was on the ocean again with Linda Greenwald, listening to her book, "Seaworthy." She had some tough luck coming out of retirement to captain a sword season. Some things are just out of our hands in life.

I got back in the early afternoon and spent the rest of the day puttering around the seascape and painting another Garnett figure in a clearing that came into my mind last night while sleeping. I received an email from a prospect in London I have not worked with who wants to buy a painting that I placed years ago, so maybe I can make a new collector.

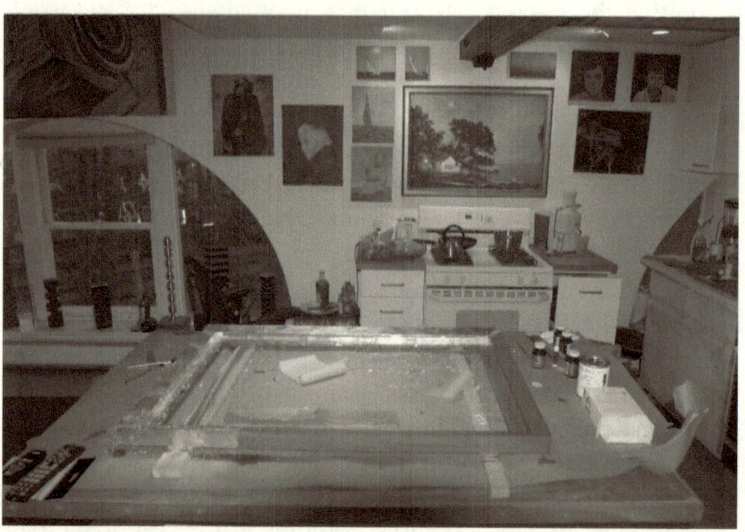

November 28 Monday

Today I did research on gold-leafing the frame I designed and had my friend Steve make last week for my recently sold 'Woman in Landscape.' She's going in a fairly formal room, but she's contemporary enough, so I created a simple floater frame which exposes the paintings edges with the thought of a traditional gold frame. I watched documentary films in the background as I often do around the studio, around the easel. I worked on the kitchen island I designed and made, which is a great work table on wheels. When I was satisfied with the gold coverage I used a satin sealant that I painted on and left for several hours to dry or cure. Then I pulled out the antiquing medium, which is the color of burnt umber. I painted this on like I was painting a picture, trying to create the vibe of an antique frame. The effect worked nicely. When this layer dried I flipped the frame over, piloted four drill holes in the back, flipped the frame back over, aligned the painting in its place, and screwed the painting into the frame. I wired the painting for hanging, then I placed the painting on the easel and shot it several times. By early evening I was looking at the first frame I had designed and gold-leafed. I don't want to do this all the time, but it's good to know how to gold leaf a frame.

November 29 Tuesday

I moved the triptych downstairs to force my own hand. It can get cushy upstairs, and although I am always working I don't putter as much in the basement studio. It's all art all day long, and with all the lights off except for the easel I can zone into the canvas at hand, let my imagination take a ride. I don't have a choice. I have to hit the ball out of the park this week. There is no let up. I feel like I just sold a bunch of work but art is asking me, "What have you done for me lately?"

I turned the easel lights on and sat in the chair, looking at my meal ticket for the next several weeks, my truth serum that I have placed it in the lion's den. The under-painting is convincing but it is flat; a pale sky tumbling around, a tree line of land on either side, Long Island shooting the gap in the distance, some boat sketches in the foreground. The painting is at once foreboding and inviting. I've been here on this side of a canvas a thousand times before, for commission or sport or passion or to woo a collector, charm a woman, cover the monthly expenses to run this old ship. The only rule is that I can't cheat myself, my studio, or my collector. I have been handed this trust to deliver, so deliver I will.

Deep space, the space that can be found in the best representational landscapes, nautical pictures, or abstract paintings for that matter, rely on a type of spatial meditation that I find most interesting. I just sold three Reconstruction paintings that are veil-like in their appearances, layers of color washing in and out of a quasi-representational narratives, so one's mind can go representational or abstract. I find plenty of parallels between Rothko, for example, and some of the best nautical pictures, regardless of the ancillary elements that might root let's say a Hudson River school painting in the 'representational' realm.

I let the triptych flow into my psyche, and herein the space began to emerge. I will be here for a week on this picture unless a blast completes it in a day. You never know. Sometimes a painting takes a day and sometimes it takes a month. I am pretty good at handicapping myself on the time-line, a lot of which requires the discipline to cut myself off from other projects in order to focus on a primary target in the studio.

November 30 Wednesday

In the morning I got over to the monument shop, brushed off a cooler that would be my seat, and started in on an etching of the Holy Family above the family name of a very large black granite gravestone. I etched half of the image quickly, holding a light in my left hand, the etching needle in my right, music playing in my earphones, my jackhammer headphones on top of the earphones to keep all the sound out. It's nice to etch or make any type of visual art for that matter with music playing in the background.

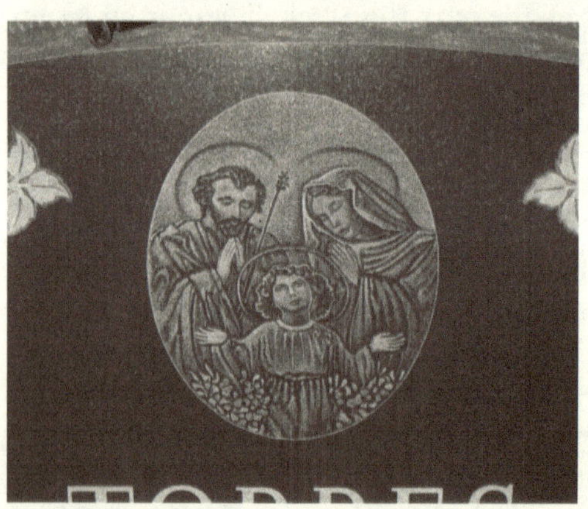

I returned to my studio and did some office work over lunch, playing with a song that has been stuck in my head for a year. The melody and the parts are all there, but I need to apply myself to get it out of me. I have an acoustic version with an intro and vocals throughout, but this one song is a raunchy sort of rock song that requires studio effort, specific passages, a bunch of instruments. Boy, it sounds great in my head, but like my song 'Busted Wing,' like any solid work, this one will require TLC.

I spent the afternoon in the basement studio, working on printing, matting and framing when I wasn't falling into the nautical painting that goes to Houston as soon as I am finished. I deepened the sky, threw the middle ground tree-line back as well, and started thinking about drawing one's eye into the picture with light sea caps in the foreground. I like the sky as it is but I will have to adjust the sky once the foreground detail is down. Tomorrow will be a detail day, when my focus will be all about the bay and the boats and the description of trees and moving water. I like where the painting is going but I want to bring a sense of urgency to the work. It's coming.

December 1 Thursday

I was up early and my brain has been exploding for several hours. Sometimes I am a laser beam of focus and sometimes I am so inspired by every idea and surrounding media that I can't settle on one thing to bite into. This is an exhilarating vibration that occurs frequently, but it is not the most productive.

I have to channel this inspiration, which sometimes feels like a bore. I have to apply this inspiration to the triptych, at least for five hours today. I have to let this inspiration find its way into the landscape and sky and boats and rolling water. I can play in the evening, but today I need to focus this thing.

This feeling, this type of inspiration, is what I live for. It's a euphoric sensation of limitless possibilities in the strictly creative sense. This sensation does not equate to the highs and lows of lets say a manic episode, which I have read about and seen with friends first hand. It's a sustained vibration that can run for hours, days, weeks in some cases. The further out financial concerns go, the longer these periods can last... where art is sitting there on every branch to pluck at will. I think a lot of this also has to do with a fluidity of mediums I have attained. I remember the absolute frustration of trying to paint something that I couldn't quite do properly. Music may be like this for me now, but I can compose and I have a computer so I don't need to be a master of instrumentation; I can piece songs together. Painting isn't like this. You can't 'piece' a nice composition together if you are not fluent in whatever it is you are trying to make. There's not really a correlation here. Welcome to the free range brain on a creative inspiration high.

December 2 Friday

Yesterday my energy could not focus. It was a fire hose and kept spraying in all sorts of directions, the velocity too strong to hold in one place for long. It was a fun ride though, and I got some sketches down. I wrote a nice set of lyrics, came up with another melody for a song, I cleaned the studio, I got a little painting in. I finished the Holy Family etching as well, so that was decent work.

I tinkered most of today like yesterday. Some days are blasts and some days are tinkering days.

December 3 Saturday

I got an email from an interior design firm that may have placed one of my paintings they have had for several years in their warehouse. They asked about the percentage and I pulled out the written agreement, which is a good note for all artists. It is important to keep written agreements handy because when you have a lot of art you are bound to have art in different places. Some art hangs around with agents for awhile, people change jobs, move around, so it is good to have the paperwork. This painting is my first Hand print Portrait from 1998, so it could be a nice sale that would fill in the blanks of December and allow me to focus on January and February art placements.

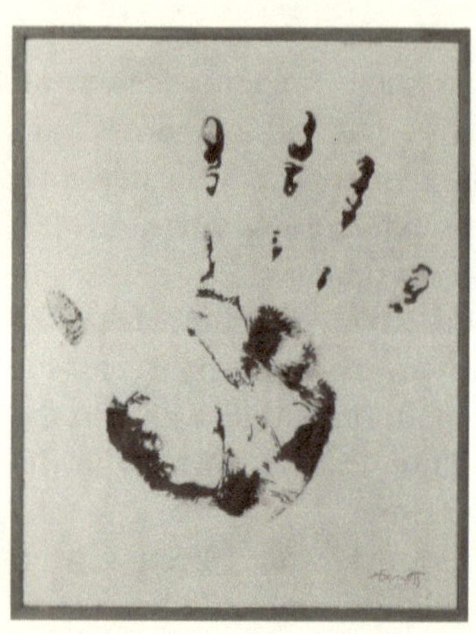

December 4 Sunday

For me the answer has always been to make a self-sufficient vessel and set sail. My job requires that I remain cautiously optimistic, that I stay healthy in body, mind, spirit, that I work hard every day, that I send out good messages and strong art that moves people to support me into the next time frame. I try to give more than I receive, I try to live simply and be prolific, I try to live in the solution always, I try to never take things personally, live by my word, and stay positive in good days and in bad. I try to be a good family member, a decent member of the community, a good friend for people to confide in, an upstanding citizen in general. I have been living my dream for decades by making art for a living. I try to live without want. I try to live in complete gratitude.

December 5 Monday

I wanted to crush the triptych, but I have learned that as an artist I cannot force my inspiration. This is the paradox of self-imposed deadlines. The closer I get to a deadline often times the more my spirit will resist it. When there is no deadline my inspiration runs free as long as I am coming from the right place.

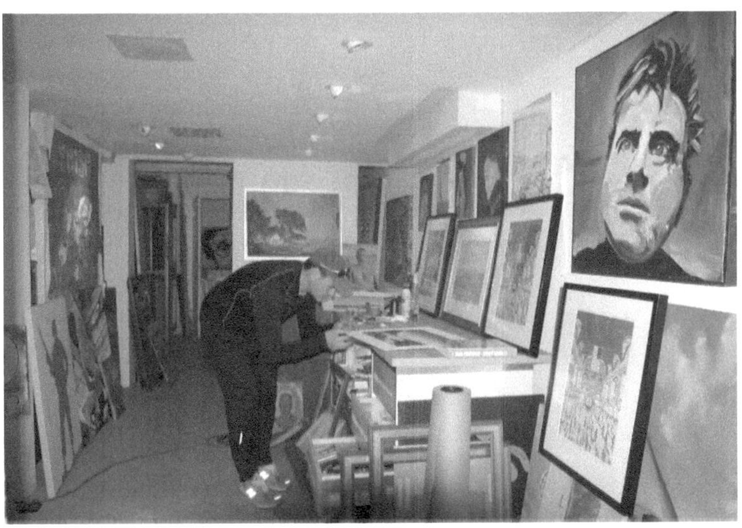

I made some archival prints, matted and framed them this morning for collectors who bought them during my open studios. I got to work on the triptych as well, making some nice progress towards the end of the day on the foreground and the water in the painting. I did not hit the ball out of the park on the painting, but I showed up, I hit some singles and doubles and a couple sparks flew. Half the battle is just showing up every day, and you never know what's going to happen. Tomorrow could be a good fireworks show if my heart is playful.

December 6 Tuesday

I split games with Matt this morning. We are both making errors but our serves and ball placements have improved this year.

I took the 'Woman in Landscape' painting whose frame I gold-leafed over to Ellen at 10:30 am and installed it quickly for her, as I always offer to do for collectors. Her painting needs a light to pop, which she brought up. Many paintings get lost without lights on them. She was happy, mission accomplished.

I got some paint on the nautical picture, darkening the water, clarifying the boats, making some new boats, pushing the background sky deeper into the recesses of the canvas. As a painting evolves all the springs of composition get pulled back one by one until a taught composition is arrived at. A cloud up here in the left corner talks to the land mass on the right, the waves in the center canvas swirl into the top right frame of the triptych, one blue affects a green, which bounces off the cloud canopy and back again onto the sea in another place. In the case of this painting, as the sky is complete, all I really have to do is focus on a one foot by five foot strip of water, bringing it alive one sitting at a time. Since my references are all over the place I have to make it up as I go along, so I'm painting my own sea, I'm tweaking my own composition, light, color, I'm making my own boats up in the bay that have to talk to each other while moving with the water on their moorings.

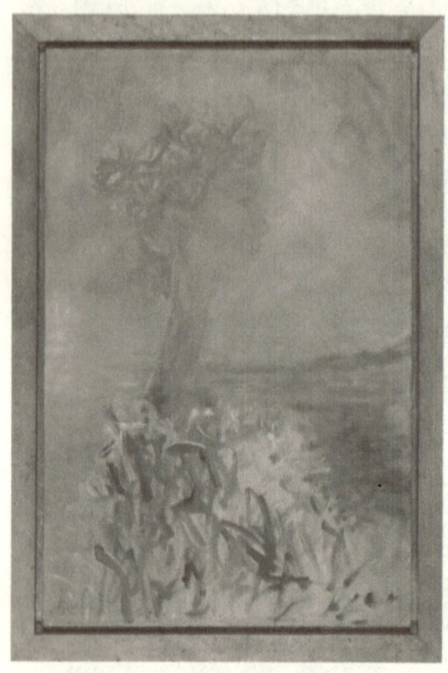

December 7 Wednesday

I spent the afternoon into evening painting the sea, making new boats, bouncing light and color around the canvas, painting the sides of the canvases. I didn't get into detail as much as spatial nuance and atmospherics today. I am fighting a cold and my energy level is low, so I'm not running at full capacity. When I am not at full capacity I let it happen, rather than forcing a square peg in a round hole. Art energy is strange stuff, so I honor the art energy or risk its wrath.

My energy is resting and meditative for something else that is coming into my world, but I don't know what this thing is. I'm burned out on editing books as I have spent probably 1000 hours doing that this year. I'd like to paint other canvases but my rule is to only paint the triptych until the painting is completed, an effective restriction I employ when I impose a deadline upon myself.

Steve brought the crate I designed over for the Houston paintings. I tried not to cough on him while I wrote a check for his crate-making time and I made him laugh before he went to dinner with his wife. If I can make someone who is helping me laugh then that person will never have a problem helping me out the next time, so long as I'm fair and respectful.

December 8 Thursday

I am sitting here looking at the water lap over the boats in the painting that is emerging. Everything feels right compositionally, so now I put detail in and continue to work the depth of the water back into the distance, where little triangular wedges of white will read like the racing sails I intend them to be. My mind is blank behind this painting, which is good. I forced myself to do nothing else, or suddenly I might be carving a piece of marble, sculpting a Twister figure, building another floor with my cousins, editing another book, painting another canvas.

Evening. The art of procrastination is an unfavorable subject for the prolific creator, yet is a common theme that binds all humans together. I milled around today, working on other things while absorbing the evolving canvases, making an effort to not paint anything else. Part of my play is that I am holding the next fruit in my hand and don't want to release it yet, because I know I have an asset and I don't know what's on the other side. Then there is the perfectionist in me, hemming and hawing about the microdynamics of composition, then there is the finishing agent in me, skittishly moving around the picture and finding the right places to dive in. Paintings can come together faster when intellect is not involved and I just get into the meat of the painting. Herein lies the distinction between strong commissioned work and strong work that I do for myself. Both creatures are equally relevant to the studio for different reasons. The best commissions are struck out upon quickly as if they are not commissions, so they can come together by riding the Id of my creative impulses. When commissions brush up against whatever else I require in life to maintain my studio, a moral dilemma ensues and intellect encroaches on the project. This does not make for a weaker painting or art object but the process becomes more difficult for me in the sense that I have to consciously evade any shortcuts or angles which might lessen the work at hand. This of course is the mind-game of a professional painter.

I have stewed about the triptych for a week now, looking, plucking away on the paintings like they are delicate flowers as opposed to sturdy spiritual supports that can absorb any blasts I toss at them. I know this feeling very well yet I am not often elucidating my sentiments and intellect on the subject. The fact of the matter is that I have time to make this work the way I want it before I ship it off. I am enjoying the creation but I want it gone at the same time. This residue will be felt in the painting's lifetime, so I have to give it respect. I have other things to do, sure, more mountains to climb, but currently I am on the endgame of this painting that has logged my journal for a week, so I might as well write about it.

December 9 Friday

I sent out an email blast to my list and spent the day doing correspondence, fielding the emails that came in from all over the place. I spent an hour painting, then an hour doing correspondence, and repeated the pattern all day. Correspondence is good energy for the studio, it inspires me, gives me new ideas, new sales. My friend R.J. checked in and wants to go ahead with a Fingerprint Portrait of his daughter. My old friend Dave checked in and wants a painting next year. Another friend is interested in a sculpture, I had some people check in about my books and music.

Towards the end of the day I lobbed an email at a potential new collector who had balked on the price of a 24 x 30 inch portrait of his wife and two dogs. Maybe we could do a smaller size, I suggested in the email. I asked what his budget was and he responded quickly. We went back and forth for two or three emails, which got friendlier and more jovial. We arrived at an agreement that I will do a 16 x 20 inch oil portrait by early January so he will be able to fulfill this birthday surprise he has in mind. Very quickly we got into all sorts of subjects; cars, planes, the Pacific Northwest, mountain climbing, a book called 'Deep Survival' I suggested he read, given to me by a collector who figured I would appreciate such a book. I did. Collectors share common interests with me and enjoy the engagement as much as I do, generally. Sure, I have to sell art, but if I'm not making art or selling it I enjoy talking about art or cool subjects with like-minded people.

By the end of the day I had done some painting, correspondence with forty collectors and friends, my website had been visited by 100 people, I had picked up two commissions, and I had run two grand in credit card transactions that came out of nowhere.

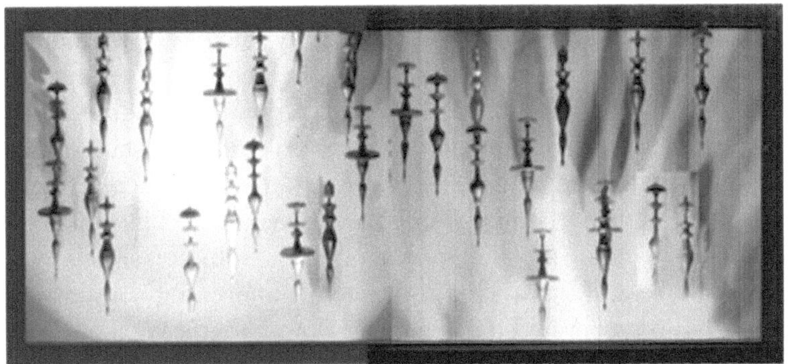

December 10 Saturday

It was my niece Emma's first birthday party, which was a blowout. Many family members have not seen her, so it was an occasion for a good-sized party at the home of my parents. I took an airplane and parachute guy over so Jackson could play with those things and not get bored by all of his sister's present opening.

Cousins Jen and Brooke brought their friend Brian over to look at art. He's interested in some of my best art objects. He likes my Field of Figures sculpture, so we talked about creating a unique environment out of steel and lighting for a particular space he has in mind. This is my favorite type of work, when collectors support the expansion of my vocabulary on more ambitious projects. He also likes some of my early Reconstructions that I don't want to part with, so we'll see where the dialogue goes.

December 11 Sunday

Last night I had seven people over and we got it going in the basement space. I pulled out a ton of work, I had three people painting on canvases, music, drinks, and good energy flowed. A handful of my brushes were left outside of water so they froze in acrylic and are done for. No matter. Brushes are a dime a dozen, even if they are ten bucks each. People will remember painting in my studio. I like entertaining once in awhile when people are in the mood with the right sorts of spirits who appreciate what I do. It's rare and good to get this type of positive energy in the studio.

December 12 Monday

I saw a job listing for an oil painting commission. I responded to the post and the poster got back to me today. He wants a 30 x 40 inch oil painting of a nude woman, I cannot take reference photos, he is not put off by the fact that my studios are 45 minutes outside of Manhattan, the subject will be here for a week at the end of January. If he books me I will prepare the painting, the under-painting, the setting, the repose. I might use a stand-in, or perhaps the subject will be fine with a photo reference if she is clothed. If I take a commission I have to make sure I have time to hammer the figure and the portrait out if the subject is sitting right there for several days. This could be an interesting commission and it would cover my studio expenses for a month. We'll see if he comes back to me.

I drove up to New Haven at the end of the day to deliver Jeffrey's 'Mother and Child' painting and the framed print he and his wife recently purchased. They are way up the line and he had a meeting in New Haven at 6 pm, so I was happy to meet him halfway, shake his hand, present him with art, and thank him for keeping me at the easel this winter. There are some other paintings they like, so I look forward to their next visit.

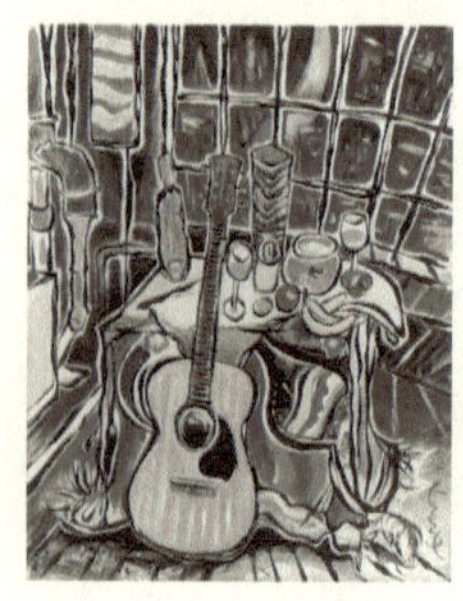

December 13 Tuesday

A collector who reserved a painting checked and wants to give me a deposit, so I might run up to Westchester and pick that up today. The sale last week cooled me out on the triptych, so I have to ramp that finish up again. I am enjoying living with my new painting, but I have to get this one off the easel to make way for the next paintings and sculptures.

There is a flow to my studio that I have not really felt all year, or for years I should say. There are people returning to me who froze projects as far back as 2007. I'm not holding my breath, but there could be a slight change in the winds.

December 14 Wednesday

Today I sat with 16 seniors around a circle of desks in my cousin Steve's English class at Brunswick and fielded questions about what it's like to be a professional artist. I talked about art making, writing, books, music, running a studio, the sacrifices, all sorts of things. I think I entertained some of the students and the hour was positive for everyone. I passed out books that they could look through while I was talking to them. I didn't have these books last year. I mean, I had some of them, but now I have a full arsenal to cover the gamut, which is empowering.

I would like to learn how to sell books eventually. If I have ten books this could begin to subsidize my studio. Rather than being far fetched, I find this goal to be practical, logical and manageable. If I have some niche perennials, like *Baloney*, like *The Rainbow Riders*, these books could continue giving back to the studio in a way that selling a painting once and only once cannot. With some decent titles in hand I might ultimately attract publishing or distribution partners, which would keep me focused on the studio as a gallerist would keep me focused on the studio.

December 15 Thursday

I picked up two games on my brother today. He was frustrated, thinking about other stuff. I just had to fend off his frustration and not buckle. It's easy for me to lose my head and let him pick up a couple points. He never does the same with me, he relishes being relentless when he's got my number, so I took a page from his book this morning and finished him off.

Yesterday I made some sense of the piles of bills, manila folders, ideas, business cards, handwritten scribbles, daily to-do lists, that have landscaped my desk for a good while. This morning I drilled down, cleared my desk and in so doing my mind. We all know what this feels like, but I can't reiterate the joy of sitting here and looking at a clean slate, an empty desk.

With my studio in order to such a degree I am thinking about organizing other thoughts, ideas, while I'm in this productive phase. My lyrics could stand some organizing, I could put together a book of my sculptures quickly enough as I have several people interested in supporting my sculpture work next year. Another book takes me back to color correcting my art catalogs and editing, detail work. When I get here I just want to hammer in some more tent poles while the energy, which is self-spun and self-perpetuating, stays around for a couple days and is hot.

December 16 Friday

People often ask me what I would do if I could do anything

I wanted, and my answer trends towards the stock response of, "I make art for a living, my art has bought my home and work place, my inventory is growing, I have built a business that has lasted for twenty years, so for the most part I already do what I want." I suppose they mean more specifically what would I focus on if I could focus my creativity on anything I wanted for an extended period of time? I'm not sure. I'd like to do larger, stranger things, but I need patronage for these sorts of institutionally and high art market-collected projects.

My archive in place for preservation and presentation, my studios bought and renovated, my small business system running even on the fumes for three years after our historic market crash, I am happy to report that I have built a small vessel with a broad beam that can take a beating and continue to move in the direction that my stubborn rudder takes it in. I continue to live the dream of making art for a living, which is about the best consolation when part of me wonders if I could be doing better, making more ambitious things, reaching deeper into the art historical zeitgeist, turning more heads to gain more support, not for my decimated ego but for the hope of making larger art statements in my time.

Larger art statements? Perhaps not. It's surprising how invigorating it feels to sit on top of the first 1000 paintings I have made, fifty a year for twenty years, 600 of which are sold, a hundred of which I have painted over or destroyed, the rest living comfortably in my inventory. Have you painted 1000 pictures by your own hand, that you did not farm out to worker bees? A lot of big guys become art producers and don't always touch their own work. I don't take issue with that so much, because taking issue with something outside of me does not reinforce the granite foundations I have created while no one else was looking. I always wanted to build a castle with turrets, a drawbridge and a moat. I have that now.

I guess I could get my swagger on and start crossing swords in larger arenas, but I have always believed that this will come in time. Will it come in my lifetime? I don't care right now, and I usually don't care in general. If I did care I would have taken the first flea-bitten share in the East Village after school, worked the music scene while I did commercial work, maybe tried my hand at modeling for five minutes because people said I could make a lot of money at that, hustle to cover a rent that was too big for my britches, chase after the art scene. I didn't do this. I resisted the urge, so perhaps I missed a glorious window of post-college youth that could have been great, working full-time 'not painting' to subsidize 10-20 weekly hours of painting for years in hopes of achieving a show that might get me in deeper.

I never looked for an 'in' that was not inside of me.

I stayed on the fringes of New York City, 30 miles away in Stamford, Connecticut, living in a commercial space, painting for every penny of my rent and existence and happiness and torture and everything else that life has to offer. My life plan has been simple in a complex world where there are temptations at every turn; fast money, beautiful women, pinning hopes on a dream of wild success which often has nothing to do with creative breakthroughs that occur in the solitude of one's peaceful space. I could have bent to the moderate pressures of society's suggestion that I ought to consider a more practical calling in order to find a nice girl and make a family, which I tried to do in my early twenties before I knew how to paint. I hammered it out, painting by painting, collector by collector, chiseling a world brick by brick that can cruise in quiet winds and survive when the shit starts blowing hard, knocking over buildings, the seas rising, taking out market segments and 401k's and family dreams. Life is simple if you make it that way, pushing the skeletons out of the closet and keeping the closet open so more skeletons don't pile up in there. I try to live by my word, by my art, by the only name I have, by honor, which might sound silly but that's in the genes. Work hard, play hard, honor, dignity, no regrets, these things burned into me since youth. This does not make the conquering kind necessarily, because I don't have a chip on my shoulder to make bigger and defend. I don't care what people think of what it is that I do. I have made one believer at a time, and now there is a pretty chorus that sings me to sleep or supports me if I need it.

With a little support my vehicle runs strong. I am a mechanic of the first rate on my engine. A lot of engines are bright and flashy and fast, but these things come with scruples. My engine does not. I try to pay as I go. I am not tortured by my past, I try to live cleanly in the present, when faced with strange energies, which fly at all of us every day in our own ways, I do my best to function with grace, humor, get through the tough spots and never burn a bridge. A strong engine, a strong mechanic, these are elements to a winning, long combination; to live well with time, to have no regrets, to seize the day and sleep well at night, to get up and do it again. I just want to get up and do it again, better, bigger, stronger, with the layers of experience and wisdom underneath me in everything that I make, in every breath I breathe. When the time comes to depart this planet I only hope that I can look back at this entry and say that I continued on this path, that this wisdom allowed me to live young deep into old age. I made friends with time many moons ago, and one thing I've learned is that the turtle can catch the hare in a marathon, even if the hare is holding the trophy.

Although my life is not one of luxury, my mind lives in the luxury of my own creation, with no boss, no system that I have to mold myself into, and the more I live the more people ask me about how I have managed to do what I have done, live a life by my creativity.

The more I live my dream the more it all makes sense to me. I have lived my dream by forging it, against many odds, casting away negative energy, running on my gut inspiration, simple living, hard working, honor bearing. The more one creates and lives one's vision, the more tangential things fall away. If I listened to all the advice people gave to me starting out I would not be making art for a living. I had to believe in myself and prove myself over and over a thousand times, ten thousand times, by living in the solution of a creative project, a personal dilemma, an emotional loss, a family tragedy, all lining the thing that is me, this thing that contains me. Now, with many inner circles and smoothly functioning mechanisms, I spin what I want. I know I am a good man, I am an upstanding citizen, I pay my way by my art, I have the love and respect of family, friends, collectors, fellow artists I respect back, art admirers, an audience. I make fun of myself every day because my ego was never the point. If I had clung to the egotistical elements that are a part of every living human I would have perished, or I would have turned out bitter by now. I stand on my own two feet, on the shoulders of my inner and outer councils, these people who love and trust what I do, these people who believe in me, these people who wonder how I stay alive in this brutal game of art making that takes no prisoners and crashes them up on the rocks in foul weather storms. One has to develop a field vision that is on this planet and not of this planet. One has to develop senses that ride underneath the surface, because this is where most of the world operates, in some spiritual realm that is much deeper than the six o'clock news stories that clutter and manipulate the mind. Who has time for these diversions? A clean spirit does not have time for these diversions. I tried it. Tracking news and arguing the perspectives gained by listening to the thoughts of others is not about making the dream.

Central Park, oil on canvas, 24x48 inches, 2011, cat20111034, ©sandygarnett.com

December 17 Saturday

I drove to Bedford to meet with my new collector Robin. Her house was tucked up a long driveway into a rambling, warm and interesting hillside home. She brought me inside and took me around to see her art. The wood stove was roaring and there was someone asleep on the couch. Robin waved this person away after I asked if this was her daughter. "No, my sister. Don't worry about her. She's covered. She worked late last night." A pillow covered her head, but I felt like I was interrupting her sleep.

In the sun room off in the corner I found my 'Woman by the Sea' hanging. The light is great on this painting. Robin gave me a deposit for the 'Central Park' painting she reserved, I handed her a receipt and was on my way. I have to frame that picture for late January delivery.

Robin was interested in my goal to make a Flag Totem, and I suggested that maybe she could subsidize a small version that I can turn around and sell in large format to a collector next year. This is a continuing example of my interest in three-dimensionalizing two-dimensional symbology, objects that talk about portraiture and identity; fingerprints, silhouettes, signatures, flags, the list is endless, a lifetime of creativity in this series alone that is universal and should already be supported on a broader scale.

I talked to my old friend and new collector Leslie via email about three Fingerprint Portraits I will be doing for her next year.

I have some nice energy in the studio right now. My studio is floating, which is different from being swept away by the current, and also different from hitting the cover off the ball. As an art survivalist in this economy I have to choose my battles carefully, not get hung up on the small stuff, not beat myself up if I'm not pressing the outer envelope of art every day. I did prepare the spec work for a Signature Totem, which was thrilling. Here is an example of a series I have wanted to make for a decade but have not been able to fund. Some day.

December 18 Sunday

I painted in the morning and received a call from my buddy Bruce's phone around lunchtime.

"Bruce?" I asked.

"No, it's Peter." Peter is Bruce's son, who is six and who I recently drew Rainbow Riders for at Bruce's dinner party.

"Do you want me to come over and draw Rainbow Riders Peter?" I asked.

"Yes, my brother and I want you to come over. I am reading this name Alexander Garnett on my Dad's phone," Peter astutely noted.

"Yes, Alexander is my proper name but friends like you call me Sandy."

Eventually Peter's mother Pam got on the phone and laughed when I told her that Peter had called me about coming over to draw. This is a simple story that made my day in between painting sessions, family visits, and Sunday football.

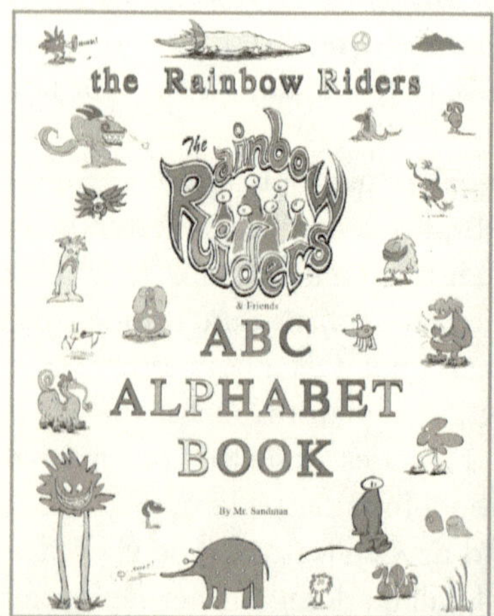

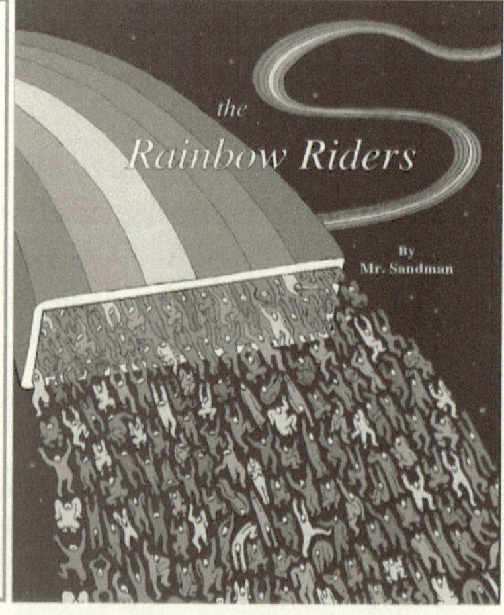

December 19 Monday

This morning I learned that my friend halfway around the world had hit his head on a hike, slipped into a coma and died. His brother Jim died five or six years ago, also a friend of mine. Life is not fair and can be very cruel. My old friend leaves a wife and family behind. There was chatter on the social networks this morning between a lot of my sad friends who were touched by Dave over the years, who had a passion for life, friendship, music, adventure. He will be missed.

I did some office work today and got a little painting in, but I was not very inspired. Some days artists are motivated and sometimes they are not. I could not catch the chain on any gears, so I waded through the day, depressed to think about all the heavy hearts I know, learning about their friend or family member who had died. I worked on the oil sketch of a woman, dabbed at two paintings on my easel, I watched a flick, did some correspondence, but nothing for the highlight reel.

December 20 Tuesday

Last night I got an email from my old friend Andy, who spends time in Hawaii every year. He was on his surfboard, waiting for a wave in line with the other guys at dusk, when something hit his board and knocked him off of it. He held onto the nose of the board and pried it away from whatever had it (presumably a shark), he took a wave in on his stomach, went over the shallow reef and paddled 200 more yards over the trough to the light beams of cars shining on the water. His ankle leash had been hit, a translucent piece of material that flashed in the light, teeth marks and everything. I'm happy to hear that Andy is alright, he will surf again today and mathematically he's had his run-in with a shark in this lifetime, from an actuarial perspective.

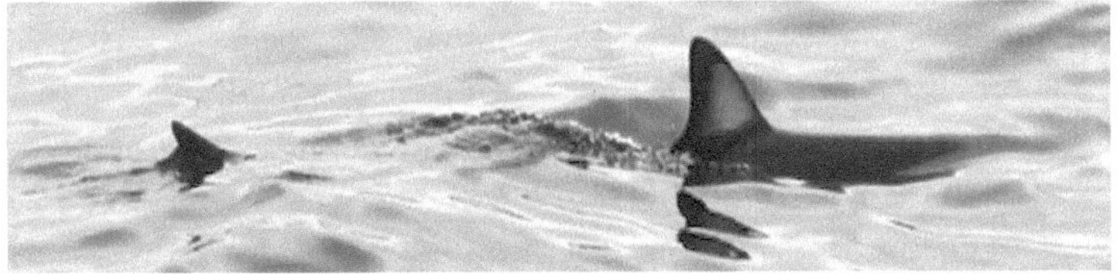

December 21 Wednesday

I was hanging around the easel all day, getting the conversation going with this painting. First the water started talking to the boats, then the boat masts started talking to the sky, then the sky was talking to the sails, corresponding with the light through the trees. A little color in the boats spoke back to the white caps in the water and so the circle continued to flow, as the boats painted themselves in and I just went along for the ride. I have a deadline, I talk to a painting, I argue with it, we bicker, I start to fall into her, stumbling around, we dance, we start to make music, I can't keep my hands off her, I'm intoxicated, I need more, nothing else will satisfy my hunger. This is how today went with my painting. She opened up, we gave each other good energy, we made a day to remember out of it. We'll still flirt tomorrow, but most of the work is done. You see, I didn't just copy something from a shoot I did. I mean, I did an informal shoot, sure, but a lot of things moved around. The sky was of my own making, Long Island had to change, the color of the water had to change, the wind had to change, and when I'm painting 50 boats I'm not looking at boats in twenty-five pictures. I make them up, for the most part. Each boat, each angulation, has to gel with adjacent shapes, colors, tones, micro-macro, small picture then big picture, from one canvas to three canvases. Here is one way to think about doing a quasi-representational work with a lot of detail involved.

This language is completely different from my approach to sculpting a Twister figure or painting a Fingerprint Portrait or composing a large Reconstruction Narrative or pre-figuring a monumental lawn sculpture with three hundred rocks or writing a page in this book. The romance can be similar, but every medium, every way of seeing, every genre has its own cadence, its own style, its own materials, its own time frame, a certain way that medium likes to be addressed, engaged with.

Mid-afternoon I went to another little portrait, which is not due until the first week in January, and got some paint on there. Unlike the triptych, which is about fussy detail and line and tonality and thin layers of paint, I unloaded paint on the 16 x 20 canvas upstairs and it made a nice vibration in my studio. There is a big difference between fudging around with 500 lines and color patches that have to ring together on a 60 inch wide triptych and a 16 x 20 portrait I have two weeks to mess around with. This is why first and foremost it is important to get familiar with a commission the moment it walks through the door. I spent an hour covering this little picture and it already has a bright, bold energy to it.

I got on a roll, so I went down to my basement studio, I took a 30 x 40 painting that just has some veils of color on it, I painted a nude figure and then washed her over three or four times. I took another canvas and painted a nude figure with large breasts leaning down. I had broken into a vibration where there was not enough canvas around for me. This energy is like a runaway train. I have spent many years living with this energy, although this year I have not exercised this daily dose rocket fuel because I focused on other priorites. More of my time has been about nipping, tucking, honing, archiving, writing, book design, editing. The energy I described just now? This energy is what I know well, what I live for, what has seen me through decades as a painter pirate.

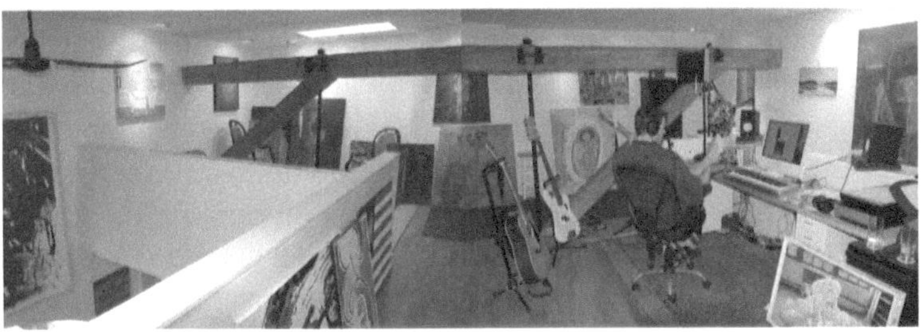

December 22 Thursday

Death is in the air of my studio this week. My friend David's birthday is today, this old friend who was a classmate of Matt's and loved by many. His life lives on in the social network, where people continue to check in and wish him Happy Birthday. I wrote a respectful email to his father, who has lost two sons.

One of my best friends from college lost his father yesterday, so a memorial is in order this weekend or next week. I remember when my grandmother died two days before Christmas when I was 13. That was a sad Christmas for my family, so I appreciate how death can add to the existing intensities of Family Holidays.

I feel like this year has been a setup year, a background year, behind the curtain, tinkering away at the studio engine that has been running full-bore for a long time. I peeled back the hood and gave the engine an overhaul of sorts, with a little more attention to the mechanics of mediums, the structure of the enterprise, some long ball that can be hard for a painter to tear himself away from the easel to focus on. Now I feel like the engine is driving cleaner and stronger, so next year I'd like to let her rip on the open road.

I picked up a Fingerprint Portrait commission today, which is coming in five years after the first three paintings from the same family. I think this painting was put on hold to weather the financial storm, another one that has come around.

December 23 Friday

I cleaned myself up and walked downstairs to my easel, wondering why it is that I belabor the finishing of some paintings. Why is this painting toying with me? Everything worked out nicely until the ending, when the painting got comfortable in my studio, in my heart, and now I don't want to see her off. I know she has to go, but there remain details I have left for the last tango, playing games with myself.

Not all paintings are like this. Some are flitty bang-outs, some are sweet, simple love affairs, some are tug-of-wars, some are catty. This painting's being catty... my creativity is playing smoke and mirrors with me. I want to put my hard hat on and bang out the problems, as I am capable of doing, but not in this compositional setup. If I take my hard hat into this type of painting the bull in the china shop will splinter the crystal vases all lined up on shelves just so. This picture is a trio of math, and you can't mess with certain equations. It's a clean, solid, well crafted picture where the detail elements beckoning me only serve to obscure the nature of the picture. This sounds complex because it is. I want the boats to be blobs of paint, simpletons, as the exercise of space is more exciting, but this is primarily a representational picture, so I can't get too abstract. When I get back ten feet the painting is done. When I am up at it from two feet away the painting is not done. So how to finish the painting from two feet that is already done at ten feet?

This is a minor example of my past 1000 paintings. Every genre has its rules for a tasteful painter, which I am. Plenty of painters out there can spin cheese on a plate to good effect. A big part of being a good painter, a good designer, architect, writer, composer... is learning what to do away with. Bells and whistles often mask the particular weaknesses of an art object, which in time bare themselves out. When you gun through an artist's arsenal, a strong eye says, "Fine, fine, great, excellent, solid, okay, understand, get the point, wow, look at that, once again," and so on... this with an exceptional talent. But when you see the weak links these weak links might go on for decades in the life of a creator. When you look at the painting I am fretting over this week there are not weak links. This is a solid case of standard composition, color and design principles coming out of my studio. If one were to break my paintings into lines and math one would see a Garnett compositional matrix come about. Some math grad in the future will enjoy this one. You've got the math, some nice movement between line and color, water and clouds, boats still and in motion. Is this the most ambitious picture? No, but it's a decent math puzzle that someone, an old friend, has prescribed to. He likes my three-panel paintings of water, several of which I have done lately. I like these paintings too, particularly because they are triptychs. Is this not edgy enough for that annoying little art school ruffian who exists within me?

No, this type of painting does not satisfy the edge in me. My new song 'Into the Sun' satisfies that edge, just like this journal entry satisfies my emotive edge, just like 'Busted Wing' in the background satisfies the edge, just like the signature sculpture I designed this week satisfies this edge, just like the woman's back I was massaging last weekend satisfies this edge. If you are an art school student you may have dropped this book a hundred pages ago, unless you realized that it is a mirror, a companion piece for fellow artists, as giving as it gets brothers and sisters. Do you think admissions of this nature are commonplace? Think again. Artists, particularly visual artists, are defensive freaks. I was going to say like deer in headlights but deer just want to stay alive. Once you find your place as an artist you don't care anymore (unless you remain petty), but the proving grounds are filled with artist carcasses, being stepped over by newbies who want to pick a fight just to show they've got big balls. Big balls don't equal long term talent and survival. What has worked for me? Aside from make original stuff, be great at it, teach yourself to sell it in order to not rely on others for money outside of the art universe you create. Be kind, be loyal to the death, be a rock of a family member and friend. These things are harder to achieve in life and these things have allowed me to be a tough ass cockroach artist for twenty years. Put that in your reindeer antler and smoke it.

December 24 Saturday

Last night was a fun, casual chili and kegger party at the home of my friends Bill and Barb, many old friends festive with their party hats full-on. Amidst heavy belly laughter I saw my friends Liege and Sarah, who mentioned that their girls want me to come over and draw with them soon.

My triptych is sitting there, taunting me. It's 10 am and all I have to do is get that one done and out. Last night I painted while listening to "The Shawshank Redemption," one of the best films ever written and created that I often listen to when there is blood in the water on a painting. I'm running out of time, but I'm also running out of work to be done. I just don't want to see the painting go, part of the game. Separation anxiety, as this painting has been my answer for a month. I have to make the next answer happen, and I don't know how today, so I don't want to let my last answer go. Maybe this is a wise observation. It feels that way as I write it. I think I just wrote myself into finishing the painting.

December 25 Sunday

Merry Christmas. I went over to my brother's house at 6 am, where I hung out until mid-afternoon. There were several rotations of parents who came through. My niece and nephew had a good day, the food and presents and egg nog and spirit of my family were warm and everyone had a nice time. Christian came back to my studio for a couple hours into the evening for drinks and some laughter.

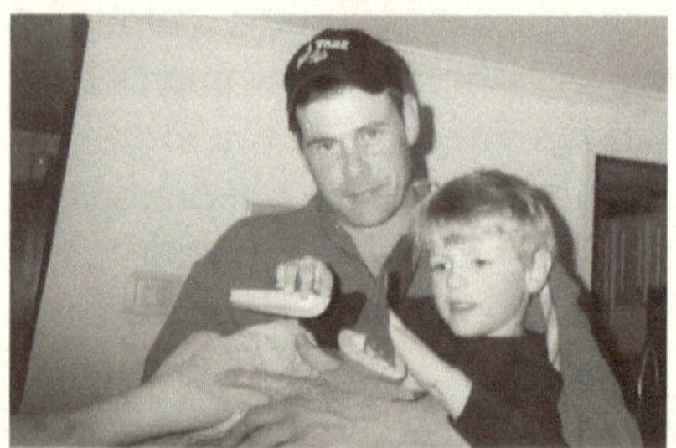

When Christian left for another party I called my friend Kevan and he asked where I was already. I drove over to see some of my favorite people. They are several generations of directors and artists and writers and photographers and filmmakers, so as always we talked late into the night about all of the above subjects. I took my Inventory book, my *1000 Paintings* book, my *Generations* book over and left them there, which will give me an excuse to go back and

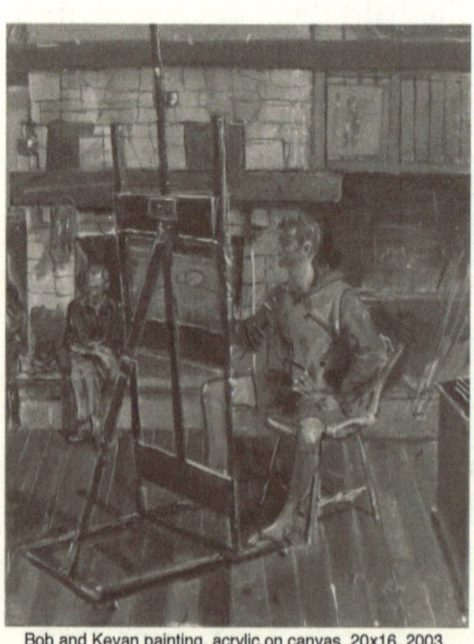

Bob and Kevan painting, acrylic on canvas, 20x16, 2003.

get some painting in with Bob and Kevan. They have a studio in the house that makes you want to paint, as art studios do.

December 26 Monday

Today I tooled around with the painting I was supposed to ship out today. I wanted to get the triptych out of my world before my collector travels on the 28th, but I can't force the finish. Every mark has to be right. My collector won't mind. I checked in with him about that today. This will give me another week to tinker.

I also worked on the portrait that is due in a week, which is coming along nicely. I just need to keep getting paint on this one and that ship will sail by itself.

December 27 Tuesday

I was sad to go to the service for my friend's father today. I wore the tie from Chris and Abigail's wedding party. I sat with my old group and listened to Chris and his siblings talk about their father during the service. Afterwards we drove to the family's house for a reception, where I spent most of my time at my friend's side.

Artists sequester themselves and when they get out life has changed around them sometimes.

Sometimes, later in the evening, the artist walks around his studio, as if on watch, surveying the grounds, this place that nobody believed in until he came to pass, walking the walls of the world he has constructed. This world that we see is a slim veil of fabric that blows away in the wind, but there are turrets from which to perch for those who build a unique life.

I peered into the eyes of spirits who lost their father today, people I love and will fight for. I listened to a son who mourned his father's passing with respect and commitment. I listened to a daughter who referenced a profound poem about the emptiness that is eternal when half of you is missing, as death goes.

I started thinking about a song along these lines, and a melody floated through the air as I scribbled lyrics down, which often start by mumbling nonsense. Half of death is living, half of life is dying. Half of life is missing, the other half surviving.

December 28 Wednesday

I spent the day fending off the two deaths I am celebrating this week and last, thinking about families who suffer and what is important in life, which is always a good thing to keep in mind. In the big moments my life makes perfect sense to others. I don't care for material things aside from tools to make art and life better I suppose, and people seem to recognize this quality in some artists. Yesterday I spoke with a woman who gardens and landscapes for her career, which must be very rewarding. The beautification and preservation of landscape as a means of income is a life well spent in my estimation. I have friends who have estates that roll for miles and generations. One of the reasons I am welcomed in these places is that I don't wish to hold the titles on properties like these. When I sit at my favorite place in the world, a little white beach house where I have spent hundreds of my favorite moments, looking out on Long Island Sound, tucked away in the New England shoreline, that place, that vision, is mine alone.

People come and go in harder ways than places change or stay the same. I went with my brother to an informal memorial for our old friend David tonight. I saw faces that I had not seen in many years. We drank and ate and reminisced with tears and laughter. The sparks recreated themselves all over again, old conversations, stories, attractions magnetizing certain people to others, as animal magnetism goes. The camaraderie was strong, the language was deep and flavored and funny and comfortable like an old shoe, like friends from one's hometown. Certain things are understood, taken for granted, don't need to be explained unless that is the joke, when communing with old friends from hometowns, until the bar lights flicker and the evening wraps itself into another end of year reflection.

Before bed I wrote some emails to friends I saw tonight. One excerpt reads, "Staying in light is a good thing to do, or helping people get there, stay there, what have you. When spending time around this flame the energy is so good that there is little room for negative energy in the long run, whatever happens. Although there is a hole in everyone's heart who cares about David and his family, the warmth of twenty or thirty people communing makes a fire that stays with us as we go forward."

December 29 Thursday

Today I painted in the morning and had lunch with cousins and my brother's family. The girls got along nicely with Jackson and Emma at lunch as the adults talked about how fast life moves along. When my plate was done I went over and ate Jackson's leftovers while wrestling with him and drawing cartoons for the kids. Beth and Michael brought Anne and Lila over after lunch to see my studios. Lila remarked that painting naked women was inappropriate, all five years of her. I started to explain that no, it was not inappropriate, that all the old sculptures in history are nudes. This was a losing battle as in some cases kids just have to see and feel the vibrations of a creative. My intentions are noble but I can't get into an intellectual gunfight with a five-year-old about why I like to paint the best bosoms on the planet.

I went over in the afternoon and spent some time with my friend Keiley, whose knee was operated on last week. Her home is filled with life; fish, a dog, Ted, her husband (who comes before fish or dogs), three kids, in-laws, siblings, cousins, neighbors. Everybody drops by and it's a warm place like the fire that was burning while we hung out. It's good for an unmarried professional artist to be an uncle of sorts, as the solitude of studio life, although very peaceful and productive, is always enhanced by frequent visits with friends and family. The answers lie within, but there is plenty of enjoyment and laughter that is important to have in watering the gardens of our relationships often. This way we help one another through good times and bad.

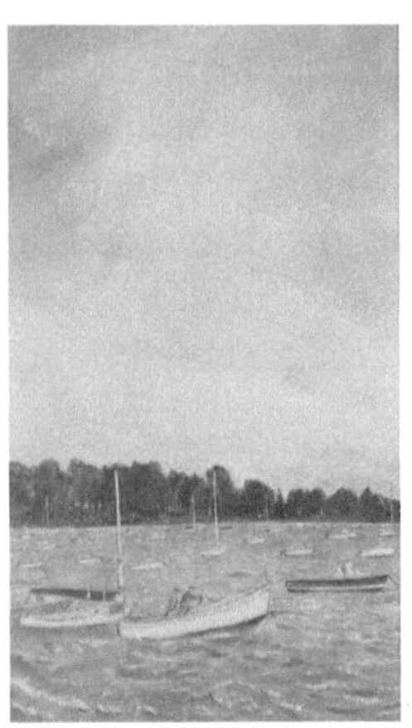
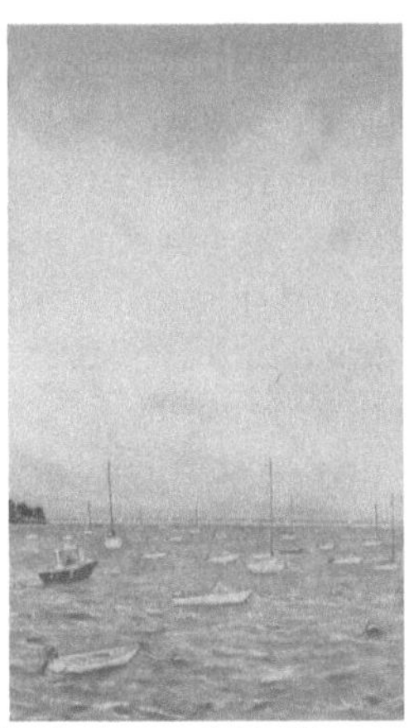
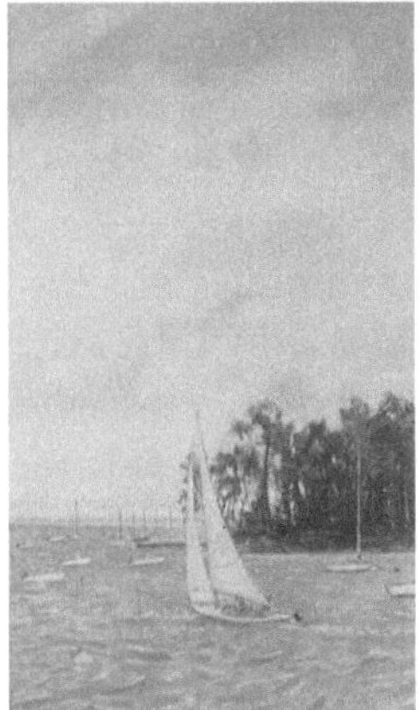

© SandyGarnett.com, Noroton Bay Triptych, oil on canvas, 34 x 20 inches each (34 x 60), 2011, Private Collection.

December 30 Friday

When I go to the art time flattens out, the burdens vanish, I feel like myself, and the energy starts to ramp. Sometimes I am away from the easel, but I always return. This is where I am at peace, at home, a boy to frolic, running through the fields of youth, burnt by the sun, tired by the swim, happy with my lot in life. Here there are no answers, only endless questions.

People say I look young for my years. I think half of this is genetics and half of this is what you do in life. I spend so much time in meditation, reflection, my face without expression, my spirit tilted towards the stars, my head cocked to take in the sound of the next inspiration, my heart on the rails trying to feel for the next rhythm. The best thing about this way of being is that it is a young way to be, to think about life, in the sense of timeless works of art, in powerful gestures of love and humanity, these things that have no time. They are meant for the ages, told, retold, revisited, lived in, lived on, taught by. I spend my life in this space, eschewing the fleeting fancies of consumer culture, media saturation, intellectual acrobatics that have a short shelf life, the complete and utter corruption of our financial and governmental systems, both based on short term gains for the few and far between.

To build a better world? I will stay in light and do my part. This time around is an interesting ride, and I am still searching for the questions. The art is now the easy part. I have trained my muscles, I have run marathons, I have scaled mountains, I have lived in the purgatory of 1000 paintings, I have seen the darkness and the light. My paintings have sustained me, they have bought my home and this computer and this keyboard that I type on. My art has kept me sane in a crazy world, loving and laughing and being the best human being that I can be. What else is the point of life? The life of an artist is unconventional by definition, but often times it is the life and output of creators who shine lights forward for the rest of humanity. Artists are satellites and they are everywhere it seems. They are in the fabric of every stratification of our culture. If the world were run by creatives the world would certainly be a messier place, but it would be a better one too.

December 31 Saturday

Today I was up early and have been enjoying a full day of creativity. I have been rotating between three easels on three different paintings, I have been working on keyboard and guitar parts for a song that is slowly turning her head to meet me, and today is the last entry of my book. These favorite days of mine are downright chipper. I slide upstairs and downstairs in my loft, moving with the currents of various paintings in translation. These projects riff off of one another and the energy starts to spark in the studio. This is finishing energy, which is delicate, not steamrolling energy..

There are a hundred sub-genres of each genre, which is one of the reasons why I enjoy genre-hopping or moving between sub-genres within one genre. The thing about most of my creative days is that the energy from one painting finds its way into another painting, often from a completely different genre. A canvas came in today for that 20 x 16 Fingerprint Portrait, which is a different genre and feeling than the other two paintings on my easels. And I am going to sculpt Picasso's Signature Totem next week, which has nothing to do with anything I'm working on today. The cycle of energy rippling through the studio is nice rhythm, it feels good, I am in the right zip code on these projects, the paintings will go out with confidence next week to make room for new energies, new creative adventures. Tomorrow is a new year and I have a pipeline of five paintings, maybe two sculptures, which is a larger pipeline than I have had since the economic meltdown over three years ago. It's been a long slog for people, but at least in my business, in my spirit maybe, I have survived and see the weather brightening a bit. I can't wait to get my hands on all the projects I'm going to dive into next year.

My second book hangs in the balance of this last entry. This year has been a good run and I threw everything I had at it. It has been a challenging year, as many years go in the life of a professional fine artist. I have worked hard, I have lived, I have excelled at many things, failed at some of them, I have loved, I have mourned, I have produced, I have created every day, I have been a good brother, uncle, son, friend, I have been a decent human being who works his tail off for his passions.

When painting deep space on a canvas one of the most important lessons that no one ever taught me was that the deep background should be painted faintly first, the closest foreground should be painted last, and the lines between geographically spatial stratification points should be blurred. It is in the blurring of the lines that space grows infinite in a canvas, contrary to Clement Greenberg's silly argument that the canvas is flat. The lines are blurred between my art and my life. Life is art to me. Art is my religion, this being stated by a happily Confirmed Episcopalian from old American Protestants. Art is the way I see, the way I think, the way I live, the way I commune with nature and with the spirit realm. Art is my sustenance, art pays my bills, puts a roof over my head, sings me to sleep often, art feeds me, clothes me, bathes me, gets me from point A to B. Art allows me to travel, to work with other original creatives, thinkers, doers, artists, writers, musicians, photographers, sculptors, ceramicists, directors, editors, collectors, friends, family members. Art is a way of life, an institution on its own. I bristle back to listening to art critic Arthur Danto explain to me in one of his pompous lectures that there is no new art, that art has arrived at its own self-definition, that everything created since 1963 is simply post-historical character. When I heard this rubbish coming from a non-creative, listening to all these sheep around him clapping, I knew my road would be a long and solitary one, swimming against the vast oceans of skepticism that can sometimes be found all around a creative person in his own world even, in his own community. Art belongs to the creators and their audience, and intellectual brokers have lost a lot of their clout in recent decades. There will always be excellent critics in every field, but for the critics who overshoot with giant egos, they are not doing artists any favors.

I am beholden to nobody, I am my own boss, I do what I want, I think in my own way. Why? Because I am a fine artist who lives by the paintbrush and will die by the paintbrush. This is not wild ego talking, rather the voice of a professional artist who has relied on his art for survival since he was an adolescent. If any cynic, and I know there are a lot of them being cranked into the art world every year, picks this book up and thinks there is a lot of ego that made this second book? Keep reading the book over and over again as it might be the right kind of medicine to knock the ego out. Ego doesn't often make great, timeless art. Or maybe it does, just not in my case. Some may learn through this book that ego is not helpful in the deepest spiritual ways, in many of the most timeless things, creations, ideas, in the life of a creative who strives for balance between making original art objects and being a decent citizen. It is by checking the ego at the door, something the above stated art critics never did, that clarity and peace can be held in the hand like a monarch butterfly. One cannot possess a butterfly's beauty or delicacy, but by allowing the monarch to be free an observer can enjoy the beauty that a butterfly ignites.

The friends and relatives of artists will always remain puzzled by the mystery which propels their loved ones to walk on burning coals again and again. At the other side of this meditation is a truth and beauty and sometimes horror so mesmerizing that creative people will build their lives around it, they will lead hard lives and suffer for this insight in the physical manifestation of their particular worlds. And there is the philosophy that souls select their paths to a certain extent, their bodies, their lives, to sort out something unresolved from past lives.

Life is short and ephemeral and intoxicating and magical and I make art for a living this time around. Art is life. Life is endless. There will always be new life, and where there is new life there will always be new art. Just look for the next burned out industrial wasteland where artists congregate and will get a rhythm going before the developers smell opportunity.

I am at the cusp of the New Year. The lights are dim as I designed them, so that I can move from one creative area to another and each creative area makes a different environment. I stroll over to my new painting, who smiles at me.

I have this nice Garnett Girl on my easel that I started today. Her hair is flowing, but her face and her hair are flat. I know what to do in paint without using words, as painting is second nature. Explaining what I am about to do to make this painting the next one I sign into the archive?

I walked upstairs to the keyboard, to this document, and I realized in a MOMENT that my last year has been studiously documenting the life of a painter in action. There is NO WAY to explain to you how I will with several brush strokes bring this sweet little picture into another Garnett painting. I'll sign her tomorrow and she will be smiling at you, but I don't know how to write that which I paint.

One thing I have learned is that if I do not honor my line, I will never know where that line might have gone...

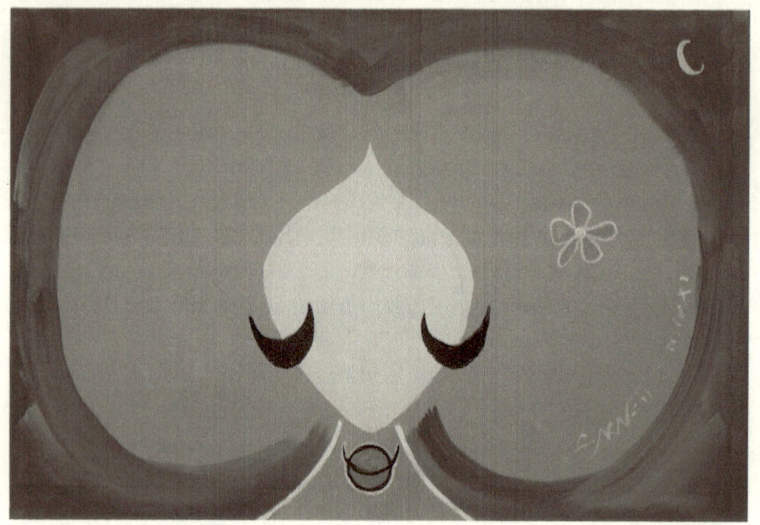

New Year Garnett Girl, acrylic on canvas, 24 x 36 inches, 2011, © SandyGarnett.com.

... Neither will anyone else.

www.ingramcontent.com/pod-product-compliance
Lightning Source LLC
LaVergne TN
LVHW091641100826
845152LV00006B/123/J

* 9 7 8 0 9 8 2 2 3 4 8 8 4 *